Lee's Tarnished Lieutenant

Lee's Tarnished Lieutenant

*James Longstreet
and His Place
in Southern History*

William Garrett Piston

The University of Georgia Press
ATHENS AND LONDON

© 1987 by the University of Georgia Press
Athens, Georgia 30602
All rights reserved
Designed by Dariel Mayer
Set in Linotron 202 ten on thirteen Baskerville
The paper in this book meets the guidelines for
permanence and durability of the Committee on
Production Guidelines for Book Longevity of the
Council on Library Resources.

Printed in the United States of America
91 90 89 88 87   5 4 3 2 1

Library of Congress Cataloging in Publication Data

Piston, William Garrett.
    Lee's tarnished lieutenant.

    Bibliography: p.
    Includes index.
    1. Longstreet, James, 1821–1904. 2. Generals—
United States—Biography. 3. Confederate States of
America. Army—Biography. I. Title.
E467.1.L55P57.L55   973.7′3′0924   86-16025
ISBN 0-8203-0907-9 (alk. paper)

British Library Cataloging in Publication Data available.

Frontispiece: Lieutenant General James Longstreet,
Cook Collection, Valentine Museum,
Richmond, Virginia.

To Thomas L. Connelly, in appreciation of his confidence and encouragement

Contents

Preface

ONE OF THE THINGS I have enjoyed about living in New Orleans is the presence of the past, particularly the Confederate past. It is possible to argue, as Charles L. Dufour does in *The Night the War Was Lost*, that the fall of New Orleans doomed the Confederacy.[1] Nine Southern generals are buried in this city, among them P. G. T. Beauregard, John Bell Hood, and Leonidas Polk. The city is rich in bronze, with statues of Albert Pike, Jefferson Davis, and others. One elaborate monument is dedicated to the soldiers of the Army of Tennessee, and a corresponding one honors those of the Army of Northern Virginia. Presiding over the scene from atop a sixty-foot Doric column at the junction of St. Charles and Howard avenues is the city's most formidable Confederate monument: a sixteen-and-one-half-foot bronze statue of Robert E. Lee. Like all the other statues in New Orleans, the Lee statue has turned a dull green.

But nowhere in New Orleans, or in all of the South, for that matter, does there stand a memorial to Lee's intimate friend and second in command, James Longstreet. Whereas the tarnish on Lee's statue does the famous Virginian's reputation no harm, the uncommemorated Longstreet is tainted by something less visible yet more enduring. The stain colors his reputation, his place in history, and it is more complex than the chemical formula which explains why bronze tarnishes.

Longstreet's place in history was shaped, first, by his membership in the Republican party after the Civil War and his cooperation with the

Radicals during Reconstruction and, second, by the fact that certain of Longstreet's fellow officers blamed him for losing the battle of Gettysburg—a defeat that by extrapolation, they claimed, cost the South its best chance for independence. Many Confederate veterans came to believe that Longstreet's alleged slowness and obstinacy in Pennsylvania, and not the Yankee fleet which captured New Orleans, best accounted for the extension of the United States' boundary below the Ohio River. Many historians of the late nineteenth and twentieth centuries have agreed.

Unlike other gray-clad warriors whose deeds are familiar to Southerners and Northerners alike, Longstreet has the image not of a hero but of a villain, even a Judas. He is the dark, brooding presence behind the saber-wielding Cavaliers. He explains how a superior people could have lost the war—for surely the Yankees never actually beat the South in a fair fight! As scapegoat for the Confederate defeat, Longstreet is perhaps the keystone of the "Lost Cause," playing a role in history which has affected our perceptions of the Civil War to the present day. His image is all the more fascinating because it is completely divorced from reality. It was artificially created by the General's postwar enemies, and it reflects his own ineptitide as a politician and writer after the war.

The present book is not a traditional biography and makes no attempt to catalogue the General's every movement. I study Longstreet's military service to set the record straight before showing how the many falsehoods about him came to form an integral part of the Lost Cause. I do not attempt to describe his every battle completely, however. I presuppose a moderate amount of knowledge about the war on the reader's part. Because my book probes Longstreet's image and his place in history in addition to the man as he was, it also analyzes his detractors and postwar Southern politics and culture.

Part 1 reappraises Longstreet's contribution to the Confederate war effort. Although he made his share of mistakes, Longstreet's skill at directing men in combat made him perhaps the best corps-level commander of the war. By advocating the use of defensive tactics and a concentration of Southern forces in the western theater, Longstreet showed himself to be ahead of many of his peers in appreciating the Confederacy's plight. His belief in such strategies led him several times to attempt to leave Lee's service despite their close friendship.

When he did so temporarily in 1863–1864, Longstreet was prompted by his views on Confederate strategy, not by an overweening desire for independent command. Part 1 shares similarities with such works as Thomas L. Connelly and Archer Jones, *The Politics of Command* (1973); Grady McWhiney and Perry D. Jamieson, *Attack and Die: Civil War Tactics and the Southern Heritage* (1982); and Herman Hattaway and Archer Jones, *How the North Won: A Military History of the Civil War* (1983). In it I challenge old assumptions about the war and study personal relationships among the Confederate high command and various theories of strategy and tactics as they affected the outcome of the conflict.

Part 2 deals with the creation, manipulation, and persistence of Longstreet's image as well as the fascinating role that this image played in his lifetime and the unique place it gave him in Southern history. By joining the "enemy" during Reconstruction, Longstreet lost his status as a Confederate hero at a time when the Southern people, responding to the shock of defeat, were transforming their heroes into veritable saints. Robert E. Lee became the dominant Confederate hero only after his own death, when a group of Virginia officers launched an intense campaign to make Longstreet publicly bear the blame for Lee's defeat at Gettysburg and for the loss of the war. Longstreet's own writings in self-defense confirmed rather than disproved his guilt in the eyes of his contemporaries, for in his prose Longstreet displayed, particularly in old age, vanity and jealousy which had not been evident during his wartime service. The deeply religious Southern people viewed Longstreet's "guilt" as accounting for the failure of a righteous, God-fearing populace in its bid for nationhood. Novels, poems, and plays reinforced Longstreet's infamy in the public eye.

Part 2 places nineteenth- and twentieth-century perceptions of the Civil War in the context of the South's larger social, cultural, religious, and literary history. In so doing, part 2 resembles Rollin G. Osterweis, *The Myth of the Lost Cause* (1973); Thomas L. Connelly, *The Marble Man: Robert E. Lee and His Image in American Society* (1977); and Charles Regan Wilson, *Baptized in Blood: The Religion of the Lost Cause* (1980). I hope that my portrait of Longstreet will provide insights not only into the manner in which history is made but also into the process by which history becomes a part of memory and written record.

Acknowledgments

THIS BOOK EXISTS only because I received support and assistance from many kind people. I gratefully acknowledge my debt to them.

My thanks go first to Professor Thomas L. Connelly of the University of South Carolina, for his invaluable advice and constant encouragement. The parallel between my approach to Longstreet and his to Lee is deliberate, although we have not always reached the same conclusions about either man.

The following individuals read one or more drafts of the manuscript and provided helpful criticism: Professors Walter B. Edgar and John Scott Wilson of the University of South Carolina; the late Henry Lee Swint, Professor Emeritus, Vanderbilt University; and Archer Jones, Professor Emeritus, North Dakota State University. I also wish to thank the anonymous reader who evaluated the manuscript for the University of Georgia Press.

I am indebted to the staffs of the following institutions for their courteous assistance during my research: the Chicago Historical Society; the Swem Library, College of William and Mary; the Perkins Library, Duke University; the Woodruff Library, Emory University; the Gettysburg National Battlefield Park Library; the Historical Society of Pennsylvania; the Henry E. Huntington Library, San Marino, California; the Library of Congress; the Louisiana State University Libraries; the Mississippi State Department of Archives and History; the National Archives and Records Service; the New York Public Library;

the North Carolina Department of Cultural Resources, Division of Archives and History; the Rutherford B. Hayes Memorial Library, Fremont, Ohio; the Tennessee State Library and Archives; the Howard-Tilton Memorial Library, Tulane University; the United States Army Institute for Military History, Carlisle Barracks; the University of Georgia Libraries; the Wilson Library, University of North Carolina at Chapel Hill; the Alderman Library, University of Virginia; the Virginia Historical Society; the Virginia State Library.

I wish to acknowledge in particular the assistance of Dr. Edward Campbell of the Museum of the Confederacy, Richmond; Dr. D'Arcy Jones of the Georgia State Department of Archives and History; Susan Floyd of the Georgia Historical Society; Betty Kondayan of the Washington and Lee University Library; and Jenni M. Rodda of the Valentine Museum, Richmond. My Metairie neighbor Stephen Morillo, creator of the cartoon strip "Cayenne," inked in the maps I drew, for which I am very grateful.

Edward M. Boagni, M.D., of Baton Rouge extended gracious hospitality to a perfect stranger and allowed me to use his private collection of Civil War letters. In this connection I must also thank Dr. John Loos of Louisiana State University, for introducing me to Dr. Boagni and for turning his office over to me for workspace.

Longstreet biographer Wilbur Thomas generously shared with me papers from his private collection for which I am very grateful.

One of the delights of this project was my contact with the late Abbott M. Gibney, author of an as yet unpublished biography of Longstreet for juvenile readers. Mr. Gibney shared with me materials from his private collection and made numerous beneficial suggestions.

Invaluable logistical support during my research trips was provided by Mr. and Mrs. Robert E. Williams of New Orleans, and by the Robert H. Belser, Sr. and Jr., families of Nashville. I also wish to thank Dr. Stephen Wise, currently director of the Marine Corps Museum at Paris Island, South Carolina, for countless favors and suggestions during our graduate student days.

I owe a special debt to Karen Orchard and Debbie Winter of the University of Georgia Press, for their patience and faith in my work. My thanks go also to Marcia Brubeck for her excellent copyediting.

    I could not have completed this project without the love and support of my family—my wife Nancy; my mother, Laura Caldwell Piston; my brothers Jim and Rob and their families; my in-laws, James and Esther Wall; and my late grandparents, Mannie Mae and Charles H. Piston. My thanks go to them above all others.

Lee's Tarnished Lieutenant

Prologue: Longstreet Antebellum

WITH A NOD OF HIS HEAD General James Longstreet sent the long, gray lines forward through the field of wheat, toward a stone wall and a clump of trees on a distant ridge. It was a hot July afternoon in 1863. The General was forty-two years old. He would live for another forty-one years, longer than almost all of the other high-ranking Confederates. Yet these hours spent in the rolling hills surrounding the sleepy Pennsylvania town of Gettysburg were to remain the focal point of his life. Indeed, the events at Gettysburg were much more than a battle. They entered the Southern psyche and afforded an explanation for the loss of the war.

Quite unwillingly Longstreet became the crux of the explanation. During the war he was a tower of strength in defense of the South. But postwar controversies surrounding his actions at Gettysburg engulfed him, exposing embarrassing weaknesses of character that were never displayed during the conflict itself. History has not treated him kindly, for reasons as complex and fascinating as Longstreet himself. Of the war's major figures, he remains one of the least understood.

Existing biographies of Longstreet provide only a sketchy account of his antebellum years. His experiences resembled those of many Confederate generals. He had a rural Southern upbringing, and a West Point education. He saw distinguished service in the Mexican War and subsequent years of drudgery in the frontier army of the 1850s. But in Longstreet's case we have few sources for details.

Existing antebellum private letters written by Longstreet can be counted on one hand. His massive autobiography is concerned solely with the defense of his military record and only very briefly mentions his childhood and family. It reveals nothing of his humanity, his passions and regrets. His military correspondence during the Civil War still exists in the National Archives in Washington, D.C., and in printed form in the familiar multivolume *Official Records,* but his personal papers were destroyed in a fire. There are no Longstreet diaries for historians to consult, no intimate letters to the folks at home that reveal his opinions of people, places, and events. Yet despite the shortage of data, it is possible to speak of Longstreet's character, to suggest the manner of man he was in 1861 and how well and in what fashion he was prepared to fight the war that came.

To an important degree, Longstreet reflected the environment in which he spent his earliest years. He was born at his grandparents' cotton plantation in the Edgefield District of South Carolina on January 8, 1821. He spent his first eight years, however, on his father's farm outside Gainesville, a small town in hilly northern Georgia. While he doubtless visited the Edgefield place many times, he never considered himself a South Carolinian, nor has the Palmetto State claimed him, although an overgrown roadside marker erected by Longstreet's second wife notes his birthplace.[1]

North Georgia was very much a frontier during Longstreet's boyhood. Indians were a recent memory, buckskins and long rifles a common sight. In these woods and ridges the genteel traditions of the Tidewater South were almost as alien as the customs of New England. Longstreet had some rough edges that never disappeared. Like Lincoln, he knew his manners but could be coarse when no ladies were present. He was sometimes casual, even slovenly, about his appearance and would never be mistaken for an aristocrat.

Longstreet was self-reliant and enormously strong. His passions were those common among rural lads of the nineteenth century. He loved to swim, hunt, and fish and was an excellent horseman and marksman. He was occasionally moody as an adult and was at his most taciturn while performing his duties as a soldier, traits which may have begun in childhood, but his basic nature was warm and generous. He made friends easily and loved fun and games.[2]

Despite his country upbringing, Longstreet was no bumpkin. He could make a favorable impression in the finest drawing rooms in the land, in part thanks to the social polish that West Point traditionally gave its cadets. Longstreet's personal flair resulted even more from the years he spent spent at Westover, a large cotton plantation near Augusta, Georgia, that was owned by Longstreet's uncle, Augustus Baldwin Longstreet, who lived there with his wife, Frances, and two daughters. Aspiring to a military career, Longstreet moved to Augusta to attend the local preparatory school in hope of going on to West Point. His residence at Westover became permanent in 1833 when his father died and his mother moved permanently to northern Alabama, probably intending to live with relatives. Augustus and Frances became Longstreet's de facto parents, and he remembered their love and warmth fondly in his old age.[3]

In Augusta, Longstreet was exposed during his formative years to one of the finest minds of the antebellum South. Augustus Baldwin Longstreet was a respected lawyer and judge. During James's stay he became a newspaper editor and publisher, a nationally known humorist (author of the classic *Georgia Scenes*), and a Methodist minister as well. As one of the South's foremost educators, he was later president of Emory College, South Carolina College, and the University of Mississippi.[4]

A friend and supporter of the famous Nullifiers Calhoun and McDuffie, Augustus Longstreet was a passionate advocate of states' rights. He made Westover a center of local political activity. James adopted his uncle's political views but apparently without deep thought. He seems to have lacked his uncle's passion on the subject.

Longstreet probably also acquired from his uncle his fondness for whiskey and card games. These were considered by many people during the nineteenth century to be terrible vices, but Augustus, who was ordained the year Longstreet left for West Point, saw no harm in an occasional dram or a friendly game.[5]

Perhaps because he had been somewhat an orphan, Longstreet as an adult became a particularly devoted parent. Shortly after the Mexican War he married Maria Louisa Garland, daughter of Brevet Brigadier General John Garland. They had met in Missouri when Longstreet, fresh from the Military Academy, was assigned to the

Fourth U.S. Infantry. Garland, then a lieutenant colonel, was second in command of the regiment.[6]

Longstreet and Louise, as he called her, had six children prior to 1861, but two died in infancy. Ben Ames Williams, a descendant, described the General as a father when he wrote two novels in which the Longstreets appear as minor characters: *House Divided* (1947) and *The Unconquered* (1953).[7] Williams, who questioned the General's living children and grandchildren during his research, portrayed Longstreet as an exceptionally caring family man and his marriage as a particularly happy one.

Longstreet seems to have benefited in several ways from having been the son-in-law of a brigadier general in the small peacetime United States Army of the 1850s. He was often stationed close to General Garland, under his indirect command. Probably because of Garland, Longstreet held minor independent positions, for example serving as post commandant of Fort Bliss, Texas. There were also rumors that Louise Longstreet's private letters to her father could make or break the careers of officers who served with Longstreet.[8]

Any benefits of nepotism were minor, however. Longstreet did not advance in rank any faster than his West Point classmates; he was a major at the time of his resignation in 1861. Furthermore, he rated family well-being more highly than his career. In 1858 he unsuccessfully sought transfer to the East in order to send his children to better schools. For their benefit he was willing to serve anywhere in any capacity. That same year he accepted a position in the paymaster's department, which gave him more time with his family and the hope of being stationed in larger towns with better schools.[9] Certainly the last thing he expected in early 1860, as he approached his fortieth birthday, was that within three years he would be commanding more men than were currently enlisted in the entire United States Army.

How well and in what manner was Longstreet prepared to defend the South in 1861? He was trained at West Point, having entered the Military Academy in 1838 with an appointment from Alabama which he obtained when he discovered that the position for Georgia had been filled. His classmates included many men who became famous. George Pickett, D. H. Hill, Lafayette McLaws, and U. S. Grant were his close friends. Grant later married one of Longstreet's cousins, and the two men considered each other kin. Longstreet's acquaintances included Richard H. Anderson, Richard S. Ewell, G. W. Smith, Earl Van Dorn, William T. Sherman, and William S. Rosecrans, who was his roommate.[10]

The goal of the Military Academy was to produce competent company commanders and engineers, not masters of the art of war. Longstreet's first two years were devoted entirely to the study of French and mathematics. The main course in his third year would today be called physics. His senior year alone was devoted to military engineering, with brief attention to strategy and tactics for infantry and artillery.[11]

Longstreet's military training was thus very basic. Whether he supplemented it later by reading any of the contemporary treatises on war is not known. Possibly more important than West Point was his cumulative service prior to 1861. Over a thirteen-year period he acquired, among other things, administrative skills which proved invaluable during the Civil War.

In Mexico, Longstreet served as a company commander and as regimental adjutant of the Eighth Infantry. In the former position he learned about the many needs of the individual soldier on an actual campaign. He was responsible for the arms, equipment, and discipline of his men. As adjutant, he learned about the workings of command at a higher level. He prepared and distributed his colonel's daily routine orders and communications and wrote all daily reports and returns.[12]

After the Mexican War, Longstreet served for six months as chief of commissary for the Department of Texas. He procured and distributed food for 1,500 soldiers as well as forage for hundreds of mules and horses. It was inglorious work, even dull, but it introduced him to the logistical challenges of a large-scale operation encompassing a vast territory. This experience certainly helped him as a Confederate general, particularly during his brief independent and semi-independent commands.[13]

As a post commander at Fort Bliss, Longstreet was by definition responsible for everything. Although his force was tiny, to sustain it he had to deal with all of the army's support services, such as the Ordnance Department and the Quartermaster's Corps. Training in ways of meeting his wants using proper channels would obviously help him later.

Longstreet also acquired skills in the art of war, mostly as they applied to the infantry. In Mexico he led men into action at the battles of Palo Alto, Resaca de la Palma, and Monterey, although at no time did he command over 100 men. As an adjutant he participated, often as a volunteer color bearer, in the battles of San Antonio, Churubusco, El Molino del Rey, and Chapultepec. He was severely wounded during the last-named battle. His conspicuous bravery won him repeated promotions, and he ended the war as a brevet major.[14]

Longstreet's record as a young officer was laudable, but it did not include experience directing large numbers of men. In fact the largest force Longstreet commanded before becoming a Confederate brigadier was a 240-man mounted infantry expedition against the Mescalero Apaches in 1855, during which no shots were fired.[15] Still, none of the men who rose to high command during the Civil War had previously commanded large numbers of men. Longstreet began the Civil War on a par with everyone else.

A more important question is the impact of Longstreet's Mexican War combat on his tactical thinking. Historians have hotly debated which European military theorists influenced America's Civil War generals and to what degree. In Longstreet's case, speculation seems fruitless, given the loss of his papers and the silence of his autobiography on the subject. While he may have read Clausewitz and Jomini, it seems likely that the greatest influence on his tactical thinking was the combat in which he himself participated.[16]

Longstreet's tactical experience was almost entirely limited to the offensive. At Resaca de la Palma, Churubusco, Monterey, and other battles he saw that a resolute offense could carry the field against an enemy who enjoyed either natural or prepared defenses—even if the enemy were superior in numbers to the attacker. Not once did Longstreet play a purely defensive role in a major combat in Mexico.

Longstreet may therefore have manifested a propensity for the offensive in 1861. But if so, various experiences exerted a modifying effect. Attacks do not always succeed. The attack of Longstreet's regiment at Churubusco was a very near thing. The Mexicans, firing from behind formidable earthworks, initially stopped the Americans cold. It took the courage of junior officers such as Longstreet, who rushed ahead as bullets literally rained down upon him, to start up the attack once more. Later, at the battle of El Molino del Rey, the brigade containing the Eighth Infantry advanced against Casa Mata. The Mexicans had fortified this large stone building extensively, and the Americans were slaughtered. Their retreat was such a rout that the Mexicans dared to counterattack.[17]

Successful or not, offensive tactics could carry a frightful price tag. At Resaca de la Palma, Churubusco, and the attack on Fort Libertad outside Monterey, Longstreet participated in hand-to-hand combat. On other occasions, such as the house-to-house struggle at Monterey, the fighting was virtually face to face, if not actually hand to hand. Longstreet was remarkably fortunate in not being wounded until Chapultepec, for casualties in the Eighth Infantry were high. After Resaca de la Palma, four depleted companies were disbanded and their survivors transferred to other units. Losses among the officers were always disproportionately heavy; at El Molino del Rey 50 percent of Longstreet's compeers fell.[18]

How did such experiences affect Longstreet in 1861? He probably viewed offensive tactics as a highly effective means by which an inferior force might defeat a superior one. But he also knew the cost. Longstreet could never order men into battle without knowing from his own past just what he was asking of the individual soldier. He could always be expected to show a high degree of empathy with his men.

It remains to be seen how a commander thus predisposed would react to the conditions of the Civil War, involving as it did much larger forces and weapons far more destructive than those of the Mexican War. Would he follow examples from the past or seek new tactics to meet new conditions?

PART I

Longstreet's Military Record:
A Reappraisal

"This is a hard fight and we had
better all die than lose it."
> Longstreet to General Roger Pryor
> at the battle of Antietam

1. From Manassas to Antietam

I N   H I S   M E M O I R S James Longstreet states that after resign-
ing as a paymaster in the United States Army he applied for
a comparable position in the Confederate forces. The error reflects
either false modesty or faulty memory. Major Longstreet was stationed in Albuquerque, New Mexico Territory, in 1860. He opposed
secession but decided after Abraham Lincoln's election that he would
side with the South if fighting broke out. In a move that his superiors
would probably have considered treasonous, he tried to obtain a commission from Alabama, as that state had sponsored him at West Point.
Nothing came of this effort, however, and Longstreet did not resign
and head for Richmond until the fall of Fort Sumter had made a
sectional reconcilation improbable.[1]

If Longstreet ever entertained thoughts of becoming a Confederate paymaster, he abandoned them quickly. On a train from New
Orleans to Virginia he fell in with a group of young Texans, and they
decided to form a company of mounted infantry. During an interview
Longstreet obtained with Jefferson Davis shortly after June 21, the
president expressed enthusiasm for the idea but indicated that Longstreet could expect to command far more than a mere company.
Elated, Longstreet made plans to organize an entire brigade from the
many Texans flocking to Richmond in search of a fight.[2]

Longstreet knew Texas well from his army service and had resided there longer than in any other state except Georgia. Texas was a
young state. Few of its residents were native born, and Longstreet had

as much right to adopt it as anyone. Had events gone a bit differently, history might tell of Longstreet's Texas Brigade as it does of John Bell Hood's. But there was no time for Longstreet to organize a command of his own choosing. Davis desperately needed qualified officers. On July 1, Longstreet received a commission as brigadier general which was to date from June 17. He was ordered to report to General P. G. T. Beauregard at Manassas Junction, a rail center some eighty miles north of the capital. There he was given command of the Fourth Brigade, consisting of the First, Eleventh, and Seventeenth regiments of Virginia Volunteer Infantry.[3] Longstreet had no connection with Virginia. The fact that he was not identified with any particular state, unnoticed at the time, would have grave consequences after the war.

Longstreet's command was part of a force of some 15,000 to 18,000 men guarding a strategic rail junction little more than a dozen miles from Washington. Beauregard, famous throughout the South for his reduction of Fort Sumter, styled his men the Army of the Potomac. He was opposed by Irwin McDowell, rumored to be building an immense Federal army. This enemy force would also eventually call itself the Army of the Potomac.[4]

On July 8, Longstreet's brigade was ordered forward to Blackburn's Ford, a key position in the line that Beauregard was organizing behind Bull Run. The steep banks of this meandering stream, a tributary of the Potomac River, offered the best position from which an army might protect Manassas Junction.

At Blackburn's Ford, Longstreet's 1,400 men guarded the route to Manassas via Centerville, three miles north. Other Confederate brigades protected strategic fords and crossings on each of his flanks, upstream and downstream. In Longstreet's rear, within easy reach of Blackburn's Ford, Beauregard placed a reserve brigade under Jubal Anderson Early.[5]

Longstreet picketed both sides of the ford heavily and, after camping his main force just behind the crossing, turned his attention to drilling his men. The raw recruits needed months of discipline, but McDowell allowed the rebels little time for training. By July 16, the Federal commander was moving his own equally inexperienced army forward. At 11:30 A.M. on the eighteenth an advance Federal brigade under General Israel B. Richardson drove in Longstreet's pickets and assaulted Blackburn's Ford.[6]

The ensuing combat gave Longstreet his first test as a field commander. He passed although not without making mistakes. As the Federals approached, Longstreet formed a heavy skirmish line on the south bank of Bull Run but kept his main force in reserve, correctly calculating that his skirmishers alone would be sufficient to repulse the enemy's initial assault. When a second, stronger attack followed, he moved each of his regiments forward in turn, placing them carefully to give real weight to his defensive line. Once he had become fully aware of the odds against him, he prudently sent to Early for reinforcements.[7]

As the action opened, Longstreet, dressed in civilian clothes, sat placidly on his horse, "chatting gaily with the officers and men," calming them by his seeming indifference to the danger.[8] But when some of his raw troops began to waver under the Federal attack, he came alive. Thomas J. Goree, one of Longstreet's Texan traveling companions and now his aide-de-camp, later told a friend that Longstreet, "amid a perfect shower of balls, rode amongst them, with his cigar in his mouth, rallying them, encouraging, and inspiring confidence among them."[9]

By the time Early's men had arrived, a third Federal advance was being driven off. Longstreet counterattacked, but crossing the ford proved so difficult that he canceled the move before it was really under way. As the Confederates withdrew to the south bank once more, the Union soldiers attacked a final time. Fortunately the arrival of Early's men persuaded the Federals to withdraw.[10]

A small disaster occurred just as the fighting ended. While still to the rear, men of Early's Seventh Virginia opened fire on the distant enemy, wounding several of Longstreet's men in front of them. Longstreet dashed to the scene when he saw that they were about to fire, but he was too late. In fact, he had to leap from his horse to avoid being killed himself. Longstreet made no mention of this accident in his battle report, nor did he censure Early. And Early, a fiesty, short-tempered Virginian who became Longstreet's bitterest postwar enemy, at the time had only praise for the General. "I am satisfied he contributed very largely to the repulse of the enemy by his own personal exertions," wrote Early in his official report.[11]

General Beauregard was also impressed, feeling that the skirmish gave the Confederates "the prestige of success." When analyzing the skirmish in his memoirs, he credited Longstreet's resolution at Blackburn's Ford with making McDowell so cautious in his subsequent movements that Joseph E. Johnston was able to reach Manassas with his forces from the Shenandoah Valley in time to unite with Beauregard for the great battle of July 21.[12]

Longstreet's first brush with the enemy may well have had a significant impact on his tactical thinking. His orders placed him on the defensive and allowed him to witness its great advantages. Although the terrain did not favor the Confederates, they repulsed their superior enemies with relative ease. Once the enemy's strength had been exhausted by his attacks, a counterattack became feasible. At Blackburn's Ford the counterattack did not succeed but only because of the terrain. Longstreet would attempt to repeat this pattern, first receiving an attack, then counterattacking, on several other occasions during the war. The faith that he developed in defensive tactics profoundly affected his career.

Fate was unkind to Longstreet during the battle of Manassas, fought three days after Blackburn's Ford. He was slated for a key role in Beauregard's attack plans, but McDowell's own assault prevented these from being implemented. Longstreet's brigade was not engaged during the famous Confederate victory. At 5:00 P.M. Longstreet was, however, ordered to pursue the fleeing Federals and cut off their line of retreat. Near Centerville he found troops under Brigadier General Milledge L. Bonham obstructing the road. Bonham, the senior officer, would not let Longstreet's troops proceed. When Longstreet finally reached Centerville and prepared to attack, Bonham again interfered. Insisting that the Federals were not retreating but launching a flank attack, he would not permit Longstreet to advance. While he was arguing with Bonham, Longstreet received orders from Confederate headquarters to withdraw, which enraged him. Slamming his hat to the ground, Longstreet stamped his feet in frustration. " 'Retreat!' he thundered, 'Hell, the Federal army has broken to pieces!' "[13]

Several days after the battle, Longstreet was ordered to occupy a now deserted Centerville. There he concentrated on drilling his men and on developing a brigade staff. Thomas Walton of Mississippi joined him as an aide-de-camp. Wealthy and cultured John W. Fairfax, a Virginian, became assistant inspector and adjutant general. Gilbert

Moxley Sorrel, a twenty-year-old Georgian, served as a volunteer aide during Manassas. He had difficulties securing a commission because he lacked military training, but he eventually became Longstreet's chief of staff and even later a brigadier under A. P. Hill.[14]

Sorrel became particularly intimate with Longstreet, whom he described in his memoirs as

> a most striking figure. . . . a soldier every inch, and very handsome, tall and well proportioned, strong and active, a superb horseman and with an unsurpassed soldierly bearing, his features and expression fairly matched; eyes, glint steel blue, deep and piercing; a full brown beard, head well shaped and poised. The worst feature was the mouth, rather coarse; it was partially hidden, however, by his ample beard.[15]

Goree was equally taken with the General, but in describing Longstreet in August 1861 to his kinfolk in Texas he noted both favorable and unfavorable characteristics.

> Genl. Longstreet is one of the kindest, best hearted men I have ever known. Those not well acquainted with him think him short and crabbed, and he does appear so except in three places: 1st, when in the presence of ladies; 2d, at the table; 3rd, on the field of battle. At any one of these places he has a complacent smile on his countenance, and seems to be one of the happiest men in the world.[16]

If Longstreet seemed short and crabbed, perhaps overwork was responsible, for his first months of command were extremely hectic. But the truth is that Longstreet was in no sense genteel or courtly except when polite company required him to be so. In his day-to-day life his manners were too rough for some people's taste.

During the summer and throughout the fall, the Virginia front was quiet. In October, Longstreet was promoted to major general and was assigned the Third Division of Beauregard's corps of the Army of the Potomac. Beauregard's esteem was such that he sought to have Longstreet designated second in command, even though other officers in the corps outranked him. The War Department denied the request, but Longstreet remained Beauregard's most trusted subordinate.[17]

Longstreet's promotion to major general also reflected the good opinion of General Joseph E. Johnston, who as Beauregard's superior had assumed command of all the forces which had been concentrated at the battle of Manassas. Johnston had earlier commanded the Army of the Shenandoah. Longstreet's acquaintance with the rather aloof and often cold Virginian began when Johnston and Beauregard made a meticulous tour of the Confederate positions. They dined together on several occasions, sometimes in the company of President Davis.[18]

After the war Johnston wrote that he had been particularly impressed by Longstreet's "promptness of thought and action" and by his ability in difficult situations to reach "correct solutions expressed with such quickness as to be termed by some intuition."[19] In October Johnston tried unsuccessfully to have Longstreet promoted to a corps-level command to replace Beauregard as second in command of the army. Their friendship was never intimate, but their admiration for each other was sincere.[20]

When Johnston became involved in a dispute with Davis over strategy, Longstreet supported him loyally. Like many others at the time, he erroneously blamed Davis for the South's failure to capture Washington following Manassas. When his aide Goree suggested that Davis might have political reasons for not attacking Washington, Longstreet scornfully remarked that inaction might be "very good politics, but it was *very poor* fighting."[21]

By November, Davis was so concerned about a possible misunderstanding between himself, Johnston, and Longstreet that he sent his close friend L. Q. C. Lamar to visit the army. Lamar, a Mississippi senator, had married one of Judge Longstreet's daughters. He arrived ostensibly as a volunteer aide, but it was well known that he was the president's unofficial representative.[22]

Lamar was particularly concerned for his kinsman Longstreet. On November 11 he wrote his wife:

> I shall probably start Monday next for General Johnston's headquarters. . . . There is some ill-feeling between the Potomac generals and the President. I fear that cousin James Longstreet is taking sides against the administration. He will certainly commit a grave error if he does. I hope to be able to disabuse his mind, as well as that of General Johnston.[23]

Unfortunately, Lamar was ill during most of his visit to the front, and we do not have details regarding his mission or its effectiveness.[24]

That he feared for "cousin James" is significant, however. To an experienced politician like Lamar, Davis's support, or lack of it, was clearly something no high-ranking officer could ignore. By siding with Johnston, Longstreet flirted with danger every bit as hazardous as shrapnel.

Longstreet had little time to worry about a rift between Davis and Johnston, for he was fully occupied training his division. He was the only commander to hold drills at the divisional level, and his ability to move large numbers of men without confusion enhanced his reputation. One observer noted that Longstreet could "manage a division of eight or ten thousand men with as much ease as he would a company of fifty men."[25] He was no martinet, but he did lament after the war that the Southern armies had never been "properly organized and disciplined."[26]

As fall gave way to winter and the army remained inactive, Longstreet was sometimes able to visit his family in Richmond and to participate in the social life there. He made quite an impression on the ladies, who considered him exceptionally handsome and agreeable.[27] When circumstances permitted, Longstreet also made the most of the pleasures a soldier could find in the field. He organized an officers' club, which included close friends such as George Pickett. There were nightly poker games, with whiskey close at hand. And in a culture which linked masculinity with horsemanship, Longstreet earned a reputation as the best fence jumper in the army.[28]

Longstreet was not always the jovial comrade, however. A December letter from Goree to his family speaks of Longstreet's rougher side:

> At home with his Staff he is some days sociable and agreeable, then again for a few days he will confine himself mostly to his room or tent without having much to say to anyone and is as grim as you please, though when this is the case he is either not very well or something has not gone to suit him. When anything has gone wrong he does not say much, but merely looks grim.
>
> We all know how to take him and do not now talk to him without we find he is in a talkative mood. He has a good deal of the roughness of the old soldier about him, more, so I think, than either Genl. Johnston, Beauregard, Van Dorn, or Smith.[29]

This combination of bonhomie and brooding silence fits our image of the stereotypical frontiersman and may reflect Longstreet's backwoods upbringing. Stereotypical too was his reaction when, while enjoying the relative ease of winter quarters, tragedy unexpectedly entered his life. In January 1862 scarlet fever swept Richmond, killing three of Longstreet's children. Only his eldest, John Garland Longstreet, survived. In reaction to this severe blow, Longstreet gave up card games and other forms of frivolous entertainment, seeking consolation in the Episcopal church. For a long time he remained somber and withdrawn; the traits that Goree had noticed were coming to the forefront. Yet good humor was too basic to his nature for the melancholy to last, and before the war ended he had learned to laugh once more.[30]

General Johnston was very sympathetic and understood Longstreet's protracted low spirits. As spring approached, bringing the certainty of action, he needed Longstreet more than ever. Beauregard had been transferred to the western theater, and the War Department suggested sending Longstreet to the Confederate army in the Shenandoah Valley. Johnston refused to consider this course of action, stating that he needed more generals like Longstreet, not fewer. Because G. W. Smith outranked Longstreet, Johnston was still unable to appoint Longstreet second in command but constantly gave him greater responsibilities and more difficult assignments than Smith. It was well known throughout the army that Johnston considered Longstreet one of his finest officers.[31]

In March, a Federal advance under Major General George B. McClellan, by way of the peninsula formed by the James and York rivers, threatened Richmond from the southeast. When Johnston shifted his forces to Yorktown in response, Longstreet handled many of the complex troop movements involved. Longstreet made an even greater contribution in May as the badly outnumbered Southern army withdrew up the peninsula in the face of McClellan's slow, methodical advance. While commanding a rear guard of some 9,000 men near Williamsburg on May 5, Longstreet fought a sharp battle with advance units of the Federal army, allowing the bulk of Johnston's men to continue their retreat safely. Johnston himself did not reach the field until 3:30 P.M. There, he reported later, "General

Longstreet's clear head and brave heart left me no apology for inter-
ference."[32]

If Longstreet's services at Williamsburg were invaluable, the
same cannot be said for his actions at Seven Pines, fought on the last
day of the same month. To the alarm of President Davis, Johnston
continued his retreat up the peninsula. By late May he was near Seven
Pines, only about ten miles from Richmond. McClellan, however,
soon committed a tactical error by placing his huge army astride the
rain-swollen Chickahominy, making it difficult for either half to reinforce the other in a crisis.

Johnston seized the opportunity, attacking the Federals on the
south side of the river on May 31. According to his plans, Longstreet
would have tactical control over the entire right wing of the Southern
army, but he failed to inform all his subordinates of this intention. As
a result, an argument between Longstreet and Major General Benjamin Huger regarding seniority and whose troops had priority over
a certain route occasioned serious delay.[33]

But Longstreet himself committed a far worse error by shifting
his troops farther south than Johnston had intended, so that he attacked over the wrong route. This mistake robbed the Confederate
advance of the power and coordination that it needed for a decisive
victory. Though driven back, McClellan's army remained a dangerous
threat to Richmond. Longstreet's mistake may have been an honest
misunderstanding; he had received only verbal orders. Such, at least,
was Johnston's conclusion. He praised Longstreet in his report on
Seven Pines and even forced G. W. Smith to modify passages of his
report which were critical of Longstreet.[34]

Johnston was too magnanimous. Seven Pines marks the lowest
point in Longstreet's military career. That Johnston's instructions to
other subordinates were equally vague does not exonerate Longstreet. One Confederate officer summarized the situation percep-
tively by noting that Seven Pines "remains a monument of caution
against verbal understandings."[35]

The battle ended Longstreet's service under Johnston, who was
badly wounded late in the day on May 31. Command devolved upon
G. W. Smith, the senior major general, rather than upon Longstreet,
as Johnston would have preferred. On the following morning the

Confederate attack continued, but no further progress was made. Johnston's wisdom in preferring Longstreet for his second in command was soon borne out. Smith, faced with the responsibilities of command, suffered a nervous breakdown within twenty-four hours.[36]

As a replacement Davis chose Robert E. Lee. Because Longstreet was castigated after the war when he dared to criticize Lee, who by then was famous, it is important to remember that Lee's reputation was actually quite mixed when he first took command. The Virginian had been appointed the third ranking general in the Confederacy. His first campaign in the mountains of western Virginia ended in an embarrassing defeat, which provoked public outcry. When Davis subsequently sent Lee to command the Atlantic coast defenses, he had to reassure the other officers there regarding Lee's competence.[37]

When Davis appointed Lee his military adviser in March 1862, the news attracted little notice. But when Lee took Johnston's place in June, the newspapers scornfully called the new commander "Evacuating Lee," "Granny Lee," "The King of Spades." Nor was concern limited to the press. Given Lee's reputation, one soldier in Johnston's army expressed a view of Lee that may have been common: "I know little about him. . . . But I doubt his being better than Johnston or Longstreet."[38]

Less than a month after taking command of the force he styled the Army of Northern Virginia, Lee initiated a series of battles known as the Seven Days campaign. Bringing Thomas J. "Stonewall" Jackson's troops down from the Shenandoah Valley and concentrating other reinforcements, Lee planned to threaten McClellan's communications by moving against his right flank. But for many reasons, including Lee's inexperience, faulty staff work, and a poor performance by Jackson, the Confederates instead launched a series of badly coordinated frontal assaults. These drove McClellan back to Harrison's Landing, twenty miles from Richmond, but his army remained intact and a threat to the capital.[39]

Longstreet's wartime reaction to his first service under Lee is not known. Contrary to legend, however, the campaign did not catapult Lee into a preeminent position among Confederate heroes. Some newspapers erroneously credited the wounded Johnston with planning it, and many others focused on Jackson in their coverage. Indeed, Jackson's reputation, founded at Manassas, augmented by his

Valley exploits, and enshrined by his death, equaled or exceeded Lee's until after Lee had died in 1870.[40]

More important for a consideration of Longstreet's impression of Lee is the fact that Lee drew sharp criticism once the casualty figures had been published and the price for pushing the enemy back less than two dozen miles had become known. Lee was particularly condemned for a bloody attack made at Malvern Hill. Within a few days his repeated assaults on McClellan cost the South some 20,000 men, a number greater than the entire strength of General Albert Sidney Johnston's army in the western theater during the fall of 1862.[41]

Not everyone considered the cost of the campaign worthwhile. One young soldier in Jackson's command lamented to a friend, "I am now of the opinion that the battles of Richmond will soon have to be fought all over again, and it is fearful to contemplate. . . . I think our killed and wounded will reach 20,000 or 25,000 . . . in the battles before this city. And nothing is done towards terminating the war."[42]

Robert Toombs, a prominent Georgia politician then recently turned brigadier, may have been prejudiced against West Pointers when he wrote his friend Vice President Alexander H. Stephens in July, "Lee was far below the occasion. If we had had a general in command we could easily have taken McClellan's whole command and baggage. . . ."[43] Toombs's remark was entirely unrealistic, but his opinion carried weight. And the important point is not whether Lee *deserved* criticism. In understanding the criticisms which Longstreet himself eventually formed about Lee's generalship, we should remember that Lee's actions met with some degree of disapproval from a variety of quarters, beginning with his earliest association with the Virginia army.

Longstreet, in contrast, won consistent praise for his conduct during the Seven Days campaign. The difference between his quick movements and Jackson's sluggish ones did not go unnoticed, and within the army his already high reputation continued to grow. The private soldiers regarded him as a hard fighter, and the sight of his staff officers scurrying about was considered a sure sign of imminent combat.[44]

Longstreet made his greatest impression upon Lee. Shortly after assuming command, Lee informed Davis, "Longstreet is a Capital soldier. His recommendations hitherto have been good, & I have confidence in him."[45] At the conclusion of the Seven Days fighting, Lee called Longstreet "the Staff of my right hand" and magnanimously gave Longstreet much credit for the South's victories when he spoke in public.[46]

Like Beauregard and Johnston, Lee soon decided that Longstreet should be his second in command. By mid-July 1862, he was moving to rid the army of all four of the officers who outranked Longstreet. G. W. Smith, Benjamin Huger, John B. Magruder, and Theophilus Holmes were soon transferred, leaving Longstreet the senior major general in Lee's army. Despite some apparent misgivings, Lee retained Jackson but gave him clearly subordinate status and reduced his responsibilities. In the reorganization following the Seven Days battles, Lee assigned Longstreet five divisions and Jackson only three.[47]

Lee and Longstreet soon became close friends. For this reason they pitched their headquarters tents near each other. They saw each other daily in the course of duty and were frequent guests at each other's camp for supper, conversation, and companionship. Contrary to popular belief, Lee never developed a friendship with Jackson anything like that which he enjoyed with Longstreet. Nor did he socialize frequently with Jackson.[48]

There is no mystery in Lee's decision to relax with Longstreet rather than with Jackson. Outwardly, it is true, Lee seemed to have much in common with the Calvinistic Jackson. Both men believed in sobriety, self-denial, and the will of Divine Providence. Compared with Jackson's headquarters, Longstreet's camp was a den of iniquity. Why would Lee seek the company of men who drank and gambled, as did Longstreet and his staff?

The answer is probably that Lee possessed a deeply repressed fun-loving streak, a naturally gregarious nature held in check by years of guilt, doubt, and feelings of unworthiness and failure. His unhappy marriage, his preoccupation with death, and his antebellum conviction that his career was a failure had led him to develop iron self-control and a strict sense of duty. But as a young man Lee had been happy and flirtatious, a gay bachelor who enjoyed social life.[49] Perhaps when Lee joined the warm, relaxed atmosphere of Longstreet's headquarters, a place full of laughter, jokes, and good spirits, he was seeking to return to something in his past.

The summer of 1862 afforded few occasions for socializing, however. In late July, Major General John Pope, commanding the Federal Army of Virginia, advanced on Richmond from the north. In response, Lee split his forces. While Longstreet guarded the capital, Jackson outflanked Pope, captured his supply depot, and forced him to retreat. A sharp fight at Groveton between a portion of Pope's command and part of Jackson's produced heavy casualties. Pope was badly confused by this turn of events but recovered sufficiently to attack Jackson on August 29. The Confederates stood firm, however. occupying a defensive position just west of the old Manassas battle-field.[50]

Lee meanwhile hurried north with Longstreet's corps, bring his army together without arousing Pope's suspicions. In their march to join Jackson, Longstreet's men proved as worthy of the sobriquet "foot cavalry" as Stonewall's veterans of the Valley. Longstreet's men began to arrive on Jackson's flank around noon on the twenty-ninth.[51]

Lee wanted to attack immediately with the troops available, but Longstreet urged caution. His commander was "urging nothing less than a piecemeal attack on an unknown force over unknown ground."[52] Longstreet declared this tactic unwise, particularly as they knew that Pope was receiving reinforcements from McClellan but were uncertain where and when these new troops would arrive. As some evidence suggested at the time that the fresh units would threaten Longstreet's flank, a thorough reconnaissance was essential. Afterward, Longstreet asserted, positions could be chosen which would allow the Confederates either to make or to receive an attack the following day.[53]

In advancing these suggestions Longstreet may have been remembering Blackburn's Ford, where he had witnessed the power of the defensive. Why not let Pope wear himself out on the morrow as he had on the twenty-ninth? It was his prerogative as second in command to offer advice, but the decision would of course be Lee's alone. Lee in this case decided to remain on the defensive for the rest of the day.[54]

When the sun rose on August 30, Lee and his lieutenants watched in amazement as hour after hour passed while the Federal army remained inactive. Not until noon did the Federals strike. Then, drums beating, the blue lines moved forward—but toward Jackson alone. The Union commander had walked into a very neat trap. His movement placed Longstreet in a perfect position for a flank assault.

Pope's advance prompted Jackson to call for reinforcements. Longstreet's artillery, placed to enfilade the enemy, opened fire, relieving the pressure on Jackson in far less time than it would have taken to send infantry to him. Anticipating orders from Lee which arrived only moments later, Longstreet ordered his entire command forward in a hard-hitting counterattack. Pope was decisively defeated.[55]

Longstreet's remarkable energy and stamina played a significant role in this campaign and in all his others. At age forty-one he was able to go for long periods without food or sleep. Often, while his young staff officers lay in exhausted repose, he would pace back and forth throughout the night, mulling over some military problem. Once dawn made reconnaissance possible, he would be off, leaving his staff to break camp and hurry after him, all hopes of breakfast dashed.[56] Service with Longstreet was demanding, but he never failed to reward good work, and his reports were filled with commendations of subordinates who displayed merit. "There was no illiberality about him," Sorrel recalled, "and the officers knew it and tried for his notice."[57]

Shortly after Second Manassas, the men and officers under Longstreet had an opportunity to distinguish themselves once more as Lee decided to invade Maryland. He believed that a bold raid would compel a Federal withdrawal from Virginia and would perhaps encourage the secessionist movement in Maryland. He also hoped to convince the nations of Europe that the Confederacy was a viable, successful government worthy of recognition. Most important of all, the move would allow him to provision his army from a region previously exploited by the enemy while sparing an already lean Virginia.[58]

Longstreet and Jackson supported Lee's plan to strike north, but both were dismayed by the proposed division of the badly outnumbered Confederate force in order to capture the Federal garrison at Harpers Ferry. Lee feared leaving this threat on his flank as he moved north, as it might prevent him from establishing a line of communications through the Shenandoah Valley. Longstreet demurred, calling the plan to seize Harpers Ferry "a venture not worth the game," while Jackson urged that Lee's army "should all be kept together."[59]

Lee was adamant, however, and split his forces into four columns. Three, under Jackson, converged on Harpers Ferry, capturing it on September 15. Once reconciled to the assignment, Jackson conducted it with characteristic enthusiasm and skill. September 15 found Lee, Longstreet, and the fourth and largest fragment of the army near Sharpsburg, Maryland, seventeen miles north of Jackson's position. Lee had counted on his swift movements to mystify and confuse his opponent, as they had until McClellan received a copy of Lee's plans that a staff officer had accidentally lost. Although he reacted with something less than lightning speed, McClellan began concentrating his troops against Lee's widely dispersed forces. Lee was soon faced with the possibility not just of defeat but also of annihilation.[60]

Fortunately, Jackson was able to reach Sharpsburg on September 16 with most of the troops that had been used in the Harpers Ferry action. These were placed on Longstreet's left flank in a defensive position behind Antietam Creek. On the following day, amid fearful carnage, Lee's army of fewer than 40,000 men barely managed to repulse a series of uncoordinated Federal attacks. Had McClellan made a concerted assault with all the forces available to him, Lee would probably have been crushed.[61]

The desperate fighting at Antietam showed Longstreet at his best and also at his most inelegant; an earlier foot injury forced him to fight the battle wearing a pair of carpet slippers. Fortunately he was still able to ride, for the battle proved to be one long series of crises, with the thin gray lines threatening to give way in a dozen different points. Confident and unperturbed, Longstreet committed his scant reserve. When these men were gone, he used his own presence at the front to bolster his weakening firing line in a display of courage, tenacity, and resolution that Sorrel termed "magnificent."[62]

At one point, General Roger Pryor sent an orderly to Longstreet, begging for more artillery support. The note Longstreet sent in reply was grim but reassuring by its very firmness: "I am sending you the guns, dear General. This is a hard fight and we had better all die than lose it."[63]

Another crisis found Longstreet and his staff with the Washington Artillery just as heavy casualties left two of the guns of the crack battalion unmanned. The New Orleans cannoneers were Longstreet's favorites. Jackson, in a rare joke, dubbed them "Longstreet's Body-guard," because he always had them camp near his headquarters. Now Longstreet ordered his staff to the guns. Unable to dismount himself, he held their horses, drinking calmly from his canteen while directing their fire. The Federals approached so close that Longstreet ordered canister. When a member of Lee's staff arrived with a message, his "eyes popped as though they would come out of his head" when he saw the measures to which Longstreet had been driven. The Federals were repulsed but not before two of Longstreet's staff had been wounded, and one of the horses the General held was killed.[64]

Despite the exertions of Lee, Longstreet, and Jackson, the battle would have been lost had not A. P. Hill arrived at about four o'clock with 2,000 men who had been delayed at Harpers Ferry. Longstreet and Jackson had been quite right in questioning the wide dispersal that Lee's plans produced; the Confederate army was fortunate to have survived the day.[65]

When darkness ended the combat, Lee's subordinates made their way to his headquarters in Sharpsburg. As time passed and Longstreet failed to arrive, Lee grew concerned for his safety until a staff officer remembered seeing the General unharmed at sundown. Longstreet arrived late because he had stopped to help a group of wounded and a family whose home had caught fire during the artillery shelling. When he finally appeared, Lee embraced him proudly, exclaiming "Ah! here is Longstreet; here is my old *war-horse!* Let us hear what he has to say."[66]

Since taking command, Lee had developed considerable affection for Longstreet and felt complete confidence in his ability. Longstreet fully reciprocated the friendship but not the confidence, a fact that is revealed in a letter he wrote to Joseph E. Johnston shortly after Antietam. Neglected in previous studies of Longstreet, it sheds crucial light on his relationship with both Lee and Johnston.

While Longstreet's friendship with Johnston was never intimate, it was warm and heartfelt. Longstreet was gratified when Johnston took the time in June, less than a month after having been wounded, to send him a gift from Richmond. In a note of thanks he promised to visit Johnston as soon as possible.[67] In October, in a letter describing

Antietam, he assured his still recuperating chief that, although the enlisted men had "fought many battles and successfully under another leader, I feel you have their hearts more decidedly than any other leader can have."[68]

In the same letter, while discussing Johnston's health and future, Longstreet wrote:

> I can't become reconciled at the idea of your going west. I command the 1st Corps in this army; if you will take it you are more than welcome to it, and I have no doubt but the command of the entire army will fall to you before spring. . . . If it is possible for me to relieve you by going west don't hesitate to send me. It would put me to no great inconvenience. On the contrary it will give me pleasure if I can relieve you of it. I fear that you ought not to go where you will be exposed to the handicaps that you will meet with out there. I am yet entirely sound and believe that I can endure anything.[69]

Longstreet's offer to go west in Johnston's place may have stemmed from genuine concern for his health, a desire for his own command—a common ambition for any soldier—or both. It may also have reflected a desire to escape service under Lee, as the letter constitutes an extraordinarily unfavorable assessment of Lee's ability. Longstreet predicted that if Johnston returned as Lee's subordinate, he would soon rise to the top at Lee's expense. Perhaps Longstreet hoped that the flattery would elicit an invitation to accompany Johnston to the west.

Whatever his motives, Longstreet's implied criticism may seem startling in the face of modern veneration of Lee. Unfortunately, further information on the subject is lacking. We can only speculate as to why Longstreet considered Johnston superior to Lee (an opinion he also expressed after the war) and why, apart from his natural desire for advancement, he was apparently anxious to leave Lee's service. Such speculation should ignore modern assessments of Lee and should consider how he might have appeared to Longstreet after only three and a half months as an army commander.

Lee's Maryland campaign accomplished only one of its objectives—drawing the Federals out of Virginia—and did so at a cost of 10,000 casualties, one-quarter of the Confederate forces engaged. This fact did not go unnoticed in the press.[70] Straggling, a chronic problem for every Civil War commander, reached nightmare proportions. Perhaps as many as 20,000 men left the ranks either before Lee crossed the Potomac or prior to the fight at Antietam. A percentage of these troops fell behind only because of exhaustion, hunger, or lack of shoes. Some refused to participate in an invasion of the North as a matter of principle.[71] But many, to Lee's embarrassment, stole away to plunder. Others, as Lee noted in his battle report, simply "kept aloof."[72] That is, they marched with the army but ducked the fight. Straggling *increased* after the return to Virginia and encompassed many officers, not just enlisted men. A large number of soldiers threw away their shoes in an attempt to avoid further service. As a result, Lee acknowledged to President Davis, the army was "greatly paralyzed."[73]

Longstreet may have wondered whether the Army of Northern Virginia had lost faith in the newly appointed Lee. In the mere seventy-odd days of Lee's command prior to Antietam the veterans whom Beauregard and Johnston forged into an army over a year's time saw some 37,000 of their comrades fall. Is it surprising that so many kept aloof from Antietam, where another 10,000 fell, or that straggling increased after the battle? Longstreet may have worried that Lee's pugnacity was bleeding the army white, destroying its morale, and he may therefore have sought to leave the Virginia army, either as an independent commander or as Johnston's subordinate.

Lack of appreciation for his efforts in the eastern theater may also have influenced Longstreet to offer Johnston his corps in October 1862. Although he never sought public accolade, Longstreet must have noticed that he received scant credit in the public eye for his accomplishments in fifteen months of service. Recognition for his victory at Blackburn's Ford was lost amid the huzzahs for the many heroes of Manassas, where fate had denied him a role. His work at Williamsburg was highly praised by Johnston but little noted in the press, probably because it ended in a preplanned retreat. By the fall of 1862 Stonewall Jackson's name seemed to be on every Virginian's lips, but if Longstreet was mentioned, it was in a manner that ranked him among lesser Confederate heroes. In fact, by January 1863 the public's lack of appreciation for Longstreet was itself deemed newsworthy by one magazine.[74]

Finally, it is interesting to note, in terms of Longstreet's future relations with President Davis, that during this period of disenchantment Longstreet was in contact with several prominent politicians who eventually opposed the administration. Foremost among these was Texas senator Louis T. Wigfall, who, like Longstreet, was a native of Edgefield District, South Carolina. Wigfall served Longstreet as a volunteer aide during the summer of 1862 and was friends with Johnston as well. He was particularly grateful to Longstreet for keeping an eye on his seventeen-year-old son Halsey, an artillery lieutenant in Hood's Division. Longstreet in turn looked to Wigfall as the army's advocate in Congress and asked him to sponsor legislation making the apprehension of deserters and draft resisters easier.[75]

Longstreet also left a very favorable impression on two powerful Georgia politicians, Robert Toombs and Alexander H. Stephens. Toombs, who was nearly chosen president of the Confederacy, resigned as Davis's secretary of state in 1861 to serve as a brigadier general. Despite an early misunderstanding over the placement of a picket line, which resulted in Longstreet's temporary arrest of Toombs, Longstreet recommended the Georgian for promotion after Antietam. A friend noted that Longstreet "always had a decided liking for Toombs."[76]

Through Toombs, Longstreet's name became well known to Vice President Stephens. Toombs wrote Stephens following the Seven Days battles that, throughout the campaign, in generalship Longstreet had exceeded his peers, Lee and Jackson not excepted. In later correspondence and conversations, Stephens noticed that Toombs always expressed a "very high regard" for Longstreet. By 1862, Stephens had become alienated from Davis, in part because of the president's military policy. Stephens believed that, instead of attempting to defend every inch of Southern territory, the Confederates should concentrate their forces against the enemy's weak points—a view of strategy that Longstreet would soon adopt.[77]

Longstreet was also associated with Alabama Congressman Jabez Curry, who had worked unsuccessfully to win him a state commission in 1861. Curry never attacked Davis openly, but he resented the president's aloofness and way of treating legislators. Curry tried to obtain a position on Longstreet's staff late in the war, and when Longstreet was unable to give him one, he served under Johnston, who was also his friend.[78]

Friendship with these men did not automatically place Longstreet among Davis's adversaries and did not necessarily cause Davis to dislike Longstreet. There is evidence, though of doubtful accuracy, that a rift occurred between Davis and Longstreet as early as February 1862, following the Confederate surrender at Fort Donelson. When asked to comment on the strategy of Albert Sidney Johnston, a man Davis admired and placed in command of the western theater, Longstreet replied with a jest that made it apparent he considered Johnston a fool. Davis reportedly took the comment as a personal insult.[79]

It is much more likely, however, that Longstreet and Davis enjoyed good relations throughout the fall of 1862. More important, Lee seems to have been unaware of Longstreet's preference for Johnston or his offer to go west. Lee's own strong confidence in Longstreet was apparent when he reorganized the army into two corps following Antietam, legitimizing the unofficial wing commands that Longstreet and Jackson had been exercising for some time. In October the two men received well-deserved promotions to lieutenant general.

Lee had some reservations about Jackson and felt the need to explain the desire to retain him. Lee reassured the president that his opinion of Jackson had been "greatly enhanced" by the Maryland campaign. Privately, however, Lee expressed the opinion that Jackson was "by no means so rapid a marcher as Longstreet" and that he had "an unfortunate habit of *never being on time.*" Longstreet, however, he endorsed without hesitation or qualification.[80]

Jackson's commission dated from October 10, 1862. Of six other lieutenant generals appointed that same day, five outranked him. Lee gave him command of the smaller Second Corps. Longstreet's commission, dated October 9, made him the senior lieutenant general in the Provisional Army of the Confederate States. To him Lee entrusted the greater portion of his troops, the First Corps of the Army of Northern Virginia.[81]

Stonewall Jackson drew the headlines and the adoration. Women begged for locks of his hair and buttons of his coat, thrusting babies into his grim visage to be kissed. But as his chief lieutenant and second in command Lee chose James Longstreet. In the months which followed Lee came to trust him more every day. But ironically Longstreet would at the same time come to doubt the wisdom of Lee's strategy and tactics and would spend considerable energy attempting to leave the Virginia army.

2. *From Fredericksburg to Gettysburg*

B Y DECEMBER 1862 James Longstreet had been in the Confederate army for almost a year and a half and had participated in five major campaigns. While Seven Pines represented a colossal blunder, Blackburn's Ford, Williamsburg, the Seven Days battles, Second Manassas, and Antietam gave him a reputation any soldier would envy. How had these experiences affected his outlook on the war? The wartime writings of the reticent Longstreet hold few clues, but it is almost certain that he either had a preference for defensive tactics or was developing one.

As a subordinate, Longstreet was not always free to chose a particular method of warfare, but if he had a preference in combat plans it was probably to allow the enemy to wear himself out attacking a carefully chosen Confederate position and then to subject him to counterattack. Longstreet's counterattacks at Blackburn's Ford and Williamsburg were ineffective, and none had been possible at Antietam. But at Second Manassas, where Lee was guided in part by Longstreet's advice, Longstreet's counterattack was powerfully destructive.

The combination of defense and counterattack was appropriate, given the South's numerical inferiority. It also suited the changes in military technology that had occurred since the Mexican War. When Longstreet fought in Mexico, the soldiers used smoothbore muskets accurate to only approximately 100 yards. A determined attacker could cover the distance rather quickly, allowing his enemy relatively few shots at him. The rifled muskets used during the Civil War, however, were accurate to some 300 yards, giving a defender in 1862 a three times greater chance of killing an attacking enemy.

Longstreet's experience with defensive tactics was strongly augmented by the battle of Fredericksburg, which for the South proved to be a welcome change from the bloodbath campaigns of the summer. McClellan, the familiar and predictable foe, had been replaced after his failure to crush Lee's emaciated army at Antietam. On November 9, 1862, Major General Ambrose E. Burnside took command of the Army of the Potomac. He shifted the scene of action some seventy miles south and east, attempting to steal a march on Lee by crossing the Rappahannock River at Fredericksburg. But a delay in the arrival of his pontoon train allowed the Southern forces time to reach the town ahead of him.[1]

Lee ordered the First Corps to Fredericksburg in mid-November. Longstreet reached the city on the nineteenth or twentieth and made preparations to repulse any Federal crossing of the river. A low range of hills behind the town, together with a sunken road that ran along their base for some distance, provided an excellent defensive position. Longstreet placed his infantry on the hills and at their base, where a stone wall bordering the road formed a natural trench.[2]

Although they were modest compared with the elaborate earthworks that both sides would routinely construct quite rapidly later in the war, Longstreet established extensive field fortifications, working right up to the morning of the battle. Parts of his line, he later informed Lee, were strengthened by "rifle trenches and abatis," and reports from his subordinates refer to rifle pits, trenches, and breastworks of logs and earth.[3]

When Jackson arrived, Lee placed his troops on Longstreet's right flank but without entrenchments. Lee hoped the Federals would so exhaust themselves attacking Longstreet's position that Jackson would be able to counterattack. The plan was thus similar to that for Second Manassas, with Longstreet and Jackson reversing roles.[4]

When Burnside's men finally attacked, on the cold, misty morning of December 13, their major thrust did indeed strike Longstreet. Viewing the mass of men arrayed in plain sight of his chief lieutenant's position, Lee felt some doubt that Longstreet could hold. Longstreet, however, confidently predicted that he could repulse the entire

Federal army with his corps alone. "I will kill them all," he said. Long-street's primary artillerist, E. P. Alexander, remarked, "We cover that ground now so well that we will comb it as with a fine-tooth comb. A chicken could not live on the field when we open on it!"[5]

Longstreet and Lee observed the enemy's advance from one of the hilltops above Fredericksburg that was bristling with Longstreet's artillery. Their position exposed them to the intense counterbattery fire of the Federals, but William Pettit, a young gunner who observed them, found the Confederate leaders seemingly indifferent to the shrapnel that filled the air. "I did not once see them stoop," he wrote his wife later, "tho' others say they sometimes did."[6]

Pettit's description of Longstreet in combat is one of the few left by an enlisted man, worth quotation in full despite its redundancies:

> Lt. Gen. Longstreet wore a gray military coat and pants, the coat with remarkably short skirts or tail. It was a frock coat, of course, and did not reach the middle of his thighs. He wore the same every day. He wore a gray or lead colored shawl wrapped closely around his neck and shoulders, and kept in place by holding it together with his hands and arms, which were generally wrapped up in it. No marks of insignia of rank were visible. His hat was plain black felt, with rather narrow brim and high crown. A plain sword hung at his side. He is about six feet 2 inches high, of strong round frame, portly and fleshy but not corpulent or too fat. His hair is dark auburn and long, his whiskers and moustache of same color and thick and heavy. His forehead is broad and full, his brows heavy. His nose, straight and rather fleshy, and his eyes, which set in close to his nose, are dark and steady in their movements and gaze. The lids come quite close together. He is about medium size and height and weighs, I suppose, 190 pounds. He was almost always walking to and fro, except when gazing upon the battlefield with his shawl closely hugged about his neck and shoulders, apparently intensely thinking. He spoke but seldom, and then in rather a low tone. He had a very intellectual appearance, is certainly a very industrious man, and an energetic, skillful officer. Next to Lee I should prefer entrusting the chief command of our armies to him.[7]

The Federal attack against Longstreet's entrenched position was marked by courage and tenacity. Longstreet was compelled to reinforce his front line at the stone wall, and shortages of artillery and small arms ammunition caused momentary anxiety. Yet the issue was never seriously in doubt. No enemy soldier got closer than thirty

yards to the stone wall, and by the end of the day the ground in front
of Longstreet's position was carpeted with prostrate men in blue.[8]
After some initial difficulty, Jackson's corps turned back a parallel
thrust. Lee's casualties of 5,309 to Burnside's 12,653 made Fredericksburg one of the great Southern victories of the war. Lee's losses were
significant, however, and though hideously mangled, the enemy army
was far from destroyed. Fearing further attacks (which Burnside did
indeed contemplate), Lee did not order Jackson to counterattack as he
had originally planned.[9]

The battle was an impressive lesson in the power of the defensive. J. E. B. Stuart, Lee's famous cavalry commander, wrote shortly
afterward: "The victory won by us here is one of the neatest and
cheapest of the war. Englishmen here who surveyed Solferino & all
the battlefields of Italy say the pile of dead on the plains of Fredericksburg exceeds anything of the sort ever seen by them."[10]

In previous combats, Longstreet had always used the terrain to
his best advantage, but at Fredericksburg he had improved upon it
with field fortifications. As a result, and also because of the fortuitous
stone wall, his corps hardly budged an inch under the most intense
assault the war had yet seen and suffered only 1,894 casualties. Some
of Jackson's forces were pushed back by the Federal advance on their
part of the field and regained their positions only after costly counterattacks. Jackson's unentrenched men took 3,415 casualties, almost
twice those suffered by Longstreet's.[11]

The implications were not lost on Longstreet. Burnside tried to
turn Lee's left (Longstreet's position) in mid-January but was stymied
by bad weather in a debacle his soldiers promptly labeled the "Mud
March." Afterward, both sides settled into winter quarters. To guard
against any further winter activities and to prepare for a Federal advance in the spring, Longstreet constructed a system of fieldworks
along his left flank, guarding the upstream fords of the Rappahannock.[12]

The system incorporated an important new feature, the traverse
trench. Earlier trenches were dug as long ditches, the earth piled up
in front to form a wall. Often they ran in straight lines, protecting
soldiers against fire from the front but leaving their sides vulnerable,
particularly to artillery shells. As these shells flung shrapnel in all di-

rections, even a near miss could be deadly. Longstreet greatly lessened the danger from artillery by building short earth walls to traverse his trenches at regular intervals. Running perpendicular to the main trench wall, the traverses separated the men into a series of compartments, covered on each flank.[13]

The idea for traverses may have originated with Longstreet himself or perhaps with one of his engineers. In any case, the General deserves much credit for incorporating the idea into his fieldworks and for bringing it into wider use. At Jackson's request he sent instructions on how to build traverses, thereby greatly increasing the effectiveness of Lee's whole force. Military historian Donald Sanger notes in his biography of Longstreet: "From this small and somewhat crude beginning grew the highly complicated modern systems of field fortifications in depth. If James Longstreet had contributed nothing else to the science of war, this alone should place him on the list of those whom posterity honors."[14]

During this period Longstreet made additions to his staff. Raphael Moses, one of the few Jewish officers in the Southern armies, became chief of commissary. Osmun Latrobe of Maryland became assistant inspector and adjutant general. When Sorrel transferred to line service in 1864, Latrobe became chief of staff. Francis Dawson, an Englishman who had served in the Confederate navy, joined the ordnance department of Longstreet's Corps.[15]

One of the most trusted members of Longstreet's inner circle was Edward Porter Alexander of Georgia, who commanded the First Corps Reserve Artillery. The General made almost daily use of Alexander's engineering and reconnaissance skills. He soon directed almost all of Longstreet's artillery; the General's appointed chief of artillery, Major James B. Walton, proved physically unfit for rigorous campaigning. Alexander was clearly more skilled than Walton as well, but Walton commanded the Washington Artillery, and the New Orleans cannoneers remained Longstreet's soft spot. He postponed the humiliating removal of their chief until 1864.[16]

Containing men from Georgia, Louisiana, Maryland, Mississippi, Texas, and Virginia, Longstreet's staff was much more of a cross section of the Confederacy than Lee's or Jackson's and lacked their clerical element. It is indicative of Longstreet's own personality and his backwoods upbringing that he chose to surround himself primarily with rough young bon vivants who gambled, drank, and played practical jokes on each other.[17]

Despite the informality of the men, Longstreet's staff has been described as the finest in the Confederacy.[18] The key was in the way he used it. As he commanded only a corps, not an army, he faced an easier task than Lee, but the difference in their methods is illuminating.

As Longstreet had learned at Second Manassas, Lee could be impatient with matters concerning reconnaissance, and once battle was joined, Lee left his corps commanders essentially on their own. Even given the difficulties that faced every commander in the nineteenth century, when armies had grown too large to be viewed in the line of sight and information still moved by horseback, Lee's battlefield control was minimal.

Longstreet's remarkable physical stamina allowed him to make personally the sort of meticulous observations that were beyond a man of Lee's age and indifferent health. The General's own observations were augmented by those of his staff, whom he often drove to the point of exhaustion in coordinating his troop movements. Because he kept such tight control, Longstreet's attacks were usually more powerful than those of his peers. By 1863, although Jackson's fame far outshone his own, and Lee, Johnston, and Beauregard were all far better known, Longstreet was considered by some observers to be the finest combat officer in the South.[19] When it came to directing troops once the fighting had begun, he probably had no superior on either side during the war.

Longstreet's first assignment of the new year 1863 involved little fighting, however. Lee found it increasingly difficult to obtain adequate supplies for his men. He was threatened not only by the Federal army across the Rappahannock but also by growing enemy forces in northeastern North Carolina. These had expanded to some 20,000, endangering his rear. Lee therefore dispatched two divisions to operate south of the James River. They would counter Federal activity and, equally important, would gather provisions for themselves and the rest of the army.[20] Probably because he wanted to keep Jackson free to operate in the Valley if necessary, he gave command of the two divisions to Longstreet.

Longstreet's reinforcements were a big help to the Confederates already operating in southeast Virginia and northeast North Carolina, but the arrangements boded ill. Longstreet was ordered to report directly to the War Department, yet he was still subordinate to Lee and subject to recall by him. Longstreet's new command was really three separate departments, two in Virginia and one in North Carolina, commanded by Major Generals Arnold Elzy, Samuel French, and D. H. Hill. He was supposed to coordinate the work in these three departments but could make no changes in them.[21]

Thanks to Longstreet's tireless efforts, Lee's men began to receive adequate food supplies once more, and for this important, if unglamorous, work he deserves much credit.[22] Longstreet's operations against the enemy were not successful, but they reflected his growing respect for the power of defensive warfare.

Longstreet supported D. H. Hill's efforts to capture New Bern and Washington, North Carolina, and mounted an offensive of his own against Suffolk, Virginia. Lee urged Longstreet to be aggressive, and Longstreet believed all three towns could have fallen before determined attacks. But with the example of Fredericksburg fresh in his mind, Longstreet was wary of the enemy's fortifications and resorted to siege tactics. Pyrrhic victories would not advance the Southern cause. He considered the casualties that would be incurred by direct assaults not worth the prizes to be gained. He was eventually forced to lift his sieges and won no great victories while detached from Lee, but he returned with two divisions that were fit and able. Secretary of War James A. Seddon praised Longstreet for his restraint, declaring that his accomplishment in supplying Lee's forces was enough to consider the campaign a success.[23]

Longstreet's men were not present for the Chancellorsville campaign against Major General Joseph Hooker, the new Federal commander. Their absence was unavoidable and did not reflect any desire on Longstreet's part to prolong his separation from Lee. The correspondence between the two men during this period shows clearly that, although his title made him department commander, Longstreet considered himself fully subject to Lee's orders.[24] Lee kept his distant lieutenant fully informed regarding the possibility of operations along the Rappahannock and explained what they might mean for Longstreet.[25] Longstreet, for his part, was careful to describe how any operations he proposed in southeastern Virginia might affect his ability to return quickly. Longstreet frequently deferred to Lee and sought his advice.[26]

A letter from Longstreet to Lee on March 19 shows how he viewed both his role on detached assignment and his professional relationship with his commander: "I know that it is the habit with individuals in all armies to represent their own positions as the most important ones, and it may be that this feeling is operating with me; but I am not prompted by any desire to do, or attempt to do, great things. I only wish to do what I regard as my duty—give you the full benefit of my views."[27] After the war, Longstreet wrote that Lee wanted his executive officer to be not a yes man but someone who would discuss problems vigorously and would offer alternatives:

> He always invited [my views] in moves of strategy and general policy, not so much for the purpose of having his own views approved and confirmed as to get new lights, or channels for new thought, and was more pleased when he found something that gave him new strength than with efforts to evade his questions by compliments. When oppressed by severe study, he sometimes sent for me to say that he had applied himself so closely to a matter that he found his ideas running around in a circle, and was in need of help to find a tangent.[28]

Lee would have been a poor commander had he ignored the benefits of his subordinate's views. But it cannot be said that he was dominated by Longstreet or that Longstreet was trying to dominate him.

Lee had no complaints concerning Longstreet's actions on detached service and in a letter on May 7 expressed awareness that Longstreet's return in time for Chancellorsville had been a physical impossibility.[29] The battle had been a tremendous victory but an expensive one, costing Lee not only 13,000 men but also his famous third in command. The wounded Stonewall Jackson died on May 10. To replace him Lee chose not one man but two, creating a Third Corps and thereby bringing more flexibility to his command structure. Late in May, Richard S. Ewell and A. P. Hill learned that they would be promoted to lieutenant general and assigned to the Second and Third corps, respectively.[30]

At the same time, though he never knew it, Lee almost lost James Longstreet. The First Corps commander was happy at the promotion of his friend Ewell, who was the army's senior major general, but was unhappy about Hill's promotion. According to a letter he wrote to Lafayette McLaws on June 3, 1863, he and McLaws were both so discontent that they had recently discussed leaving the Army of Northern Virginia.

> You spoke of going South the other day. If you wish to go I expect that I may make the arrangements for you that I was speaking of for myself. That is for you to go there and let Beauregard come here with a Corps. . . . I understand that Beauregard is anxious to join this army, and if he is I believe that I can accomplish what I have mentioned. I do not know, however, and can only promise to make the effort if it is desirable to you.[31]

A letter that McLaws later wrote to his wife indicates that Longstreet had had in mind a straight swap with Beauregard.[32] He was thinking of offering the First Corps to Beauregard, just as he had offered it to Johnston in October 1862, eight months earlier.

The deal Longstreet contemplated for McLaws was similar. McLaws would take Beauregard's position as commander of the Department of South Carolina, Georgia, and Florida; Beauregard would come to Virginia as commander of an entirely new corps, drawn largely from troops presently defending the Atlantic seacoast. Longstreet hoped that Beauregard would not merely play a supporting role, operating elsewhere in Virginia, but would officially join Lee's army. This point is significant, for Beauregard outranked Longstreet. It indicates that Longstreet was not jealous of his position as Lee's second in command.[33]

It is easy to understand why McLaws would want to part with Lee, for he had been next to Ewell in seniority. Powell Hill had been promoted over his head and over that of D. H. Hill as well—an apparent sign of gross favoritism. McLaws promptly complained. Lee's response is not known, but as McLaws was thinking of transferring, he could not have found it satisfactory.[34]

Possibly Longstreet was considering a transfer to the coast because Confederate activity there would be largely defensive. His motive may also have involved a perfectly natural desire for advancement; the coastal command would mean independence and quite possibly promotion to full general.

It is certainly not likely that Longstreet resented Hill's promotion over McLaws strongly enough to make him consider leaving Lee in protest. On the other hand, Hill's move up the ladder did prompt Longstreet and others to wonder whether his main qualification lay in being a native Virginian.[35] Longstreet may have felt that a sort of "Virginia-ism" pervaded the army. In April 1862, for instance, Johnston appointed as his chief of artillery the inept William Nelson Pendleton, an Episcopal minister who led the Rockbridge Artillery. Some officers from the Deep South saw this move as an example of the favoritism usually shown Virginians.[36] In April 1863, two months prior to Longstreet's contemplated transfer, Brigadier General William Dorsey Pender despaired of promotion, believing that his North Carolina origins would prejudice Stonewall Jackson and President Davis against him.[37] Pender was eventually promoted, but his fears were shared by others. Wade Hampton of South Carolina believed that Virginians received too many promotions in the cavalry corps. Virginia did contribute more troops to Lee's army than any other single state, but the majority of its forces came from other states. Yet in the spring of 1863 six of the army's division commanders and two of its three corps commanders were Virginia born.[38]

Virginia-ism did not involve the president and the army's high command alone. A few months before Jackson's death and Hill's promotion, McLaws wrote to Ewell, whom he and Longstreet had known since West Point:

> Do you know there is a strong feeling growing among the Southern troops against Virginia, caused by the jealousy of her own people for those from every other state? No matter who it is may perform a glorious act, Virginia papers give but a grudging praise unless the actor is a Virginian. No matter how trifling the deed may be which a Virginian performs it is heralded at once as the most glorious of modern times.[39]

Longstreet, McLaws continued, "has no superior as a soldier in the Southern Confederacy," yet the press never gave him proper credit, simply because he was not a Virginian.[40]

A desire to escape the bias and receive the recognition he unquestionably deserved may have been part of the reason Longstreet contemplated leaving Lee. But probably more significant was the growing divergence of their views on the overall war effort. In general terms, Longstreet believed that the main peril lay in the western theater, necessitating a reinforcement of the armies there with men from Virginia. Lee did not always agree.

One of Lee's great contributions in the East lay in persuading Davis to apply the principle of concentration of force, taking advantage of the South's railway network to exploit its interior lines of communication. According to the theory, the South's limited manpower should be concentrated where it was most needed and most likely to produce results rather than spread thin in a vain attempt to protect every inch of territory. Lee therefore frequently called for reinforcements from the West, the Deep South, and the seacoast to defend the capital. He made good use of those he got; Union prospects in the Eastern theater in early 1863 were no better than they had been two years previously.

Lee agreed that the principle of concentration of force might necessitate sending troops from his army to other locations to meet particular crises. In practice, however, he vigorously resisted almost every attempt to diminish his force, employing arguments that revealed his limited knowledge of Southern geography, climate, and the scope and aim of the enemy's various advances. Historians Herman Hattaway and Archer Jones explain Lee's resistance to troop transfers in terms of any commander's natural tendency to magnify his own perils and reluctance to reduce his forces in the face of grave dangers. Thomas L. Connelly, however, argues that Lee's concern for defending Virginia amounted to an obsession which warped his strategic thinking.[41]

Longstreet believed that the fate of the Confederacy lay across the Appalachians, and it is easy to see why in the spring of 1863 he thought the region demanded immediate attention. Early in the war Albert Sidney Johnston was driven out of Kentucky and Middle and West Tennessee with embarrassing ease. His unsuccessful attempt to recoup Confederate fortunes at Shiloh in April 1862 cost him his life. His army, later the nucleus of the Army of Tennessee, passed briefly to Beauregard and then to General Braxton Bragg. Bragg enjoyed Davis's firm admiration and support, but his defeat at Stones River in January 1863 caused many to question his ability and sparked rumors that he would be replaced. While Longstreet was operating around Suffolk, Bragg's forces occupied a line south of Murfreesboro, near

Tullahoma, Tennessee. A Federal advance against Bragg could threaten vital rail connections at Chattanooga or Decatur, Alabama. If either city fell, the heartland of the Confederacy would be open to invasion.[42]

Another threat lay at Vicksburg, the last major Southern stronghold on the Mississippi. The garrison there under Lieutenant General John C. Pemberton faced a determined advance by Longstreet's kinsman, Ulysses S. Grant. Joseph E. Johnston had the task of coordinating the defense of Middle Tennessee and the river city. Spring found him at Jackson, Mississippi, heading a small force that sought to succor Pemberton.[43]

Longstreet kept close track of these events. His concerns made him a member of an important informal organization which Connelly and Jones have labeled the "western concentration bloc." This complex group of army officers and politicians was bound by family ties, long-standing friendships, common strategic views, and personal ambitions. It came into being in 1862, when Sidney Johnston's cordon defense of the West failed disastrously. Although they were concerned about the entire trans-Appalachian region, by early 1863 the members of the western concentration bloc particularly feared a Federal thrust against Bragg, as this would threaten vital war industries, particularly munitions, in East Tennessee, Georgia, and Alabama. They therefore advocated a reinforcement of Bragg from Lee's army.[44]

Longstreet's concern for the West may have reflected purely military judgment, but he must have worried for his relatives in northern Georgia and Alabama. More important, leadership of the western concentration bloc centered on three friends he greatly admired: Joseph E. Johnston, P. G. T. Beauregard, and Louis T. Wigfall. He not only matched their calls for a western reinforcement, he hoped to lead it himself.

Less than a month after Fredericksburg, Longstreet suggested to Lee that "one army corps could hold the Rappahannock while the other was operating elsewhere."[45] In February 1863 he wrote Wigfall that he was anxious to be sent west with reinforcements, as there appeared to be "opportunities for all kinds of moves to great advantage" there.[46] While operating in southeastern Virginia that spring, Longstreet discussed strategy with Secretary of War Seddon, who routinely

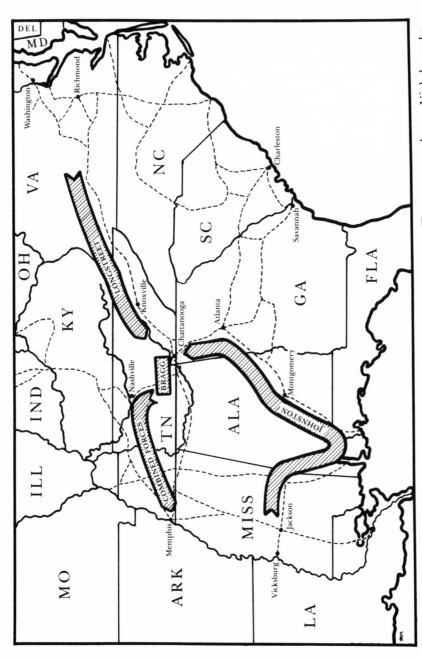

In May 1863 Longstreet proposed a western concentration to recover Tennessee and save Vicksburg by threatening the enemy's communications.

heard the views of high-ranking officers.[47] During their talk Seddon suggested that Longstreet, with part of Lee's forces, unite with Johnston in Mississippi to save Pemberton's besieged army. Longstreet suggested instead that all or part of his corps, together with Johnston's men, reinforce Bragg at Tullahoma. The Army of Tennessee thus greatly enlarged could defeat the Federals in Middle Tennessee (commanded, incidentally, by Rosecrans, Longstreet's West Point roommate). Afterward, the Confederates could force Grant to retreat from Vicksburg by threatening his line of communications. Seddon liked the idea but doubted that Lee could be persuaded to part with any troops, and Davis was unlikely to go against Lee's wishes.[48]

While Longstreet's plan was strategically sound, his motives in offering it must be questioned. Given the recent criticism of Bragg, Longstreet may have hoped to replace him, an idea he knew Senator Wigfall favored. He would have known, however, that Wigfall was politicking primarily to have Johnston take Bragg's place, to take direct control of the Army of Tennessee.[49] Although he may have hoped for more, Longstreet's plan indicated his willingness to serve as a mere corps commander under Johnston. This is hardly surprising, given his earlier evaluation of Johnston relative to Lee. Not until March 1863 did Longstreet's service under Lee exceed that which he had done under Johnston, who as a leader of the western concentration bloc continued to elicit Longstreet's admiration. Longstreet may even have looked upon his former chief nostalgically, remembering the early days when the war had seemed simple, even gay.

Whatever Longstreet's interest in the western theater, Lee effectively blocked any concentration there by convincing Davis that he might soon be forced back into the entrenchments surrounding Richmond. To avoid this possibility, Lee argued for an advance into Pennsylvania. This tactic would draw the Federals out of Virginia and perhaps North Carolina as well, sparing agricultural regions essential to the war effort. In Pennsylvania Lee would supply himself at the enemy's expense. Any apparent threat to Washington would certainly disrupt the Federals' summer plans and might erode civilian support for the war.[50]

Longstreet supported Lee's plan fully, although it meant temporarily shelving his interest in the West. On May 13 he explained to Senator Wigfall: "When I agreed with the Secy [Seddon] & yourself about sending troops west it was under the impression that we would be obliged to remain on the defensive here. But the prospect of an advance changes the aspect of affairs to us entirely."[51]

Perhaps Longstreet thought a northern thrust would cause the Federals to divert troops to the East, relieving pressure on Bragg and Pemberton. It is likely, too, that he was loath to leave Lee soon after Jackson's death, realizing that so great a change in the command structure might hurt the army.[52] His interest in the move may also have stemmed from Lee's apparent commitment to defensive tactics.

Longstreet discussed the forthcoming campaign with Lee throughout the remainder of May, after his forces rejoined the main army at Fredericksburg. Drawing on his past experiences, he urged Lee to combine his proposed strategic offensive with defensive tactics. Once the Army of Northern Virginia was on enemy soil, the Federals would be virtually compelled to attack by public pressure, if for no other reason. A careful selection of ground, perhaps a position across the enemy's line of communications, might allow Lee to win another relatively inexpensive victory like Fredericksburg.[53]

Lee agreed that the suggestion was sensible. As historians Hattaway and Jones note, Lee envisioned the invasion of Pennsylvania essentially as a foraging raid; he was not seeking a climactic battle to end the war. Lee's later report of the campaign, some of the earliest histories of it, the memoirs of his military secretary, and a wartime letter by one of Longstreet's division commanders all indicate that Lee originally planned to avoid an offensive battle in Pennsylvania.[54]

Longstreet believed that Lee's commitment to defensive tactics was firm, but he apparently did not believe in 1863 that Lee had *promised* to remain on the defensive. He never made a direct statement to that effect, although he did imply it in some of his postwar writings. As the Army of Northern Virginia marched north, Longstreet merely expected Lee to fight a defensive battle if a favorable opportunity arose.[55]

The campaign that followed has become the most controversial of the war. It was marked by courage and valor so intense that it is still breathtaking more than 100 years after the fact. It also severely stretched the friendship between Longstreet and Lee and brought into sharp focus the difference between their methods of generalship.

3. "The Best Fighter in the Whole Army"

LEE BEGAN HIS PENNSYLVANIA campaign on June 3, sweeping far west of the main Federal forces in Virginia, using the Shenandoah Valley to cover his advance into Maryland and Pennsylvania. Ewell's Second Corps spearheaded the advance, capturing Winchester, Virginia, on the fourteenth. Ewell then moved into Pennsylvania, turning east at Chambersburg, dispersing his corps to capture York and Carlisle. Longstreet and Hill followed a few days behind, reaching Chambersburg on the twenty-seventh.[1]

Although Lee had ignored Harpers Ferry, by June 28 his army was as widely scattered as it had been during the Antietam campaign. Nonetheless, Lee felt secure, for Jeb Stuart, his trusted cavalry commander, had been instructed to protect the army's flanks and to bring word if the Union army left Virginia. Exercising the discretion granted in his orders, Stuart had broken free of Lee's army, passing completely around the Army of the Potomac. As he had not yet heard from Stuart, Lee naively assumed that he was in no danger.[2]

This assumption was rudely dispelled on June 28 when Henry Thomas Harrison, a spy in Longstreet's employ, accurately reported the position of the Federals, also bringing the news that Hooker had been replaced by Major General George Gordon Meade. The enemy was actually dangerously close, some units being as near as South Mountain, only a few days' march away. Lee therefore issued orders for a concentration at or near Gettysburg, a small village where the roads from Chambersburg, York, and Carlisle converged.[3]

Lee was not panicked, however. Indeed, it would be difficult to exaggerate the confidence he felt in the Army of Northern Virginia. Only a month before he had written in a private letter: "The Country cannot overestimate its worth. There never were such men in any Army before & there never can be better in any army again. If properly led they will go anywhere & never falter at the work before them."[4]

Lee took steps to prevent the sort of looting and pillaging that marked the Maryland campaign, and according to legend the behavior of the Southerners in Pennsylvania was almost saintly. While wanton destruction was rare, individual soldiers nevertheless foraged freely. Hood's Texas Brigade lived up to its reputation for collecting everything edible for miles around. An officer in the Third Corps confessed that there was "a general uprooting of gardens and depopulation of hen houses." A Maryland soldier was more explicit in a letter home: "We gave the old dutch in Penn. fits. Our Army left a mark everywhere it went. Horses, cattle, sheep, hogs, chickens, spring Houses suffered alike."[5] Such activities were expected, given Lee's intention of living off the country.

There was certainly no shortage of food at Longstreet's headquarters, which was always noted for the quality of its mess. Perhaps as a result, a number of foreign visitors more or less attached themselves to the First Corps during the campaign. The memoirs of these men provide an invaluable objective view of Longstreet during his most controversial campaign.

The most prominent visitor was Arthur Fremantle, a British lieutenant colonel, who found Longstreet "a particularly taciturn man." He noted that Longstreet was "never far from General Lee, who relies very much upon his judgement. By the soldiers he is invariably spoken of as 'the best fighter in the whole army.' "[6] Colonel Fitzgerald Ross of Austria-Hungary also commented on the closeness between Longstreet and Lee. Other observers who attached themselves to the General included Major Justus Scheibert of Prussia and two British newspapermen, Frank Vizetelly and Francis C. Lawley.[7]

Shortly after Lee ordered his concentration, these foreign visitors witnessed enough carnage to make their respective transatlantic crossings worthwhile. On the morning of July 1, Major General Harry

Heth's division of Hill's corps marched southeast along the Chambersburg Pike (also called the Cashtown Road) toward Gettysburg. About eight in the morning the troops encountered dismounted Federal cavalrymen just outside the village. A skirmish developed which escalated into a pitched battle as reinforcements arrived on each side. When A. P. Hill joined the battle with the bulk of his corps, he discovered that he was facing not just cavalry but the First and Eleventh corps of the Army of the Potomac. Around noon, brigades from Ewell's corps began arriving from Carlisle, threatening the enemy's right flank and rear. In the early afternoon the Federal line slowly collapsed, the troops retreating through Gettysburg in some disorder.[8]

Although losses had been heavy, the Confederates had matched their recent performance at Chancellorsville. Decisive victory escaped them, however, thanks in part to the caution of Ewell and one of his division commanders, Jubal Early. The fleeing Federals were observed rallying on Cemetery Hill, an 80-foot rise south of the town. Just east of this was Culp's Hill, a rocky knob rising to a full 100 feet. But although several hours of daylight remained, no attempt was made to dislodge the enemy from this strong defensive position before he could receive reinforcements.[9]

The Confederate troops closest to Cemetery Hill were commanded by Early, whose timely arrival had contributed greatly to the victory thus far. There was nothing to prevent Early from continuing his advance across the strategic Cemetery Hill while Federal resistance was still embryonic. One of Early's four brigades had not been engaged, and losses in the other three had been light. Early, however, halted his troops and rode into Gettysburg in search of Ewell.[10]

Ewell, meanwhile, was showing even less initiative than his subordinate. He was new to corps-level command, and he had difficulty in interpreting Lee's orders. The need to seize Cemetery Hill was obvious to him, but Lee had instructed him not to bring on a major action until the army was well concentrated. Under such circumstances, what should he do? In the end he did nothing, to the amazement of his staff. Several of them argued, with heat bordering on mutiny, that as a general battle had already been fought, it was ridiculous not to follow it up by driving the enemy from the hills overlooking and commanding the town.[11]

When Early at last located Ewell in Gettysburg, a precious hour had been lost. By halting his troops, Early had missed a magnificent opportunity. But now that he could shift responsibility to his chief, he argued for an advance. While the two men discussed the matter, new orders arrived from Lee. The Confederate commander ordered Ewell to take Cemetery Hill "if he found it practicable, but to avoid a general engagement until the arrival of the other divisions of the army," which were hurrying forward.[12]

These instructions confused Ewell even further. A general engagement had already been fought, but Lee seemed to want to avoid a second one. In Stuart's absence Ewell had no way of knowing the position of the rest of the Union army and could not determine whether an immediate attack on Cemetery Hill would produce the sort of contest Lee feared. As Lee did not seem to want Cemetery Hill badly enough to fight for it, it is not surprising that the vacillating Ewell finally decided not to try to take it. Years later, with humility rare in a professional soldier, Ewell admitted that his hesitation was a major blunder.[13] Yet it is hard to fault him for exercising the discretion that Lee's orders granted. The real fault lay with Lee; a single positive word from him would have placed Cemetery Hill in Southern hands before dark.

Lee was on the battlefield by late afternoon, viewing the field from Seminary Ridge, a line of low hills just west of Gettysburg which ran roughly north-south. Longstreet was with him, both men having been drawn to the conflict by the sound of the guns.[14] Longstreet had begun the day as he so often did, riding with General Lee. It was a day of frustrations and delays. Longstreet's men did not break camp until 9:00 A.M., not from laziness, but because the road they were supposed to use was blocked, making an earlier start impossible. As Lee's scattered forces drew together, too many men were attempting to use the same route, and the efficiency which usually marked Lee's movements was missing. The First Corps was on the Chambersburg Pike, which ran east through Fayetteville and Greenwood, passing through the mountains just before it reached Cashtown. From that point, where it began to dip south toward Gettysburg, it was usually called the Cashtown Road. Longstreet's men, moving east, halted frequently to let troops from Ewell's and Hill's commands pass by. One of his divisions did not begin its march until 4:00 P.M., although it had been standing in ranks, waiting for the other corps to pass, since 8:00 A.M. This pace was too slow for Lee, who soon rode ahead to check on the army's advance elements.

Longstreet remained behind for a while with his corps. He now commanded three divisions. Two of these were under old friends, Lafayette McLaws and George Pickett. The third was in the hands of John Bell Hood, a Texan with a high reputation as a combat officer. Pickett's division had been left behind at Chambersburg as the army's rear guard, but even reduced to two-thirds of its normal strength, Longstreet's column, marching in good order with its ranks well closed, occupied some seven miles of roadway. An army corps occupied a great deal of physical space, especially when its logistical support is considered as well. Ewell's wagon train, which had to pass before the First Corps could begin its day's march, was estimated by McLaws to have been fourteen miles long.[15]

The late start and frequent halts meant that for Longstreet's men, Gettysburg was still more than a day's march away. Fremantle, the British visitor, noted that Longstreet was impatient to press forward. The General moved through the rear of Hill's and Ewell's columns. As he did so, the young Briton had an opportunity to gauge Longstreet's standing among the enlisted men outside his own command. In his diary, Fremantle recorded the reaction of the famous Stonewall Brigade.

> As they have nearly always been on detached duty, few of them knew General Longstreet, except by reputation. Numbers of them asked me whether the General in front was Longstreet; and when I answered in the affirmative, many would run on a hundred yards in order to take a good look at him. This I take to be an immense compliment from any soldier on a long march.[16]

Later in the afternoon, Fremantle recorded a similar incident which illustrates Longstreet's reputation as a fighter: "After passing Johnson's division, we came to a Florida Brigade which is now in Hill's corps; but as it had formerly served under Longstreet, the men knew him well. Some of them (after the General had passed) called out to their comrades, 'Look out for work now, boys, for here's the old bulldog again.'"[17]

Longstreet soon spurred his horse ahead toward the front of the column. As he neared Gettysburg, the echo of artillery fire revealed that a major fight was in progress. According to Fremantle, who accompanied Longstreet, they reached Seminary Ridge at 4:30 P.M.[18] Although the chronology is difficult to establish, Lee had probably just sent his orders to Ewell concerning Cemetery Hill as Longstreet rode up.

After studying the Federals on the distant knob, Longstreet was impressed with the potential strength of the enemy's position, particularly if the Army of the Potomac was concentrating rapidly. Just south of Cemetery Hill, Longstreet could see Cemetery Ridge, which ran due south for over a mile, roughly parallel to Seminary Ridge. Almost eighty feet at its northern tip, the ridge descended gradually along its length, giving way to a stretch of relatively open terrain. Beyond rose two high knobs, known as the Round Tops. The closest of these, Little Round Top, caught the eye, as a recent logging operation had left its rocky crest bare. To walk these two hills north along Cemetery Ridge to Cemetery Hill, and across to Culp's Hill, would be to trace a path four miles long, shaped like an inverted J or fishhook.[19]

If the approaching Federals occupied any portion of this position, they would be difficult to dislodge. Longstreet therefore suggested that they be content with the day's splendid victory. If the Confederates moved south and east across Meade's line of communications, they might find a strong defensive position of their own, and Meade would be forced to do the costly attacking.[20]

To Longstreet's surprise, Lee announced his intention of attacking the enemy where they stood on the following day. A flanking movement, he explained, would expose the long Confederate baggage train to attack. He also believed that only a portion of the Union forces was present, giving him an opportunity to destroy the Army of the Potomac piecemeal. Lee considered an attack on the following day to be "in a measure unavoidable, and the success already gained gave hope for a favorable issue."[21] With contact established, the Confederates could no longer forage at will. Lee may have worried that he would not be able to remain on the defensive long enough had he adopted Longstreet's suggestion.

As soon as Lee announced his decision to attack on July 2, Longstreet dispatched couriers back along the Cashtown Road to hurry his divisions forward as rapidly as possible. More he could not do, as Lee had yet to issue orders, verbal or otherwise, indicating *when* or *where* he intended to attack. Such a decision could not possibly be made until daylight on the morrow revealed what positions the fleeing Federals had occupied during the night and whether they had received reinforcements.[22]

At about sunset Longstreet and his staff moved back down the Cashtown Road toward the approaching columns of the General's divisions. Soon they met Dr. J. S. D. Cullen, the First Corps chief surgeon, who spoke confidently of fresh victories on the following day. Cullen was surprised to find Longstreet concerned about the strength of the Union position. Fremantle also noticed Longstreet's concern. During supper that night the younger officers spoke contemptuously of their foes, but the more experienced Longstreet remarked that the enemy's position would be difficult to carry.[23]

After Longstreet's departure, Lee rode to the position of the Second Corps to discuss what might be done on that flank for the next day's operations. He spoke at length with Ewell and two of his subordinates, Jubal Early and Robert E. Rodes. An outspoken Early convinced Lee that it would be impossible for the Second Corps to attack Cemetery and Culp's hills successfully because of the difficult terrain and the strength of the enemy. Lee suggested shifting the Second Corps to the right to shorten the Confederate line, but Ewell, Early, and Rodes all believed that such a move would damage the men's morale.[24]

Having reached an impasse, Lee returned to his headquarters without giving Ewell any orders at all, but he soon summoned Ewell and they discussed tactics once more. Now separated from his naysaying division commanders, Ewell agreed that an attack was feasible. He left Lee's camp at about midnight but still had no orders concerning the *time* he was expected to attack on July 2. The issue could not be settled, now that it was dark. As Colonel Charles Marshall of Lee's staff recalled, Lee had already "examined the ground," on the Confederate right, but as yet he "had found no favorable point to attack." Further reconnaissance after daylight would be necessary before all plans could be finalized and coordinated.[25]

Longstreet did everything possible to ready his two divisions for

Lee's instant use the next morning. McLaws's men marched until midnight, sleeping at a campsite that the General had selected for them two or three miles west of Gettysburg. By dawn they were en route once more. Yet their march was easy, compared with that of Hood's division. Passing McLaws's camp during the night, Hood's men reached Gettysburg at sunrise, having halted for only two hours' rest during the whole night.[26]

Longstreet himself did not retire until long after midnight, yet rose between 3:00 and 3:30 A.M. on July 2. Leaving his staff breakfasting, he rode ahead, apparently alone, to meet Lee on Seminary Ridge. Fremantle, who arrived at 5:00 A.M. with Longstreet's staff, saw Longstreet, Hill, Hood, and Lee in conference. Longstreet and Hood whittled sticks as they talked.[27]

Many who saw Lee on July 2 remembered him as nervous, irritable, and restless. Major Scheibert, the Prussian observer, was struck by the contrast between Lee's demeanor at Gettysburg and at Chancellorsville. During Chancellorsville Lee had been calm, but in Pennsylvania Lee displayed an "uneasiness" which Scheibert thought unsettled all the officers about him.[28]

Lee may have felt ill.[29] If so, he spent an active morning nevertheless. He dispatched an aide-de-camp to confer with Ewell once more, for he had not entirely abandoned the idea of shifting the Second Corps to the right. To explore the terrain in that direction, and to determine what ground the enemy occupied along Cemetery Ridge and in the direction of the Round Tops, Lee ordered a reconnaissance by Captain Samuel R. Johnston of his staff and Major J. J. Clarke, one of Longstreet's engineers. They were accompanied at least part of the way by Pendleton, Lee's chief of artillery, and some of Pendleton's aides. Johnston gave an oral report on his return; Pendleton sent notes to both Lee and Longstreet following his observations.[30]

Disturbed by Lee's determination to attack, Longstreet on the morning of July 2 proposed a flanking movement. Lee was not interested. Confident of a Confederate victory with the troops on hand, he also refused a request by Longstreet to delay operations until Pickett's division could reach the field.[31] When McLaws arrived at the head of his column at 8:00 A.M., Lee sent for him immediately, and together they reviewed a map of the region, discussing Lee's plans for

the day. Lee had decided to attempt a surprise attack on the Union
left flank, hoping to repeat his success at Chancellorsville. Hood and
McLaws were to move by a circuitous concealed route to a position on
the Emmitsburg Road, which ran in front of Cemetery Ridge. Forming a battle line perpendicular to the road, their two divisions would
sweep north, catching the Federals on Cemetery Ridge in the flank.[32]

Longstreet spoke up, questioning the proposed angle of
McLaws's line. Lee overruled him on this issue but made no objection
when Longstreet denied McLaws permission to make his own reconnaissance. Both Lee and Longstreet assumed that Johnston's observations would be sufficient. Throughout this discussion, McLaws noted
that Longstreet was "irritated and annoyed" but did not speculate
upon the cause. Longstreet may have been upset because Lee was not
going to use defensive tactics or because the jittery Lee had ignored the
usual chain of command by issuing orders directly to McLaws. In any
case, Longstreet made immediate preparations to obey Lee's orders.
McLaws's division was placed under cover to rest until Captain Johnston came to act as a guide. According to McLaws, Lee witnessed this
move and approved.[33]

Having finalized his plans for the right flank, Lee turned his
attention to the left. At approximately 9:00 A.M. Lee reached Ewell's
headquarters, located in a house near the Hanover Road, which provided an exit from Gettysburg to the east. Ewell was absent on a
reconnaissance, and while waiting for his return, Lee examined the
surrounding terrain from the window of a nearby building. According to Brigadier General Isaac R. Trimble, who accompanied Lee, the
Southern commander still contemplated moving Ewell's Corps to the
right. Lee remarked, "The enemy have the advantage of us in a
shorter and inside line, and we are too much extended."[34]

Soon after Ewell's return, however, Lee abandoned any remaining thoughts of shifting the Second Corps and made his final battle
plans. He informed Ewell that the main attack would be delivered by
Longstreet's men, supported by those of A. P. Hill. Longstreet was to
attack en echelon from his right. Hill's first brigade would therefore
go into action immediately following Longstreet's last one. Ewell, however, was instructed to advance the moment he heard Longstreet's
opening guns, "to make a simultaneous demonstration upon the en-

emy's right, to be converted into a real attack should the opportunity offer."[35]

Lee did not tell Ewell when the battle would commence, but "report circulated that the attack of Longstreet would be delivered at 4 o'clock."[36] While it was a late hour for the beginning of a major battle, Longstreet's men would need time to get into position. Their destination was only three miles distant, but the concealed route they were to follow doubled the distance. Lee did not give Longstreet the order to proceed until 11:00 A.M., and there was an immediate half hour delay as Longstreet, with Lee's permission, waited for Law's Brigade of Hood's Division to reach the field. Lee could have had no misconceptions concerning the time it would take to implement his battle plan. Only two months earlier, using similar tactics at Chancellorsville, Jackson's flank march had consumed a full eight hours.[37]

The foreign observers waiting on Seminary Ridge also realized that Confederate preparations would consume most of the day. Ross, the Austrian, noted, "As evidently a long time would elapse before Longstreet's corps, which would do the chief fighting that day, could be placed in position, I determined meanwhile to ride into the town of Gettysburg with the doctors."[38] Ross rejoined Longstreet at his attack position at about three o'clock, which suggests that someone told Ross when he should return if he wanted to view the combat.[39]

The assault might have begun somewhat earlier but for problems involving Captain Johnston, the officer of Lee's staff who had made the early morning reconnaissance. Lee ordered him to guide the First Corps to its position. He rode with Johnston and Longstreet part of the way, and had there been any misunderstanding concerning Johnston's duties, it would have been discovered immediately and corrected.[40]

Unfortunately, the route followed by the First Corps proved to be visible to the enemy, forcing Longstreet to make a long countermarch in order to find a substitute, hidden path. The delay irritated Longstreet greatly. He was particularly anxious to place his artillery and ordered Alexander to make a detailed reconnaissance. Lee returned to the right flank while this was in progress, although the exact time of his arrival cannot be determined. Longstreet's dispositions were made under Lee's eyes and with Lee's approval. Between 3:30

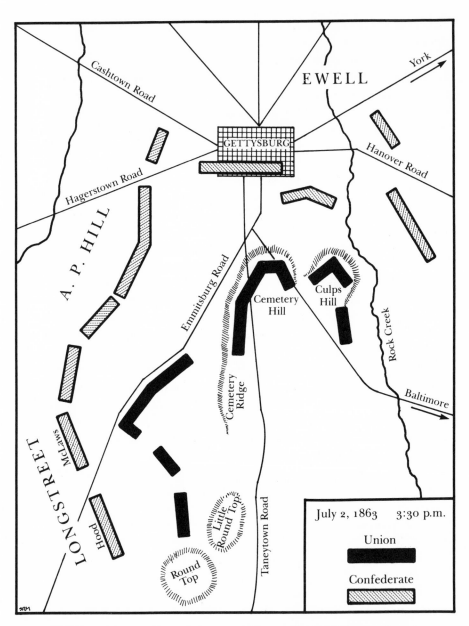

This map shows the outline of the opposing armies' positions prior to
Longstreet's attack on the second day at Gettysburg.

and 4:00 P.M. Longstreet completed his arrangements and gave orders for the attack to begin. Given the route, his men had made the flank march with admirable speed.[41]

At the last moment, however, Hood and McLaws balked, sending messages to ask that the assault be delayed and rearranged. They did so with good reason, for in deploying their divisions Longstreet's subordinates discovered that the Federal lines did not actually end on Cemetery Ridge, as Lee and Longstreet had assumed, but ran along the Emmitsburg Road until they reached a peach orchard just west of the ridge. From there the Federal line bent backward, toward the east, running through a wheat field and into a region of boulders and tangled undergrowth known as Devil's Den, not far from Little Round Top.

The discovery was a major revelation and a severe embarrassment, for it meant that the information collected that morning was completely out of date and that the Federal positions had radically changed. Longstreet's own subsequent reconnaissance work had obviously been grossly inadequate, for it had not revealed this fact. At first, Longstreet refused to admit that he could have made so great an error. But once persuaded of his mistake, he saw no alternative to ordering the attack to proceed unchanged. This could not have been a happy decision, for he was now facing exactly what he had hoped to avoid—a major frontal assault—but he had no other choice. Lee was present on the right flank, aware of the changed situation and expressing annoyance at the last-minute delays by his lieutenant's division commanders. The attack therefore went forward, despite Longstreet's reservations—reservations actually stronger than anything he indicated in print after the war. In a letter to McLaws written more than a decade later, Longstreet said of July 2, "It was my intention not to press this attack if [it] was likely to prove the enemy position too strong for my two Divisions."[42] Longstreet was willing to risk Lee's censure rather than wreck his divisions as he had seen Burnside do at Fredericksburg.

Hood objected strongly to the frontal assault, wanting instead to send a brigade to circle Round Top and strike the Federal rear. He requested permission to do so no less than three times, but each time it was denied. As soon as his troops started forward, Hood made a fourth request directly to Lee, who was now present. Lee, however, wanted no further maneuvering. "I cannot take [the] risk of losing a brigade," he informed the Texan. "We must do the best we can."[43]

No one would ever guess Longstreet's dislike of Lee's tactics from his performance on July 2. He timed his en echelon attacks carefully. He even led Barksdale's Mississippi Brigade against the peach orchard in person, riding well ahead of the attack and waving his black hat instead of a sword. A captured Federal officer remarked ruefully, "Our generals don't do that sort of thing."[44]

When night fell, Longstreet's troops occupied Devil's Den, the peach orchard, the wheat field, and the ground in front of the Round Tops. But the Federal line remained intact, running now from Cemetery Ridge to the Round Tops. The Confederate success would have been greater had Longstreet's divisions not fought virtually alone. Although three brigades of the Third Corps had fought valiantly on Longstreet's flank, the bulk of A. P. Hill's men rendered no assistance. Ewell, ordered to make a demonstration that would prevent Meade from shifting any troops to his left to face Longstreet, did not attack until late in the day. This assault was badly mismanaged and was generally ineffectual.[45]

In short, there had been no concert of action between the three corps. The fault lay with Lee, the only person who could attempt to coordinate the action once the fighting began. After witnessing Longstreet's opening movements, Lee returned to Seminary Ridge, where he and Hill viewed the fighting. If Lee had thought Longstreet's attack warranted the support of Hill's full corps, he could have ordered it forward. He did not do so, nor did he take any action to hasten Ewell's attack. Once the battle had begun, Lee's lieutenants received no assistance from their chief.[46]

Viewing the events of July 2 as a limited success, Lee determined to renew the contest for a third day. Longstreet understood that on the morning of July 3 he was to attack again as soon as possible. He spent most of the night of July 2 searching for a way to outflank the Federal position and to avoid the sort of costly frontal assaults that he, Hood, and McLaws had all opposed in the afternoon.

By morning Longstreet was convinced that a flank move was practicable. He had just given orders for it to begin when Lee arrived and canceled them. Lee was annoyed at Longstreet for contemplating such a move. Lee apparently wanted exactly what Longstreet feared, namely another series of frontal assaults, the only difference now being that, in contrast to the situation on the previous day, Longstreet would be reinforced by Pickett's division and would begin earlier in the day. Longstreet's orders for a flank attack spoiled the alignment Lee desired and made a delay necessary. Meanwhile, on the far left, Ewell had been attacked by the Federals.[47]

Faced with these frustrations, Lee adopted a new set of battle plans. He now decided to assault Cemetery Ridge directly with Longstreet's entire corps, preceded by a massive artillery barrage. When Longstreet noted that such a move would expose Hood and McLaws to counterattack on their flank, Lee ordered these two divisions to remain in position. Pickett's fresh division would be reinforced by men from the Third Corps instead: Heth's Division (commanded by Brigadier General James Pettigrew, as Heth was wounded), plus two brigades from Pender's Division, placed under the command of Major General Isaac Trimble.[48]

Lee considered the matter settled, but Longstreet did not. Four months earlier, while serving in southeastern Virginia, Longstreet had expressed to Lee his concept of his duty as second in command: "I only wish to do what I regard as my duty—give you the full benefit of my views."[49] He stuck to this principle on July 3 by suggesting that a frontal assault was unwise. Given the width of ground that the Southern troops would have to cover, he told Lee, it was simply not possible for the attack to succeed. But as Lee was adamant, Longstreet began his preparations.[50]

At 1:30 by the watch of Colonel Walton, the First Corps chief of artillery, a note arrived from Longstreet, reading, "Let the batteries open, order great care and precision firing." With a signal gun from the Washington Artillery, the great barrage began. As on the day before, tactical control of Longstreet's artillery was in E. P. Alexander's hands. According to the young Georgian's watch, the guns opened at 1:00, not 1:30, and continued firing for some forty minutes.[51]

"That day at Gettysburg was one of the saddest of my life," Longstreet later wrote.[52] He carried out his orders with great reluctance. Just before the cannonade began, the General exchanged a series of notes with Alexander which did him little credit and reveal his disturbed state of mind. These communications concerned the timing of Pickett's advance, which was to initiate the general assault. Alexander felt that Longstreet was seeking a way to cancel the assault or to place the responsibility for it on someone else's shoulders. His interpretation seemed correct when Longstreet arrived to speak with him just after the infantry advance began. Learning that Alexander lacked the ammunition needed for proper follow-up support for the attack, Longstreet nearly canceled the entire movement. According to Alexander, Longstreet "then spoke slowly and with great emotion: 'I do not want to make this charge. I do not see how it can succeed. I would not make it now but that Gen. Lee has ordered it and is expecting it.' "[53] John Cheves Haskell, who was standing nearby, reported that Longstreet shrugged his shoulders and said, " 'It is all wrong, but he will have it,' or words to that effect referring to Gen. Lee's decision to charge the enemy on Cemetery heights."[54] In his official report of the battle, Longstreet boldly wrote, "The order for this attack, which I could not favor under better auspices, would have been revoked had I felt that I had that privilege."[55]

The attack upon which Lee placed his remaining hopes therefore lay in the hands of an officer utterly opposed to it. Yet despite his reservations, Longstreet had devoted his full talents and energy toward its success. He was particularly concerned with the morale of the men who would make the attack. Unable to protect them from the fearful Federal counterbarrage, he ordered them to lie down and take cover.[56] James L. Kemper, one of Pickett's brigadiers, remembered how the General shared their danger:

> Longstreet rode slowly and alone immediately in front of our entire line. He sat his large charger with a magnificent grace and composure I never before beheld. His bearing was to me the grandest moral spectacle of the war. I expected to see him fall every instant. Still he moved on, slowly and majestically, with an inspiring confidence, composure, self-possession and repressed power, in every movement and look, that fascinated me.[57]

Beneath his calm exterior Longstreet, who unlike Lee knew what it meant to fight hand to hand, felt deeply for his men. When the moment came to order the advance, he was unable to speak. When

Pickett inquired, "Shall I go forward, General Longstreet?" he could only nod.[58]

It was approximately two o'clock when the advance began, and by all accounts it was magnificent. With iron discipline the gray ranks marched slowly across the valley, braving shell, grapeshot, and canister. They broke into a run only as they neared the crest of the ridge. Pickett himself kept quite close to the rear of his division much of the time. Men from his command, Pettigrew's division, and Trimble's brigades pierced the Federal lines but were soon driven back. During the assault there were problems with alignment, and artillery support was inadequate because of shortages of ammunition. But even without these the assault was doomed. As Longstreet remarked to Lee, "The fifteen thousand men who could make successful assault over that field had never been arrayed for battle."[59]

Arthur Fremantle, the British observer, left a vivid account of the Southern retreat. He described the valley between the Union position and Seminary Ridge as being "covered with Confederates slowly and sulkily returning toward us in small broken parties, under heavy artillery fire." But in the face of this disaster, he noted, "No person could have been more calm or self-possessed than General Longstreet. . . . I could now thoroughly appreciate the term bulldog, which I had heard applied to him by the soldiers."[60]

Longstreet feared a Federal counterattack. He rode out among the returning men to rally them and prepare for it. Lee was at the front as well, encouraging the fugitives. For three days of heat, misery, and death the Virginian had sought a decisive victory at Gettysburg, one that would make all the hardships and suffering worthwhile. He had failed, and more than 20,000 Southerners lay scattered about the Pennsylvania countryside as testimony to the high stakes of war. To his troops Lee announced, "It is all my fault."[61]

Although Longstreet brought to the contest all the skill and energy which marked his successes on other fields, he had fought the battle of Gettysburg against his better judgment. He had objected to Lee's tactics in the strongest terms, and the Confederate commander was plainly annoyed. But there was no bad feeling between the two men. Lee still had confidence in his "Old War Horse." Whether the Army of Northern Virginia and the Southern people still had confidence in Lee, however, was another matter.

4. The Bull of the Woods at Chickamauga

REACTION TO THE DEFEAT at Gettysburg was severe, beginning even as the remnants of Longstreet's assault force retreated from Cemetery Ridge. Although most of the army was prepared to repulse any Federal counterattack, there was significant demoralization.[1] When General Pettigrew reported that he could not rally his men, Longstreet replied sarcastically, "just let them remain where they are; the enemy's going to advance, and they will spare you the trouble."[2] General Pickett, upon meeting one of Longstreet's staff officers, wept and cried, "Why did you not halt my men here? Great God, where, oh! where is my division?"[3] Longstreet and Lee both tried to console Pickett, Lee remarking that his men had earned a place in history through their gallantry. Pickett supposedly replied that "all the glory in the world could never atone for the widows and orphans this day has made."[4] His language may not actually have been as dramatic, but there is no question that Pickett never forgave Lee. After their only postwar meeting, Pickett said, "That old man . . . had my division massacred."[5]

Pickett was not alone in his criticism. One of McLaws's brigadiers, William T. Wofford, had warned Lee much earlier that, even if it was penetrated by an attacking column, the Federal position could never be held by the Southerners. James F. Croker, adjutant of the Ninth Virginia Infantry, observed after viewing the enemy's position that the battle would be "another Malvern Hill."[6] Reflecting on Pickett's advance long after the war, E. P. Alexander wrote, "It seemed madness to order a column in the middle of a hot July day to undertake an advance of three-fourths of a mile over open ground against the centre of that line."[7]

Some of the letters and diaries written by participants were also critical. Moxley Sorrel referred in his diary on July 4 to the "disasters of yesterday."[8] General Wade Hampton concluded on the fifteenth that the battle had been "terrible & *useless*."[9]

Enlisted men were also quick to judge the campaign. One soldier referred to the invasion of Pennsylvania as "ill-fated," while another believed it to be "as clear a defeat as our army ever met with."[10] James Pleasants, writing on July 17, concluded, "The campaign is a failure and the worst failure that the South has ever made. Gettysburg sets off Fredericksburg. Lee seems to have become as weak as Burnside. And no blow since the fall of New Orleans has been so telling against us."[11]

Some accepted the battle fatalistically and turned their thoughts toward the future. "If we are to invade the North again," wrote a member of the Jeff Davis Legion, "I sincerely hope that we may succeed in accomplishing a little more than was accomplished in our last invasion."[12] Thomas Rosser, a Virginia cavalryman, was less forgiving: "This trip to Penn. has done us no good—indeed I feel it is quite a disaster so far." Another young soldier concluded that Gettysburg had "prolonged the war for two years at least."[13] One Texan felt that Lee had simply placed too much confidence in the army's ability "to accomplish anything he chose to attempt."[14]

Lee agreed. On the night of July 4, standing around a campfire in the rain with his staff, Longstreet, and some of the foreign visitors, Lee blamed the debacle on his own overconfidence.[15] Yet he was loath to admit the extent of his defeat. His first battle reports portrayed it as merely a setback, calling his casualties "large" and "heavy" when they were clearly disastrous. The total loss was approximately 20,000. Lee also concealed the truth from his wife, writing her in July that "our success at Gettysburg was not so great as reported." After returning to Virginia he wrote her that he was back from Pennsylvania "rather sooner than I had originally contemplated."[16]

Demoralization and desertion before, during, and after battle were problems for every Civil War general, but after Gettysburg Lee's difficulties were acute. On July 4, while the army was still in the presence of the enemy, 5,000 physically fit Confederates left the ranks without permission to join the train of the wounded who were heading for Virginia. Lee feared that most were captured.[17] As had happened before when Lee incurred major losses, desertions *increased* after the army returned to Virginia. Lee was forced to issue a public appeal for the absentees to return. On July 27 he informed President Davis that there were "many thousand men improperly absent from the army." Expecting his personal entreaties to be futile, he suggested the president offer a general amnesty for deserters.[18]

Combined with the news of Vicksburg's surrender on July 4, the Gettysburg defeat caused profound disillusionment throughout the South. Blame fell upon both Lee and Davis. Although early newspaper reports often distorted details of the battle, they were critical of Lee's tactics. While some papers such as the *Daily Richmond Examiner* downplayed the defeat, boasting that Meade had been fortunate to escape "annihilation," others adopted the tone of the *Charleston Mercury,* which concluded that the invasion could not have been "more foolish or disastrous."[19]

Some of Longstreet's friends outside the Virginia army also criticized the campaign. D. H. Hill predicted disaster in June, from the moment when he learned that Lee was heading north, as he feared "Lee's scattering method." Beauregard thought the invasion wasted 20,000 good men who could have been put to good use in the western theater. Johnston made no comment, but one of his aides, Richard Manning, denounced Lee vociferously.[20] Lee was also criticized by some observers within the Confederate War Department. William Preston Johnston, one of the president's most trusted aides, received reports that Lee had fought without a coherent battle plan and had exercised little control over his army. He concluded that the "disastrous" campaign had been a waste of precious manpower.[21]

The battle could not have improved Longstreet's opinion of his chief, yet he did not join those who criticized Lee. When writing his Uncle Augustus on July 24, Longstreet *did* state that he felt his plans would have stood a better chance of success than the ones Lee followed, but he stressed that Lee deserved the South's full support. He felt that all of Lee's subordinates should share the blame for the army's setback.[22]

Longstreet also supported Lee when corresponding with his friend Louis T. Wigfall. This powerful opponent of the administration had concluded that Lee's resignation was necessary, but Longstreet disagreed. When he wrote the Texan on August 2 he did not mention his own disagreements with Lee, stating simply that Federal superiority in numbers had been the main cause of the defeat.[23]

Some of Wigfall's contacts were not as generous toward Lee. While recovering from wounds received in Pennsylvania, Wade Hampton wrote, "We could better of stormed the Heights of Stafford [the hills opposite Fredericksburg] than that at Gettysburg. I am thoroughly disgusted & nothing but a sense of duty would take me back to my unpleasant position."[24]

Wigfall himself could not understand why a flanking move had not been attempted.[25] Unaware that Lee had already offered to resign as the price of failure,[26] Wigfall wrote a fellow congressman:

> His blunder at Gettysburg, his wretched handling of his troops, & his utter want of generalship have only increased Davis' admiration for him. I was in Richmond soon after his defeat & was told that Davis was almost frantic with rage if the slightest doubt was expressed as to [Lee's] capacity & conduct. He was at the same time denouncing Johnston in the most violent . . . manner & attributing the fall of Vicksburg to him & him alone.[27]

Gettysburg and Vicksburg, Wigfall and Johnston, Lee and Davis—all were on Longstreet's mind following the army's return to Virginia, as he contemplated the Confederacy's worsening plight. Pemberton's surrender left the South with little more than Johnston's small force in Mississippi and Bragg's understrength army in Tennessee to defend the vast region between the Mississippi River and the Appalachians. Longstreet concluded that Bragg must be reinforced by troops from Lee's army. He had made this suggestion twice, in January and in May 1863. With Lee's influence at a low ebb after Gettysburg, he now found that the idea of a western concentration was being seriously considered by the government.

Discussing some of his concerns in a letter to Wigfall, Longstreet wrote on August 18:

> I have just sent a private letter to Mr. Seddon asking him to send me to the West. If you can give the time and inclination to it, I would like to ask you to go to Richmond to urge this. . . . If I remain here I fear that

we shall go, little at a time, till all will be lost. I hope that I may get west in time to save what there is left of us. I dislike to ask for anything, and only do so under the impression that if I do not our days will be numbered.[28]

Longstreet approached Wigfall because their views on strategy were similar, and they shared a firm admiration of Joseph E. Johnston. Wigfall was one of Johnston's leading advocates in Congress and wanted him to replace Bragg and to assume direct control over the Army of Tennessee. Wigfall also considered Longstreet a likely candidate to replace Bragg. Johnston himself believed Bragg should be retained, but saw Longstreet as the only choice to replace him, and had heard gossip that he wanted Bragg's position. Johnston wrote Wigfall in March: "It is, indeed, a hard case for him, the Senior Lieut. Genl. & highest in reputation, to be kept in second place. . . ."[29]

In addition to asking for Wigfall's support, Longstreet tried to pursuade Lee of the wisdom of a western concentration. He wrote Lee that far more could be accomplished if Bragg's forces advanced than would be achieved by another Virginia offensive.[30] Lee should quickly send at least three brigades west, "putting me in Bragg's place and giving him my corps."[31]

This frank statement and the gossip Johnston passed to Wigfall raises the question of Longstreet's motives. Was the desire for an independent command the primary reason Longstreet advocated a western concentration? Not if we may believe a letter he wrote Lee on September 5: "I feel that I am influenced by no personal motive in this suggestion, and will most cheerfully give up, when we have fair prospect of holding our Western country."[32]

Many historians believe that Longstreet's letter was insincere and self-effacing, one reason being that he informed Lee that he was "willing to go West and take charge there."[33] Longstreet's subsequent displeasure while serving under Bragg is well documented. Together these would seem to indicate that Longstreet coveted Bragg's position.

While Longstreet may have hoped for independent command (what soldier would not?), self-advancement was probably not his primary motive in seeking western service. When Longstreet wrote Lee on September 5, he explicitly offered Bragg the First Corps. In October 1862 he had offered it to Johnston, and in June 1863 he had discussed with McLaws a previously contemplated scheme for swapping places with Beauregard. Now, for a third time in less than twelve months, and in the wake of Lee's poor performance in Pennsylvania, Longstreet was seeking an honorable way to transfer from the Virginian's command.

Longstreet evidently feared the tactics that Lee would employ in the coming Virginia campaign and sought to avoid a repetition of the situation at Gettysburg, where he was forced to carry out orders very much against his better judgment. On September 2 he had written Lee of his continued dislike of frontal assaults: "I don't know that we can reasonably hope to accomplish here by offensive operations, unless we are strong enough to cross the Potomac. If we advance to meet the enemy on this side, he will in all probability go into one of his many fortified positions. These we cannot afford to attack."[34]

Longstreet knew that another campaign was forthcoming, for on August 31 Lee had instructed him to prepare the army for "offensive operations" in which they would "crush" Meade's forces.[35] Lee had used offensive tactics in Pennsylvania, and the wording of his orders suggested that he was about to do so again. This was Lee's prerogative, of course, and Longstreet never questioned that it was. But rather than participate in operations he considered ill suited to the South's resources, Longstreet apparently chose to seek service under Johnston, his former chief.

Although he had written of replacing Bragg, Longstreet was not seeking complete independence. When soliciting Wigfall's assistance in August, he stated: "I have no personal motives in this for with either Bragg's or Pemberton's army I shall be second to Johnston and therefore in the same relative position as I am at present. I am not essential here, on the contrary, I am satisfied that it is a great mistake to keep me here."[36] While an army command would have meant great freedom, Longstreet expected to work under Johnston's close supervision. He was apparently not troubled by Johnston's difficulties and disputes with the War Department or by the question of whether Johnston's department command still embraced Bragg's army.[37]

Longstreet's presumption that he could save the West appears egotistical, but he never contemplated going alone, realizing that reinforcements were crucial. When Longstreet informed Wigfall that his presence in Virginia was "not essential," he was actually showing remarkable humility for a man who, since Blackburn's Ford, had been perhaps the greatest source of continuity at the high-command level in the army presently commanded by Lee.

In the wake of Gettysburg, President Davis decided to initiate the western concentration which Wigfall, Beauregard, Johnston, Longstreet, and others had long advocated. Lee had reservations and hoped that Longstreet's absence would be brief. When writing Lee on September 12, Longstreet promised a quick campaign and a speedy return to Virginia if he found no hope of success. Disputes over tactics had not blinded him to the debt that he and the First Corps owed their commander. Longstreet assured Lee; "All that we have to be proud of has been accomplished under your eye and under your orders. Our affections for you are stronger, if it is possible for them to be stronger, than our admiration for you."[38]

The movement began on September 9. Longstreet's force consisted of McLaws's and Hood's divisions, plus Alexander's reserve artillery, a total of only nine infantry brigades and nine batteries. The trip was unexpectedly time consuming, for Rosecrans's Army of the Cumberland had advanced against Bragg only a few days earlier, forcing the Confederates back into Georgia. Because Chattanooga was now in Federal hands, Longstreet could not go through East Tennessee as planned but had to send his men south through the Carolinas, west to Georgia, and then north toward Bragg.[39]

En route to Bragg, Longstreet penned a letter to Wigfall which revealed lingering frustration over his attempts to have his strategic views appreciated by the War Department. "I have learned after much experience," he wrote, "that one must after expressing views, fight for them if he hopes to have them adopted. So I shall hereafter contend with more pertinacity for what I know to be right." Of his new assignment Longstreet noted, "I don't think that I should be under Bragg. And would fight against it if I had any hope of setting anyone in the responsible position except myself. If I should make any decided opposition the world might say that I was desirous of a position which would give me favor."[40] Such a frame of mind boded ill for Longstreet in terms of his future cooperation with Bragg and with the authorities in Richmond.

Longstreet arrived at Catoosa station, near Ringgold, Georgia, on the afternoon of September 19. Hood's Division, which had preceded him, had already joined Bragg, but through an oversight no one had been sent to guide Longstreet to his new commander. It took him seven hours to locate the headquarters of the Army of Tennessee, and he was nearly captured during his search. Long before he reached his destination the echo of cannonfire told him that a major battle was in progress. Thanks to the hesitancy of the War Department and Lee, and to the poor condition of the Southern railroads, Longstreet had arrived almost too late. The western concentration bloc's plan to utilize the Confederacy's interior lines of communication to concentrate against Rosecrans before he attacked Bragg had failed, but through no fault of Longstreet's.[41]

Longstreet was not too late to affect the course of the battle in progress, however. Hood had been in time to participate in the indecisive contest that Bragg and Rosecrans fought in the wooded country along the west bank of the Chickamauga on December 19. If the rest of Longstreet's forces, which arrived during the night, were a smaller reinforcement than Bragg could have used, they were timely nevertheless.[42]

Bragg had already retired when Longstreet rode up, but he rose to greet the General. Bragg was fifty-four years old and a native of North Carolina. His grizzled beard, thick, knitted brows, and piercing glare gave him an antagonistic appearance which matched his personality. Although he was a stern disciplinarian and careful organizer, he was indecisive, argumentative, and greatly disliked by most of his subordinates. Bragg gave no indication that he welcomed the presence of Lee's lieutenant but turned immediately to the business at hand. After discussing his battle plans for the morrow very briefly, he retired once more.[43]

Despite the brevity and lack of cordiality that characterized Longstreet's conference with Bragg, it resulted in important decisions. In deference to Longstreet's rank, Bragg divided his forces in two. Lieutenant General Leonidas Polk, the senior corps commander prior to Longstreet's arrival, took charge of the right wing, which contained some 20,000 men. Longstreet was assigned the left, five divisions of more than 22,000 infantrymen and attached artillery. Polk was ordered to advance at dawn, the attack proceeding en echelon along the line of the entire Southern army.[44]

As Longstreet would be making a frontal assault not unlike the ones which had drawn his protests in Pennsylvania, one must wonder why he voiced no objections to Bragg. The situations at Gettysburg and Chickamauga were hardly parallel, however. The field at Gettysburg had been relatively open and easy to inspect. Longstreet's suggestions had been based on his intimacy with Lee and his knowledge of Lee's army and its foe. The field at Chickamauga was thickly wooded. Longstreet's late night arrival precluded an inspection of it until dawn. He was not intimate with Bragg, and both Bragg's army and its enemy represented unknown factors to him. Under the circumstances it is hardly surprising that Longstreet made no objection to his assignment and voiced no suggestions to Bragg.

Polk's attack, which was to start the battle, did not begin at dawn as ordered. The delay was fortunate for Longstreet, who was supposed to advance as soon as the last of Polk's men did so, for daylight revealed chaotic conditions within his new command. The Virginia reinforcements had become jumbled in their haste to reach the scene. Bragg's own troops and Hood's division, which had fought with him, were disorganized from the fight. Worst of all, the entire wing under Longstreet's command overlapped Polk's by a considerable margin.[45]

Longstreet was expected to bring order to this chaos and to launch a major assault even though he had been placed in command only hours before. While the Tennessee army contained a few old friends such as D. H. Hill and Simon B. Buckner, most of Longstreet's new subordinates were complete strangers. Prior to dawn, the General's knowledge of the field and the enemy's positions was based entirely on a map that Bragg had given him during their conference.

It would be difficult to imagine a more inhibiting set of circumstances than those facing Longstreet, but he did not hesitate. At first light he gathered information about the Federal positions and began readjusting his lines for the attack. This was time-consuming business, and he was fortunate that Polk did not attack on schedule. Even so, probably no other officer in the South could have taken control as quickly and smoothly or with such self-confidence as Longstreet at Chickamauga on the morning of September 20.[46]

Longstreet arranged his assault formation three divisions deep in places, thereby giving it great power, although the potential for misalignment and confusion in the wooded terrain was great. When the gray lines moved forward at 11:30 A.M., they struck the Union army with tremendous force. In a spirit of friendly rivalry Longstreet's and Bragg's men strove to outperform each other, and luck was with them. A gap accidentally opened in the enemy's lines just as the Confederates advanced. After intense fighting, Longstreet's wing was able to smash through the Federal position and drove Rosecrans and half his army from the field in one of the greatest routs of the war.[47] Throughout it all, Longstreet puffed complacently on a meerschaum pipe, his businesslike calm effectively conveying his own confidence to the soldiers.[48]

In midafternoon, Longstreet's wing of the army pivoted northward, joining Polk's in an assault upon Major General George H. Thomas, behind whom the remaining Union forces had rallied. This Virginia-born Federal officer's stout defense so occupied Longstreet's attention that he failed to do everything he might have done to cut off the retreat of his enemy. Nor at the end of the day did Longstreet adequately convey to Bragg the magnitude of the victory his wing of the army had achieved.[49]

Although Bragg was later criticized by Longstreet and others for failing to follow up his triumph at Chickamauga, the truth is that the Confederates were virtually paralyzed by their success. Over a two-day period Bragg lost some 18,000 men. Longstreet's own casualties on the twentieth were approximately 8,000. On the positive side, his wing captured 3,000 prisoners, 40 artillery pieces, almost 18,000 muskets, and well over 250,000 rounds of small arms ammunition. Such prizes were invaluable, but they also demanded attention, and much time was consumed in sorting things out. Bragg's inactivity immediately following the battle is understandable.[50]

At Chickamauga the cynical, hard-bitten soldiers of the Army of Tennessee gave Lee's War Horse a new nickname. They called Longstreet the "Bull of the Woods."[51] Because of the extreme difficulties he faced—he had taken command at the last minute of disorganized forces; he fought an unfamiliar enemy on unknown ground; he was unsure of the capabilities of some of his own troops—Chickamauga was the greatest achievement of his career. A lesser soldier might not have been able to launch an attack of any kind; Longstreet's action gave the Federals one of their worst defeats of the war. Luck, in the form of an accidental gap in the Union lines, played a major role. But if we describe this as the primary reason for the victory we ignore the valor and skill of both Longstreet and his men. Longstreet's accomplishment was exceeded only by that of the common soldiers who fought with such determination under his adroit leadership.

5. *From East Tennessee to Appomattox*

INSTEAD OF CONCENTRATING on a method of evicting his enemy from Chattanooga, whence they fled following the battle of Chickamauga, Braxton Bragg wasted time quarreling with his subordinates. Personality conflicts and petty jealousies had plagued the Tennessee army for some time, and Bragg did not enjoy a cordial relationship with any of his subordinates. He often seemed more concerned with stifling dissent within his own forces than with defeating those of the enemy. Given the depth of these problems and Bragg's irascible temperament, Longstreet probably could not have oiled troubled waters had he attempted to do so. It is hardly to his credit that he never tried. For the first time in his career Longstreet was forced to operate under a commander he thoroughly disliked, and he soon joined the growing clique of anti-Bragg officers within the army.[1]

Energy was tragically misdirected after the Chickamauga victory. On September 22 Bragg demanded that Polk account for the right wing's failure to attack at dawn on the twentieth. That same week Polk, who considered Bragg "an imbecile," arranged a meeting with Longstreet, Hill, and Buckner to discuss ways of ending Bragg's connection with the army. Longstreet agreed to write both Secretary of War Seddon and General Lee.[2]

In his letters Longstreet expressed the hope that Beauregard or Lee could be sent to replace Bragg. He certainly would have preferred working under either man to remaining under Bragg, and he may even have felt some nostalgia for Beauregard, his first commander, who like Johnston was a leader in the western concentration bloc. Lee's reply was negative. He hoped that Longstreet would soon return to Virginia rather than going west. "I missed you dreadfully," he wrote Longstreet on October 26. "Your cheerful face and strong arm would have been invaluable. I hope you will soon return to me."[3]

Longstreet knew that Lee did not want to serve outside his native state and that Davis disliked Beauregard. He may therefore have written the letters as a gesture while hoping Davis would turn to him as a logical succesor for Bragg. Whatever his motives, Longstreet bears major responsibility for the shabby squabbling which subsequently engulfed the Tennessee army's officers. His open criticism of Bragg fueled rumors that he would soon replace the North Carolinian and damaged the unity that the army desperately needed.

On October 4 Longstreet asked Hill and Buckner to meet with him to discuss the situation once more. Polk was not present, as Bragg had relieved him of command on September 28. At this semimutinous meeting a petition was drawn up asking Davis to relieve Bragg from command. Twelve officers eventually signed the extraordinary document, but it never reached the chief executive's hands. By early October the president was on his way to meet with Bragg, fully aware that dissent within the army had reached crisis proportions.[4]

Davis arrived on October 9, determined to uphold Bragg. He held to this resolution despite an embarrassing meeting at which, in Bragg's presence, each of his corps commanders recommended to Davis that Bragg be replaced. On the following day, Davis and Longstreet discussed the situation in the western theater at length. Neither the president nor Bragg seems to have realized that since Polk's departure Longstreet had become the leader of the faction that opposed Bragg.[5]

In his memoirs, written in old age, Longstreet claimed that Davis had offered him the Army of Tennessee and that he had declined, suggesting instead a further concentration of forces: "The army was part of General Joseph E. Johnston's department, and could only be used in strong organization by him in combining its operations with his other forces in Alabama and Mississippi. I said that under him I could cheerfully work in any position. The suggestion of that name only served to increase his displeasure, and his severe rebuke."[6]

Davis's offer of the army to Longstreet was probably apocryphal, but the rest of his statement is quite believable. Longstreet knew that Davis disliked Johnston. Yet he was not showing false modesty, as he may have in suggesting Lee or Beauregard, hoping that Davis would actually turn to him as Bragg's logical successor. Longstreet's original suggestions for a western concentration would have allowed him to serve as Johnston's subordinate in some capacity. And Longstreet, as we shall see, continued even after his meeting with Davis to offer plans which would reunite him with his former chief and would further the western concentration they both advocated.

The president's visit was followed by a thorough purge of the command structure of the Army of Tennessee. Polk was transferred, Hill relieved, and Buckner reduced to a division commander. While the army was wracked with bickering, Southern fortunes continued to deteriorate. Bragg was not able to make up all of his losses at Chickamauga, which had reduced his force by some 30 percent. Too weak to assault the Federals in Chattanooga and lacking supplies and transportation necessary for a campaign of maneuver, Bragg laid siege to the river town.[7]

General Thomas now led the Army of the Cumberland, but Grant, appointed overall Union commander for the West, arrived to direct operations. The Federals were not cut off from outside assistance for long, thanks in great part to serious errors made by Longstreet, who was in charge of the Confederate left flank on Lookout Mountain. Longstreet was convinced that the enemy was planning a wide sweep around his left flank. He ignored evidence of Federal activity at the base of the mountain, even though it was presented to him by some of his most trusted subordinates. Thanks to his carelessness, the Federals made an attack which reopened their supply lines, setting the stage for a complete reversal of the roles of besieger and besieged and leading ultimately to the disaster at Missionary Ridge.[8]

While Longstreet and Bragg were barely on speaking terms during this period, there is no evidence that Longstreet deliberately neglected his duties in order to make Bragg look bad, as Bragg later claimed. Longstreet was fooled into believing that a Federal advance would come elsewhere. He was outgeneraled and his errors cost the South dearly, but his poor relations with Bragg were not responsible. The animosity between Longstreet and Bragg did affect the course of the war, however, by leading to the East Tennessee campaign. Ambrose Burnside commanded a large Federal force occupying Knoxville. The authorities in Richmond contemplated having Longstreet make a move against him as early as September 23, when Lee suggested the possibility to Davis as a means of speeding Longstreet's return to Virginia. If Longstreet took Knoxville, he might also be able to advance westward, threatening Thomas's communications and forcing him to abandon Chattanooga. Davis made the same suggestion to Bragg on October 29, and Bragg discussed it with Longstreet on November 3.[9]

Bragg and Longstreet soon agreed upon an invasion of East Tennessee, probably as much from a desire to part company as anything else. Despite ever-increasing Federal strength in Chattanooga, Longstreet's men were detached from Bragg in November. As Bragg's force was considerably weakened by this split, the mutual dislike between Longstreet and Bragg did in fact contribute to Bragg's later defeat at Missionary Ridge.

Longstreet started north for Knoxville on November 5. Enormous transportation difficulties, supply problems, the rough terrain, and skirmishes with the enemy reduced what had been planned as a swift movement to a slow one. Not until November 11 did the First Corps veterans find themselves confronting the extensive fortifications that surrounded Knoxville.[10]

Neither the siege that followed nor the subsequent winter campaign in the mountain region was successful. After long delays, Longstreet attacked Knoxville on the twenty-ninth, only to be repulsed with heavy casualties. Doubting that a second assault could succeed unless he was reinforced, and learning of Bragg's defeat at Missionary Ridge, Longstreet withdrew.[11]

The First Corps remained in the vicinity of Knoxville from December 1863 to April 1864. Although Longstreet made several attempts to advance and a number of small skirmishes occurred, he was not able to initiate a major campaign. His decision to go into winter quarters in forage-poor East Tennessee rather than return to Virginia meant lean times for the troops, but subsistence was scarce in Virginia also. Withdrawal would have placed upper East Tennessee in enemy hands, and the surrender of more territory right after Bragg's disaster would have hurt Southern morale. Occupation of the region, on the other hand, left more options for the spring.

Much of Longstreet's attention during this period of independent command was devoted to internal problems. His disharmony with Bragg continued despite the distance between them, ending only when Bragg resigned in late November. Johnston replaced him, which doubtless pleased Longstreet, but he was fully preoccupied with problems of his own concerning Generals McLaws, Law, Jenkins, and Robertson.

Lafayette McLaws was a native of Augusta, Georgia, and had been Longstreet's childhood friend and West Point classmate. He had served under Longstreet since the reorganization following the Seven Days campaign, but on December 17, Longstreet relieved McLaws from command on the grounds that he had "exhibited a want of confidence in the efforts and plans which the commanding general has thought proper to adopt, and he is apprehensive that this feeling will extend more or less to the troops under [McLaws'] command."[12]

The major issue was the November 29 assault upon Fort Sanders at Knoxville, where McLaws's lack of spirit and energy had contributed to the repulse.[13] But the trouble between the two old friends had been a long time brewing. McLaws had originally considered Longstreet the equal of any general in the South, but Gettysburg had changed his opinion. Shortly after the battle he wrote his wife concerning the events of July 2:

> I think the attack was unnecessary and the whole plan of battle a very bad one. General Longstreet is to blame for not reconnoitering the ground and for persisting in ordering the assault when his errors were disclosed. During the engagement he was very excited, giving contrary orders to everyone and was exceedingly overbearing. I consider him a humbug, a man of small capacity, very obstinate, not at all chivalrous, exceedingly conceited, and totally selfish. If I can it is my intention to get away from his command.[14]

McLaws may have been overwrought by the strain of battle or even jealous of Longstreet's position as second in command, for he was certainly blaming the wrong person. While Longstreet's reconnaissance had been wretched, the faulty battle plan was Lee's, as was the decision to attack once the changes in the Federal positions had been made known. Nevertheless, McLaws's conduct as a division commander began to degenerate from this point.

After Gettysburg, McLaws lost his nerve as a combat officer. On September 21, after Chickamauga, he angered Longstreet by expressly refusing, in the General's absence, to attack an exposed portion of the retreating Federals. When Bragg suggested that McLaws be promoted, Longstreet criticized his lack of zeal in battle, favoring instead the promotion of Hood, McLaws's junior. McLaws's conduct during the East Tennessee campaign was so lethargic that Longstreet reprimanded him. And at Fort Sanders Longstreet had to send his friend a last-minute message urging him to show "heartiness and determination."[15] Longstreet should have relieved McLaws much sooner and probably would have done so but for their long friendship.

At the same time that McLaws was relieved, Brigadier General Evander McIvor Law tendered his resignation, requesting permission to deliver it in person to the War Department in Richmond. Longstreet granted this unusual request, for his relations with Law had been strained since Hood, Law's superior, had fallen at Chickamauga. Law had served with Hood's division longer than any other brigadier and resented the fact that command automatically passed to the senior in rank, in this case a relative newcomer named Micah Jenkins. A young South Carolinian with an excellent war record, Jenkins was Longstreet's protégé, and when Davis visited the army in October, Longstreet asked that Jenkins be promoted and that his position as division commander be made permanent. Davis refused, for reasons not known. When Longstreet then asked that Law be promoted and given the post, Davis refused once more.[16]

The president's refusal to name a successor for Hood sparked intense rivalry between Jenkins and Law which imperiled the effectiveness of the division. Longstreet's continued favoritism toward Jenkins only made things worse and may have contributed, directly or indirectly, to the exceedingly poor generalship Longstreet displayed at Lookout Mountain.[17]

By mid-December, Law had decided to resign rather than serve under Jenkins any longer, and as noted above, he went to Richmond. Law's actions must have awakened Longstreet to the morale crisis in the division, for he now took steps to restore harmony, specifically asking that the War Department give Hood's old position to an outsider. He suggested Major General William H. C. Whiting.[18] The War Department did nothing, however, and Longstreet's attention was soon diverted by other controversies.[19] Because of difficulties involving Brigadier General J. B. Robertson, Longstreet had asked the War Department in late December to grant him the authority to conduct courts-martial and boards of review. A board of review had been held to determine the competency of Robertson in November, while the First Corps was with the Army of Tennessee, but events had disrupted the proceedings and they had not been rescheduled. When in December Robertson declared to his regimental commanders that the war was lost, Jenkins, his superior, arrested him for "conduct highly prejudicial to good order and military discipline."[20]

Longstreet was so distressed by his failure to capture Knoxville and the disharmony in his command that he asked the War Department either to transfer him or to send another officer to supersede him.[21] It must have been painful to do so, but the request demonstrated Longstreet's willingness to place the war effort above personal considerations.

Instead of replacing Longstreet, the Richmond authorities finally granted him full powers as an independent department commander. This change solved few of his problems, however. In February a military court, Major General Buckner presiding, met to consider Longstreet's removal of McLaws. McLaws, who had circulated letters proclaiming his innocence and accusing Longstreet of seeking a scapegoat for Knoxville, promptly contacted Bragg, who needed a scapegoat of his own for the disaster at Missionary Ridge. Together they sought Longstreet's downfall.[22]

McLaws gained another ally in McIvor Law, who had gone to Richmond to submit his resignation in person. Changing his mind, Law abruptly returned to East Tennessee on the bold assumption that, since he had technically not sent in his resignation, he was still a brigade commander. He circulated a petition asking that his brigade be transferred to either Virginia or Mobile, and sent it to Longstreet.[23] The General immediately arrested him, charging him with obtaining leave under false pretenses, creating dissension through his petition, and, by tearing up his resignation, destroying government property.[24]

Law returned to Richmond, where at McLaws's request he tried to discover who among the government officials and the press might side with Longstreet in a power struggle. In April the War Department refused to entertain Longstreet's charges and restored Law to his brigade command.[25] When he returned, however, Longstreet arrested him again. The General explained his actions in a letter to Lee dated April 22: "If my efforts to maintain discipline, spirit, and zeal in the discharge of official duty are to be set aside by the return of General Law and his restoration to duty without trial, it cannot be well for me to remain in command."[26]

Lee quickly contacted the War Department, suggesting that Law be tried as soon as possible and relieved of command until then. President Davis was not impressed. He rebuked Longstreet in the strongest possible terms, stating that he had "offended against good order and military discipline, in rearresting an officer who had been released by the War Department, without any new offense having been alleged."[27]

McLaws's exoneration occurred almost simultaneously. In April (the exact date is unknown), the court found McLaws guilty of only a minor fault rather than the gross negligence that Longstreet had alleged. Law immediately sent congratulations, observing that "Longstreet is certainly on the wane both in, and out of the army."[28] This assessment seemed accurate when in May a review board overturned even the minor conviction against McLaws. Longstreet was censured for granting leaves of absence to key witnesses and personnel in an apparent attempt to slow down the proceedings during McLaws's trial.[29]

Moreover, fresh controversy arose over a replacement for Hood. Lee had suggested that Buckner, who presently commanded troops in Longstreet's Department of East Tennessee, might be acceptable for the position, if only temporarily, but Longstreet took no action at the time. He still preferred Jenkins and believed that Joseph B. Kershaw, a competent and popular South Carolina brigadier, was best suited to replace McLaws.[30]

On February 12 the slow-moving War Department finally assigned Major General Charles W. Field to command Hood's troops. When Field arrived, however, Longstreet gave him Buckner's position, shifting Buckner to Hood's division as Lee had suggested earlier.[31] Longstreet probably intended Buckner's assignment as temporary, his real purpose being to sidetrack Field so that both Jenkins and Kershaw could move up the command ladder in the future.

The War Department soon overruled these arrangements. Apparently still hoping to keep Hood's job open for Jenkins, Longstreet next requested that Field take McLaws's division instead. This request too was refused.[32] Longstreet would still not admit defeat. With the trial of McLaws yet in progress, he asked that Kershaw be promoted and given the command that McLaws had unwillingly vacated. He also wrote a highly impolitic letter questioning Field's assignment in a most sarcastic manner. When Adjutant General Samuel Cooper received this missive, he replied with some heat. He reminded Longstreet that appointments of general officers were made by President Davis, and he observed that Longstreet's questioning of their propriety constituted an insult to the chief executive.[33]

Alarmed by the disharmony in Longstreet's command, the government dispatched Lieutenant Colonel Archer Anderson to make a secret investigation of conditions and morale in East Tennessee. For reasons he never explained, Anderson made only a sketchy inquiry and did not consult any of the officers in McLaws's former command. He informed the War Department that "General Longstreet possesses the confidence and affection of his officers and men."[34]

This assessment apparently satisfied the government; no further investigation seems to have been made. Despite the many important feathers he ruffled, Longstreet was never in danger of losing his command. In the technical aspects of directing soldiers, he had few, if any, equals and probably could have handled an army as easily as he did his corps. The personal frictions which arose in East Tennessee revealed significant limitations in him, however.

Longstreet was only one on a long list of people who failed to get along with Bragg, but it cannot be said that he tried very hard to do so. The causes of his difficulties with McLaws, Robertson, and Law were complex. The problems did not originate with him, and such disharmony did not characterize his command over the course of the war. Nevertheless, his handling of the situation was poor. He was too partisan toward protégés like Jenkins and Kershaw and downright petty and vindictive toward those who opposed him.

Longstreet's main concern while he was in East Tennessee was not these internal difficulties but the problem of operating in a mountainous region populated by Unionist sympathizers. After failing to capture Knoxville, he established a strong defensive position at Bull's Gap, near Greeneville, Tennessee. The railroad provided communication with Virginia once it had been repaired, but he received no supplies from there. December and January he spent largely in collecting subsistence from the surrounding countryside. In early February he advanced on Knoxville once more, but when his request for reinforcements was declined, he decided a siege would not be practical, and he retired. Despite acute privations, his troops remained in good spirits.[35]

Although weather precluded larger activities, Longstreet's mind was not idle. As winter progressed he discussed prospects for the spring campaigns, corresponding with Lee, Johnston, Beauregard, Bragg, and Davis. He met with Lee, Bragg, and Davis in Richmond in March to review strategy. The views of the western concentration bloc prevailed, for no one suggested at this time that Longstreet should rejoin Lee. The question was how Confederate forces could best be brought together to regain Tennessee and Kentucky.[36]

As a result of the general exchange of ideas among the high command, Lee, Bragg, and Davis came to favor a conjunction of Johnston's and Longstreet's forces in East Tennessee for an advance on Nashville. It was hoped that this merger would cause the Federals to abandon Chattanooga and Knoxville. Nashville itself might be captured by battle or by simply threatening the enemy's line of communications, compelling the Northern forces to withdraw.[37]

Longstreet's thinking was greatly influenced by the fact that subsistence in East Tennessee was almost exhausted and none was available from other sources. The sooner his men left, the better.[38] Although he wrote Johnston confidently that "we could work out great results" in Middle Tennessee, both men had reservations about a campaign there. The retreating Federals would destroy the railway from Chattanooga to Nashville, forcing the advancing Confederates to operate without a supply line, to live off a region already stripped of forage.[39]

Longstreet was very enthusiastic about two plans of his own, however. The first, which he developed in February, called for him to mount his two divisions on mules and horses for a gigantic raid across the mountains into Kentucky. His men could live off the country, avoiding combat and destroying the Louisville and Nashville Railroad so thoroughly that the Federals in Tennessee would be forced to retire. Johnston would then be free to advance.[40]

The plan had some merit. Crossing the mountains would have been extremely difficult, yet Kirby Smith's men had used the same route in 1862 as part of Bragg's Perryville campaign. The privations that Kirby Smith's men encountered could be no worse than those facing Longstreet if he remained idle in East Tennessee, and so daring a penetration of enemy-held territory would have sent Southern spirits soaring.

But Longstreet was optimistic, to say the least, in thinking that his small force could hold Kentucky long enough for Johnston to make substantial gains. Worse, he ignored the fact that the Tennessee and Cumberland rivers gave the enemy an alternate supply route for their Middle Tennessee forces; in a pinch, they could dispense with the Louisville and Nashville Railroad. There was certainly no chance that the Confederacy could collect enough mounts for Longstreet's men before the Federals began their own spring moves, and the prospect of transforming Longstreet's foot soldiers into horsemen overnight seems dubious.

Longstreet persistently held to his plan for a mounted raid, even suggesting that Lee take a brief leave of absence from Virginia, bring reinforcements, and lead it himself.[41] When the idea failed to arouse interest in either Lee or Davis, he made a second proposal. He suggested instead a complete invasion of Kentucky, not just a raid. Beauregard could raise a force of men from troops stationed in Mississippi and along the seacoast, meeting Longstreet in Abingdon, a small town in extreme southwest Virginia, near the Tennessee border. Beauregard would then lead their combined forces into Kentucky by way of Pound Gap. After seizing central Kentucky they would unite with Johnston either in that state or farther south in Tennessee, depending on the progress he was able to make.[42]

Davis rejected Longstreet's second plan on the grounds that stripping the lower South to supply Beauregard with troops for the

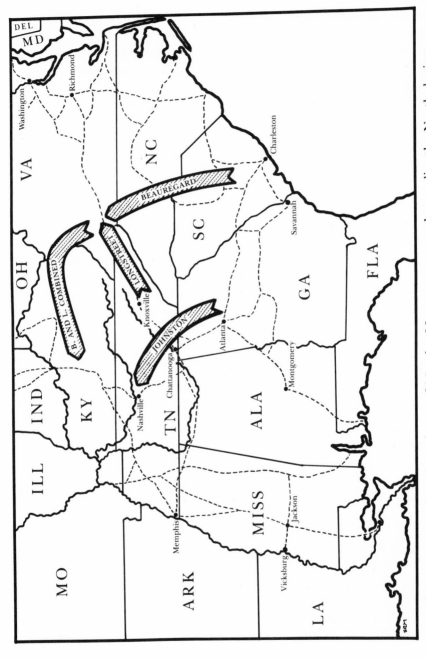

Longstreet's Kentucky invasion scheme of March 1864 was meant to demoralize the North during Lincoln's re-election campaign.

invasion invited disaster on other fronts.[43] This argument made little sense, as Davis had taken such risks previously to reinforce Bragg and Lee. More likely he thought the plan too daring or disliked the idea of reuniting formidable administration critics like Beauregard and Johnston. Lee expressed only very cautious support for the plan, warning Longstreet against overconfidence.[44]

Longstreet's second plan shared all the drawbacks of his first. It was essentially a repeat of Bragg's 1862 Kentucky invasion, which had failed to accomplish anything. Yet there was a crucial difference between them, and had Longstreet done a better job of explaining it, his scheme might have provoked much more interest. For the target of Longstreet's proposed invasion was not territory or even the enemy's army. It was nothing less than the defeat of Abraham Lincoln in the presidential campaign of 1864.

In letters to his peers Longstreet stated boldly that his Kentucky schemes could end the war, but he only hinted at the political reasons why. His strategic views were never fully appreciated because he explained them fully only in a March 27 letter to Brigadier General Thomas Jordan, Beauregard's chief of staff:

> If we had an abundance of supplies it seems to me that we should go into Kentucky as a political move.
>
> If we retain our present positions the enemy will, in the course of a few months, be able to raise large additional forces, and when entirely ready he will again concentrate his forces upon some point, and will eventually get possession, and he will continue to proceed in the same way to the close of the chapter. If we go into Kentucky, and can there unite with General Johnston's army, we shall have force enough to hold it. The enemy will be more or less demoralized and disheartened by the great loss of territory which he will sustain, and he will find great difficulty in getting men enough to operate with before the elections in the fall, when in all probability Lincoln will be defeated and peace will follow in the spring.
>
> The political opponents of Mr. Lincoln can furnish no reason at this late day against the war so long as it is successful with him, and thus far it has certainly been as successful as anyone could reasonably expect. If, however, his opponents were to find at the end of three years that we held Kentucky and were as well to do as at the beginning of the war, it would be a powerful argument against Lincoln and against the war. Lincoln's re-election seems to depend upon the result of our efforts

during the present year. If he is re-elected, the war must continue, and I see no way of defeating his re-election except by military success.[45]

Longstreet's understanding of the plight of the Confederacy was as acute as that of any other Southern leader. The American experience in Vietnam serves as a reminder that the will to victory can be as important as industrial resources and that it is difficult at best to wage a war without public support. Longstreet realized that by the spring of 1864 the Confederacy could no longer hope to win a military decision. But he hoped the South might still make strategic maneuvers of such dazzling proportions that Northern morale would collapse and peace negotiations would begin. If he underestimated the difficulties of reaching and holding Kentucky, he nevertheless showed remarkable breadth of vision.

It is also clear that Longstreet gave no thought to retaining his independent command. Indeed, if one considers the effect Longstreet's proposals would have had on his own status had they been adopted, it is impossible to sustain the idea that he was a man of inordinate ambition, as some historians have claimed.[46] If his actions between January 1863 and April 1864 reveal a pattern, an ulterior motive, it involved the concept of western concentration and reunion with Johnston. Indeed, his favorite plan for invading Kentucky would have produced the same Johnston-Beauregard-Longstreet command structure that existed in Virginia in 1861.

Under the circumstances, Longstreet could not have been happy when Lee in April persuaded the War Department to send Longstreet's men back to Virginia. But he relinquished independent command without regrets. Sorrel overheard Longstreet remark that, "while it was more honorable, possibly, to have a separate command, he preferred being under General Lee, as it relieved him of responsibility and assured confidence."[47]

Longstreet's support for the idea of a western concentration and his leadership at Chickamauga had been important contributions to the Southern war effort. His accomplishments in East Tennessee were modest. One can only wonder how Confederate history might differ had he been made a corps commander under Johnston or commander of the Army of Tennessee or had his politically oriented Kentucky plans been adopted.

Longstreet's two divisions, now led by Field and Kershaw, assembled at Charlottesville, Virginia, on April 21. Lee sent word that he would inspect the troops as soon as possible. His adjutant-general, Walter H. Taylor, sent Longstreet a message which reflected the very cordial relations which existed between the General and Lee's staff during the war. "I really am beside myself, General, with joy of having you back," Taylor wrote. "It is like the reunion of a family."[48]

On the same day Taylor was writing to Longstreet, the General was making plans to be confirmed in the Episcopal church by Bishop John Johns of Richmond. The date set for this event was Sunday, May 1, and it presumably occurred as scheduled at Orange Court House, Virginia. Nothing is known of Longstreet's motives for taking this step beyond the fact that he had turned to the church for solace after his children's deaths in 1862. Sandie Pendleton, the nephew of Lee's artillery chief, believed that Longstreet's decision was prophetic. "I am glad of it," he wrote. "It is an excellent sign for our army, & will, I trust, be another proof of the favor of the Almighty to our cause."[49]

Lee arrived for a formal dress review of Longstreet's troops on April 29. As he rode down the double columns of Kershaw's and Field's divisions, the rebel yell greeted him. E. P. Alexander recalled that "the effect was as of a military sacrament."[50] Elated at leaving the failures of the winter behind them, Longstreet's men apparently remembered only Lee's victories, not the bloodbaths which had resulted in mass desertions.

As the war entered its fourth year, Longstreet's friend Ulysses S. Grant was promoted to lieutenant general and was appointed Federal general in chief. Meade retained command of the Army of the Potomac, but as Grant made his headquarters with that army, the Confederates rightly assumed that Grant would actively direct it. As Longstreet knew Grant well, he probably discussed him with Lee on many occasions. In April he wrote Lee that he did not believe Grant would perform "any better than Pope. . . . His chief strength is in his prestige."[51] But when an officer at Lee's headquarters expressed contempt of Grant's ability, Longstreet warned prophetically: "We must make up our minds to get into line of battle and to stay there; for that man will fight us every day and every hour till the end of this war. In order to whip him we must outmanoeuver him, and husband our strength as best we can."[52]

As it developed, Longstreet was not destined to play a lengthy role in the initial struggle against Grant. When the Federal advance began on May 4, the First Corps was still on the far left flank of Lee's army, out of direct contact. Lee moved to block Grant, the two armies crashing together in a tangled forest known as the Wilderness, where Hooker had met defeat a year earlier. Marching rapidly, Longstreet's divisions arrived on May 6, in time to prevent the rout of A. P. Hill's corps.[53]

In the battle which followed, Longstreet's assistant adjutant-general Osmun Latrobe was wounded almost immediately. Shortly afterward, while passing a group of wounded soldiers, Longstreet and his trusted aide Goree discovered that one of them was Goree's brother. Watching the young man's grief, Longstreet himself was moved to tears.[54]

Then, while he was aligning his troops for an advance through the dense undergrowth, Longstreet's own men accidentally fired upon him. With him at the time were Generals Jenkins and Kershaw and a number of staff officers and couriers. The unexpected volley killed two of Kershaw's staff instantly and mortally wounded Jenkins. Longstreet reeled in the saddle, but his aides lowered him gently to the ground before he fell. Thanks to Kershaw, who shouted "friends!" repeatedly in his booming voice, and an aide named Peyton Manning, who rode bravely into the face of the erring infantry, a second volley was narrowly averted.[55]

Francis Dawson, the English staff officer, galloped to a nearby field hospital and sent a surgeon back to the General, but the First Corps chief surgeon, Dr. Cullen, arrived first. Cullen found Longstreet dangerously wounded by a minié ball that had struck him in the throat, exiting from his right shoulder. Although Longstreet was bleeding profusely, with bloody foam spilling from his lips, he gave General Field careful instructions to complete the counterattack he had been organizing. Shortly after Field departed, Major General Richard Anderson arrived, drawn by the news that the First Corps chief was stricken. Correctly guessing that Lee would name the more experienced Anderson his successor, Longstreet painfully repeated to him the instructions just given Field. Only when he was certain that he had done his duty did the General allow himself to be carried to the rear.[56]

In a few moments the ambulance carrying Longstreet, surrounded by his staff, encountered Lee. Less than an hour earlier, in
one of the most famous incidents of the war, the Texas Brigade had
refused to allow Lee to lead them in a charge, shouting "Lee to the
rear!" Longstreet, with what one of Lee's staff recalled as "affectionate
bluntness," had also "urged General Lee to go farther back." Now
Longstreet himself had fallen, in the very manner and in the same
area that Jackson had. Watching the ambulance pass, Lee wrung his
hands in despair.[57]

Robert Stiles, a young artilleryman who chanced upon the party,
later recalled the extreme grief displayed by Longstreet's staff:

> I never on any occasion during the four years of the war saw a group of
> officers and gentlemen more deeply distressed. They were literally
> bowed down with grief. All of them were in tears. One, by whose side I
> rode for some distance, was himself severely hurt, but he made no allu-
> sion to his wound, and I do not believe he felt it. It was not alone the
> general they admired who had been shot down—it was, rather, the man
> they loved.[58]

Longstreet's fall was recognized as a grave blow to the South and
a stroke of luck for the North. Many believed the battle would not
have ended in a draw had Longstreet been able to direct his counterattack in person. The press initially reported his wound as slight
and predicted his early return to the field, but that was not to be. The
formerly indefatigable Longstreet was moved to tears by his help-
lessness, and his recovery was slow. He was taken initially to the Virginia home of his quartermaster, Erasmus Taylor, and then to Lynchburg. Later he lodged with friends and relatives in Augusta and
Union Point, Georgia.[59]

The chief delight of Longstreet's convalescence was his new son,
Robert Lee Longstreet, born the previous October. He wrote Lee of
the ten-month-old's antics, and the Virginian replied that he was
"glad to hear such good accounts of my little namesake." Lee hoped
Longstreet would soon return to the army. "Do not let Sherman capture you," he warned. "I will endeavor to hold Grant til you come."[60]

Tom Goree accompanied Longstreet to Georgia and kept in
touch with the staff members who had remained at the front to assist
Anderson in running the First Corps. He was naturally anxious for

the General to resume his command and wrote his mother in the summer of 1864: "I hear from everyone that his services are *very much* needed. . . . Genl. Lee needs him not only to advise with, but Genl. Longstreet has a very suggestive mind and none of the other Lt. Genls have this."[61]

In July 1864, Longstreet's former division commander Hood was given the temporary rank of full general and replaced Johnston as commander of the Army of Tennessee. Longstreet was offered a corps command under Hood, but his slow recovery eliminated any need to consider service under someone so recently his junior.[62]

By October, Longstreet was able to mount Fly-by-Night, a horse Lee sent him from Virginia, and within a few days of his first exercises in the saddle he reported for duty once again. But because his once clear voice was now husky and his right arm paralyzed, he realized that Lee might consider him more of a liability than an asset. He therefore offered to serve anywhere in any capacity if Lee had no assignment for him. Lee was delighted at Longstreet's return, however, and immediately restored him to command of the First Corps.[63]

While his offer to serve anywhere was doubtless sincere, Longstreet was apparently interested only in rejoining Lee. By late 1864 his options were quite limited. The much admired Johnston was in eclipse, sacked by Davis for failing to stop Sherman's penetration of Georgia. Beauregard had no desire to leave his coastal command, although he might have accepted Longstreet as a subordinate. Edmund Kirby Smith's Trans-Mississippi held few attractions, and serving under someone who had been promoted over his head (Kirby Smith was made full general in February 1864) might have caused problems. The same circumstances applied to Hood, whose bloody tactics in attempting to defend Atlanta, reminiscent of Malvern Hill and Gettysburg, were the sort of thing Longstreet hoped to avoid. Lee, on the other hand, actively sought Longstreet's return, and his current plight forced him to use the defensive tactics Longstreet had long advocated.

The Army of Northern Virginia was now pinned down to a series of entrenchments south of Richmond which protected the vital railway connections at Petersburg. Longstreet took control of the left flank, a line which stretched north of the James River. The portion of the Confederate line on the river's south bank facing the region known as Bermuda Hundred was also under his command. When Longstreet made his first inspection tour, the men went wild with joy at the sight of their old leader. Leaping on top of the breastworks, they yelled that the Old Bull of the Woods had returned.[64]

Because it would have been easy for the War Department to retire him on the basis of physical disability, Longstreet viewed his return as a vindication. His aide Goree sensed this feeling of triumph when he wrote to his homefolk, "It is gratifying to Genl. L. to know that though he is no favorite with the President & Bragg, yet he has what is much better, the unbounded confidence of Genl. Lee, and the officers and troops in his command."[65]

Lee's confidence in his Old War Horse *was* unbounded, and in the waning days of the war he relied on Longstreet more than ever. Shortly before being appointed Confederate general in chief in February 1865, Lee wrote to Longstreet to thank him for the "earnestness and zeal" he displayed in his operations, stating that "were our whole population animated by the same spirit we would be invulnerable."[66]

Nevertheless, the military situation worsened daily. By late February, Lee admitted to Longstreet in a confidential letter that he could do little to prevent collapse. Neither man was dispirited, however. An officer who observed Longstreet and Lee on April 2 noted, "As usual they both looked confident."[67] But that very day Grant broke through the Petersburg lines, forcing Lee to abandon Richmond in his retreat. When A. P. Hill was killed, Longstreet took charge of the remnants of the Third Corps as well as his own troops. During the nightmare withdrawal, the First Corps retained a remarkable degree of the discipline and order for which it was famous.[68]

On April 8, as the army literally melted away with every mile of the march, Pendleton, Lee's chief of artillery, approached Longstreet to make an unusual request. The night before a group of officers had met and determined to counsel Lee to surrender. Knowing that Longstreet had a special friendship with Lee, and recognizing his position as second in command, Pendleton felt that the suggestion might be better received if Longstreet delivered it. Longstreet refused to speak of defeat, however, reminding Pendleton that under the Articles of War, the penalty for making such a suggestion was death. The First

Corps, he indignantly informed Pendleton, could still hold its own against twice its numbers. "If General Lee doesn't know when to surrender until I tell him," Longstreet said, "he will never know."[69]

Yet Longstreet was frank when discussing the military situation with Lee that night. Lee hoped to launch an attack on the morrow. Longstreet noted that the odds facing them were enormous but assured Lee, "You have only to give me the order, and the attack will be made in the morning."[70] The following day brought no hope, however. With Longstreet's reassurance that Grant was not the sort to deliberately humiliate anyone, Lee rode to meet the Federal commander at Appomattox Court House.

Longstreet headed the commission which worked out the details of the surrender on the Confederate side, but he apparently followed Lee's example and did not attend the surrender ceremony itself on April 12. His proud First Corps was the last portion of the Army of Northern Virginia to lay down its arms. Longstreet did not issue a farewell order similar to Lee's famous one but sent as many of his subordinates as possible an official letter of thanks.[71]

Lee and Longstreet parted company on April 12. Lee went to Richmond; Longstreet planned to visit relatives in Virginia and Georgia and then possibly to accompany Goree to Texas. Goree later recalled their final goodbyes:

> When Genl. Lee was about to take his departure for Richmond, a great many of his old officers called at his Head Quarters to bid him "good-bye." As Genl. Lee passed around, he had some pleasant remark to make to each one whom he bade good-bye. I was standing next to Gen. Longstreet, and he warmly embraced the Genl., and then turning to me, and shaking my hand said—"Captain, I am going to put my old War Horse under your charge. I want you to take good care of him."[72]

PART II

Longstreet's Place in Southern History

"Arma virumque cano."
—Vergil, *The Aeneid*

6. Setting the Stage

TWO MONTHS AFTER PARTING with Lee at Appomattox, James Longstreet began his journey to Texas, moving at a leisurely pace and stopping frequently along his route to visit relatives. He traveled only as far as New Orleans, however. Although the war was barely over, the Crescent City had already captured the imagination of many prominent former Confederates, including Beauregard, Hood, and a host of lesser generals. Longstreet joined this community of veterans, settling in New Orleans with his wife and family and devoting himself to business.

Longstreet became a cotton factor in partnership with a wartime friend, William Miller Owen of the Washington Artillery, and Owen's brother Edward. Within two years he was a successful businessman and a respected figure in financial circles. He became president of the board of an insurance firm and took an interest in large-scale railroad investments. During his evening hours, he and Louise mixed with the city's social elite. For recreation, he and Owen purchased a hunting cabin not far from town. One Louisiana resident described the General at the time as "a candid, sensible man. Everybody appears to like him."[1]

Longstreet made a speedy transition from a lifetime of military service, accepting defeat without bitterness. If the tragic deaths of his three children still preyed on his mind, his grief did not show. Longstreet's friend D. H. Hill described him in 1867 as "a genial, whole-souled fellow, full of fun and frolic."[2] No one would have guessed, as the second year of peace began, that Longstreet would soon become one of the South's most controversial figures.

To understand the controversies which later engulfed Longstreet and affected his place in Southern history, it is important to examine briefly the public image of the man during the war and in the immediate postwar period. This exercise gives one a taste of history as it might have been, for the Longstreet of the 1860s was not the Longstreet of the 1870s, 1880s, and beyond. The difference lay not only with the General but in the perceptions of the people viewing him as well.

In 1867, Northerners and Southerners alike considered Longstreet one of the key figures of the rebellion, and newspapers followed his postwar movements with interest. The new president, Andrew Johnson, hated Longstreet because he had occupied Johnson's native East Tennessee during the war. He declared that Longstreet was one of three Southerners (the other two being Lee and Davis) who had caused "too much trouble" ever to receive a Federal pardon.[3]

The first Northern histories of the war paid little attention to Longstreet or any other Southern generals, intent as they were on creating Federal heroes.[4] A notable exception was the writing of William Swinton, who obtained information from Longstreet which he used in two books, *Campaigns of the Army of the Potomac,* published in 1866, and *The Twelve Decisive Battles of the War,* published in 1867. The author attributed to Longstreet a statement (but not a quotation) that Lee had *promised* to remain on the defensive during the Gettysburg campaign. Longstreet himself never made such a claim, although he implied it in his later writings and never denied the accuracy of Swinton's works.[5] Except in the work of Swinton, however, the picture of Longstreet in the North remained unbalanced. Although newspapers considered him important, he was largely ignored in the books just beginning to appear chronicling the war.

In the South, the picture was reversed. As previously noted, the Southern press took little notice of Longstreet during the war. Confederate newspapers were highly provincial, each tending to portray the closest war zone as the most important. Thus Western newspapers focused on the Army of Tennessee, not that of northern Virginia. This was unfortunate for Longstreet because Virginia newspapers were highly partisan toward native sons and gave him scant attention.

Only when Longstreet went west to fight at Chickamauga did he receive the coverage and praise his efforts merited.[6]

Longstreet was therefore never a figure of great public adoration as were Jackson and such cavalier figures as Stuart, Mosby, or John Hunt Morgan. Nor did he possess the popularity of army commanders such as Beauregard, Johnston, or Lee. But among officers who had exercised only limited independent command, and who spent their careers at corps level, Longstreet's reputation was exceeded only by that of the martyred Stonewall. He towered over the rest of his peers—Ewell, Hardee, Polk, Buckner, and both Hills—and also over Hood and Kirby Smith, who had been promoted above him. As the Confederacy's senior lieutenant general and veteran of both of the major theaters of war, Longstreet's name was well known throughout the South and he was greatly respected, especially by the common soldiers.

In February 1863, when Jackson's fame was at its zenith, a private serving under the famous Virginian wrote, "Longstreet is a bully general; he is a real bulldog fighter [and] he drives the Yankees whenever he meets them. He is a favorite of mine; I think he is next to Gen. Lee. Gen. Lee calls him his old war horse."[7] In October of that same year a young Texan observed, "Longstreet is a bulldog soldier . . . and can whip any army on earth if he has men enough to fight until he is tired of it."[8] Fremantle, the British observer, noted in the diary he published in 1864 that he frequently heard the term "bulldog" applied to Longstreet by the soldiers, who invariably spoke of him as "the best fighter in the whole army."[9]

Fremantle's Austrian companion, Fitzgerald Ross, also published an account of his Confederate tour. This appeared in 1865 in *Blackwood's Edinburgh Magazine*, a journal widely read in the South. Ross lauded Longstreet's military skills, declaring that Longstreet seemed to see and hear everything. He believed Longstreet deserved more credit for the Southern victory at Chickamauga than did Bragg.[10] Another European visitor, Bela Estvan, was equally impressed with Longstreet. His *War Pictures from the South,* published in New York in 1863, described Longstreet as "one of the ablest generals of the Confederate army."[11] Other books and articles written by Europeans made similar statements.[12]

Works published by American authors prior to 1867 were

equally generous in their assessments of Longstreet. W. P. Alexander, writing for the *Southern Literary Messenger* in 1863, stated that "as a fighter, General Longstreet stands second to no man in the army."[13] William Parker Snow's *Southern Generals: Their Lives and Campaigns,* published in 1866, contained a lengthy sketch of Longstreet's service record, including his fine performance at the often overlooked battle of Williamsburg. The author noted that Beauregard, Johnston, and Lee all esteemed Longstreet highly.[14]

The most penetrating account of Longstreet published just after the war came from the pen of Edward A. Pollard, a leading figure among early Southern historians of the conflict. Pollard was an editor of the antiadministration *Daily Richmond Examiner* and an admirer of Johnston, Jackson, and Lee but very bitter toward generals he considered to be the "President's Pets."[15] His *Lee and His Lieutenants,* published in 1867, was the first detailed study of the personnel of the Army of Northern Virginia.

In *Lee and His Lieutenants,* Pollard frequently referred to Longstreet's conduct as "conspicuous" and "brilliant," portraying him as a commander of great skill and energy. Possibly from a perception that Longstreet was a fellow anti-Davis man, he discussed the General's difficulties with Bragg and Davis in some detail. He also noted Longstreet's difficulties with McLaws. Pollard concluded that Longstreet was "trusted, faithful, diligent, a hardy campaigner, a fierce obstinate fighter, an officer who devoted his whole mind to the war."[16]

Longstreet fared even better at the hands of James Dabney Mc-Cabe, Jr., a Richmond-born author and playwright who was one of the earliest biographers of Jackson and Lee. McCabe devoted considerable attention to Longstreet in his 1866 work, *Life and Campaigns of General Robert E. Lee,* a book which mixed praise and admiration of Lee with substantial criticism of his tactics. Like Pollard, McCabe portrayed Longstreet as a commander of great skill and energy, a rapid marcher whose troops were never late, a soldier hard hitting in the attack and resolute in the defense. Lee, McCabe noted, considered Longstreet "his most trusted lieutenant." The author was critical of Lee's actions at Gettysburg, but praised Longstreet's work on that and other battlefields.[17]

The same year McCabe published his biography of Lee, the Reverend Robert Lewis Dabney produced *Life and Campaigns of Lieut.-*

Gen. Thomas J. Jackson, (Stonewall Jackson). Dabney had served on Jackson's staff, and his account exaggerated the Virginian's role in the war, making little mention of either Lee or Longstreet. His few comments regarding Longstreet were highly complimentary, however.[18]

Longstreet's image in the immediate postwar period was thus both favorable and creditable. The General was also recognized during this period as Lee's intimate friend and confidant. Fremantle described their friendship as "quite touching" and noticed that it was "impossible to please Longstreet more than by praising Lee." Longstreet was "never far from General Lee, who relies very much upon his judgment."[19] W. P. Alexander described Lee's confidence in Longstreet as "unlimited" and stated that Lee considered Longstreet's generalship to be the best in the world.[20]

That Longstreet was one of the keys to Lee's success was a view not interpreted by anyone prior to Lee's death as a threat to the Virginian's greatness. Unlike Jackson, Longstreet was portrayed never as a rival to Lee but instead as a no-nonsense fighter, unambitious and oblivious to public opinion. This reputation was not surprising, for there was little about Longstreet to attract or hold public attention. He was taciturn, undemonstrative in public, and decidely unheroic in appearance. Pollard described Longstreet as fierce but somber, intelligent but cold, and habitually unkempt.[21] When Louise was not present and he mixed in exclusively male society, Longstreet paid scant attention to either his dress or his manners. An Englishman left the following revealing description of the General in 1862:

> Longstreet sat in an old garden chair . . . busily engaged in disposing of a lunch of sandwiches. With his feet thrown against a tree, he presented a true type of the hardy campaigner; his once grey uniform had changed to brown, and many a button was missing; his riding boots were dusty and worn. . . . Though the day was warm, the General's coat was buttoned up as well as it could be, and as he ate and conversed freely with those around him, it was evident that his sandy beard, moustaches, and half-bald head had latterly had but distant dealings with a barber. He is . . . thick set, inclined to obesity . . . though thoughtful, and slow of motion, he is remarkably industrious.[22]

It is small wonder that the newspapers covering the war in the East chose to focus on such cavalier types as Jeb Stuart, or Turner Ashby, or Jackson, whose own disheveled appearance could be excused as reflecting the eccentric genius of a martyr. They made much better copy. Even so, there was ample reason to predict, in 1867, that the popularity of such men might soon recede in the public mind and that Longstreet would gain full credit for his services. Both Longstreet and Lee were involved in book projects which, if completed, would accurately portray Longstreet's contributions to the war effort.

Longstreet's close friendship with Lee continued after the war, despite the distance between New Orleans and Lexington, Virginia, where Lee had settled as president of Washington College. As soon as the firm of Longstreet, Owen & Company opened for business, Lee sent a letter expressing his "great affection" for the new partners, wishing them "all happiness & prosperity." Knowing that Longstreet was out of town and that Owen would open the letter, Lee wrote, "I do not consider my partnership with him [Longstreet] yet dissolved & shall not let him go during life."[23] The two corresponded sporadically thereafter, always expressing concern for each other's health, family, and general welfare. In March 1866 Lee wrote Longstreet, "I hope your home in New Orleans will be happy & that your life, which is dear to me, may be long & prosperous."[24]

Both Longstreet and Lee were interested in the history of the recent rebellion. On July 31, 1865, less than two months after the surrender of the last organized body of Confederates, Lee issued a circular letter to his former comrades in arms, soliciting official papers and documents to assist him in writing a history of the Virginia army. Longstreet sent his son Garland to Lexington with the few papers he had salvaged from the debacle and began searching for more.[25]

Lee never set pen to paper, however. He felt limited by the paucity of available Confederate documents and discouraged by the North's continued hostility. By mid-1868 he had apparently abandoned the project, although his interest in it might well have revived had he lived past 1870.[26]

Longstreet was equally interested in Confederate history, but he approached it by proxy, possibly because his wound made writing painful and difficult. He became the semiofficial sponsor of a history of the First Corps to be written by E. P. Alexander, his trusted artillerist. The thirty-one-year-old Georgian had become a professor of mathematics at the reorganized University of South Carolina following the war. Like Lee, Alexander issued a general appeal through form letters.[27]

Alexander received information only very slowly, however, and his professional interests left him little time for writing. He, Longstreet, and many others remained enthusiastic about the project, but found, as Lee had, that official documents were extraordinarily difficult to obtain.[28] In August 1869 Longstreet advised Alexander to suspend work on the volume until they were allowed "access to the captured Confederate papers." Alexander continued to correspond on the subject with comrades for almost three decades, however. Although he published a few articles, the bulk of his collected material did not see light until his *Military Memoirs of a Confederate* was published in 1907.[29]

Thus two works of enormous potential influence, Lee's history of the Army of Northern Virginia, and Alexander's history of the First Corps, were never written. How might they have affected Longstreet's place in history? Both books would unquestionably have presented Longstreet in a favorable light, as both Lee and Alexander shared Longstreet's friendship and genuinely admired his military talents. But this is not to say that either would have been inappropriately laudatory or completely so. Alexander did not hesitate to criticize his former chief in his later articles and in his memoirs. He particularly resented Longstreet's attempt on the third day at Gettysburg to shift the responsibility for Pickett's advance onto his shoulders. Nor would Lee have any reason to restrain his judgment, as he had ample reason during the course of the war to criticize something about each of his subordinates. Lee was reported to have remarked in a private conversation that Longstreet was slow and in another conversation that Jackson was slower than Longstreet.[30] Such views might have been stated forcefully in his book.

But although Alexander and Lee would have portrayed Longstreet as less than perfect, by virtue of the very subject their books would have presented a more accurate picture of the General than existed in 1867 or has emerged since. The war had created many heroes, as all wars do, and these were already widely celebrated in print. Within two years of the conflict's close, James Avirett had published *Memoirs of General Turner Ashby.* An English translation of *Memoirs of the Confederate War for Independence,* by Heros von Borcke, a Prussian who served on Stuart's staff, was produced in Philadelphia. These combined with such works as John Scott's *Partisan Life with Col. John S. Mosby* and John Esten Cooke's *Wearing of the Gray* to eulogize the Confederate cavalry and greatly exaggerated its importance during the war.

Of these authors, Cooke was by far the most widely read, and his rambling, entertaining sketches of the war proved so popular that in 1870 he published a companion volume, *Hammer and Rapier*. Born in Winchester, Virginia, Cooke had by the 1850s written a number of novels and possessed something close to a national reputation. During the war he served on Stuart's staff. He saw Lee, Jackson, and Longstreet frequently but took no interest in the latter because he was not a Virginian. Writing after the war, he filled *Wearing of the Gray* and its successor with scenes that focused almost exclusively upon natives of the Old Dominion who fit the cavalier image already popular in the romantic literature of the period.[31]

At the same time that Cooke and his compatriots were emphasizing the cavalry, Stonewall Jackson was the subject of five major biographies (including one by Cooke) and numerous pamphlets.[32] Most of these treated Jackson as a separate army commander and barely acknowledged Longstreet's existence. Although Longstreet was consistently portrayed as a gallant member of Lee's team, utterly capable and dependable, his actual role in the war was never shown in its proper perspective, as accuracy in this regard would have seemed to diminish Jackson's heroism. None of the works on Jackson even hinted that Longstreet outranked him and was, in Lee's absence, Jackson's superior officer. All conveyed the erroneous impression that Jackson and his men, not Longstreet and the First Corps, were the mainstay of the Virginia army.

Thus as early as 1867 Longstreet's image was in danger of being obscured in popular history by books which favored martyrs, glorified the cavalry service, and gave preference to Jackson and the Second Corps. Whatever their limitations as assessed by future historians, the books Lee and Alexander planned to write would have given the public a more accurate view of Longstreet's contributions to the war and of his relationship with Lee. Jackson's reputation would probably have declined, despite his acknowledged genius, as it became clear that his role and status had been secondary. Through Alexander and Lee the South might have known Longstreet as he really was: the man Beauregard, Johnston, and Lee each sought as his second in command, Lee's principal lieutenant, trusted adviser, and intimate friend.

This view of history as it might have been, relative to Longstreet, sharply contrasts with the General's image only a decade later. For in 1867 Longstreet became embroiled in a long political controversy which, in the eyes of most Southerners, detracted from his hard-won laurels. The placid, comfortable life he had followed in New Orleans evaporated, and he found his military reputation under attack. In anger and frustration he lashed out at his accusers, but the blunt fury which had carried the field at Chickamauga proved inappropriate in the war of words which engulfed Confederate veterans in the ensuing decades.

7. Scalawags, the Lost Cause, and the Sunrise Attack Controversy

THE TRANSFORMATION OF Longstreet's image from hero to villain began innocently enough with the *New Orleans Times*, one of the city's leading Democratic newspapers. The passage of the Military Reconstruction bills by Congress on March 2, 1867, prompted its editor, W. H. C. King, to publish a list of prominent former Confederates residing in New Orleans. He appealed to these men to submit their views on Reconstruction to the public, to offer guidance and leadership in the present crisis as they had during the war.

Longstreet was among the first to respond. In a letter published on March 18, he counseled patient submission to the new, harsher legislation. Looking forward to a full restoration of constitutional government, under which the South's traditional leaders could represent the section once more, Longstreet argued, "let us accept the terms as we are in duty bound to do, and if there is a lack of good faith, let it be upon others."[1]

Many of Longstreet's comrades in the late rebellion held similar views on Reconstruction. His former staff officer Raphael Moses wrote an anonymous letter to the *Richmond Enquirer* expressing sentiments quite close to those of his chief. Robert E. Lee refused to make any political statements for publication. But since 1865 he had been advising friends through his correspondence to submit peacefully to all Northern legislation and to seek redress by reentering politics as soon as possible, even if in so doing they seemed to yield to the conqueror too quickly.[2]

In fact, a mood of pragmatism, patience, and calm prevailed among the South's leaders at the time. General Beauregard wrote to the *New Orleans Times* expressing views quite close to Longstreet's. Alabama's Governor Robert M. Patton, Wade Hampton of South Carolina, ex-Governors Henry A. Wise of Virginia and Joseph Brown of Georgia, and many newspaper editors throughout the South issued statements similar to that of Longstreet.[3]

The North viewed this moderation on the part of former Confederates as a good sign. When Longstreet wrote a second letter to the New Orleans press, arguing that cooperation would reduce the unavoidable Reconstruction period to the minimum possible length, the *New York Times* reprinted it in full.[4] Unlike most of his contemporaries, however, Longstreet carried the theory of cooperation a step further. In the spring of 1867 he visited his Uncle Augustus at Oxford, Mississippi, showing his former guardian a letter he intended to release to the New Orleans press. In it Longstreet stated that as the principles of the Democratic party stood in the way of reunion, the South should cooperate freely with the Republicans. "The war was made upon Republican issues," Longstreet wrote, "and it seems to me fair and just that the settlement should be made accordingly." Judge Longstreet needed but a glance at this letter to predict grimly, "It will ruin you, son, if you publish it." He could not dissuade his nephew, however, and the letter appeared in the June 8, 1867, issue of the *New Orleans Times.*[5]

Longstreet's letter touched off a debate which raged from Texas to Massachusetts. As one might expect, Republicans lauded his views, while Democrats condemned them. When Southern Republicans began to speak of Longstreet as one of their own, the ire of their Democratic opponents increased accordingly.

To understand the severity with which most Southerners reacted to Longstreet, one must remember that most blamed the recent devastating war directly upon the "Black Republicans." For Longstreet to advocate cooperation with the Federal occupation troops was acceptable, as the valor shown by Union soldiers during the war had been acknowledged and the soldiers were only doing their duty. But the slightest hint that Southerners themselves might join the abolition party was another matter entirely. The Republican party was seen as nothing less than a threat to Southern civilization. As one historian has noted, "In every ex-Confederate state a new Republican party—biracial in makeup, nationally rather than sectionally oriented—constituted a presence as unsettling to traditional southern life as the Union army or the Freedmen's bureau."[6]

Longstreet's friend and business partner William Miller Owen had warned him as early as May that any appearance of cooperation with the Republicans would be misconstrued by the public as self-serving. Longstreet dismissed the possibility. "I am not a politician or officeseeker," he wrote Owen, "but I think it my bounden duty to assist the people."[7] When his friend's prediction, like that of Judge Longstreet, proved only too true, Longstreet felt acute distress.

Longstreet expressed his anxiety about the political situation fully in a letter to R. H. Taliaferro on July 4. Heretofore unavailable to historians, it merits quotation at length:

> My politics is to save the little that is left of us, and to go to work to improve that little as best we may. I believe that the course that some politicians have pursued, tends to increase our humiliation and distress, and leads us to greater trouble, until we finally shall have confiscation & expatriation. Since the negro has been given the privilege of voting, it is all important that we should exercise such influence over that vote, as to prevent its being injurious to us, & we can only do that as Republicans. As there is no principle at issue now that should keep us from the Republican party, it seems to me that our duty to ourselves & to all our friends requires that our party South should seek an alliance with the Republican party. . . .
>
> Congress requires reconstruction upon the Republican basis. If the whites won't do this, the thing will be done by the blacks, and we shall be set aside, if not expatriated. It then seems plain to me that we should do the work ourselves, & have it white instead of black & have our best men in public office.[8]

Longstreet feared more than just confiscation of property and forced exile, however. He feared a resurrection of the rebellion, and he wanted no part of it. He informed Taliaferro:

> No one has worked more than I, nor lost more. I think that the time has come for peace & I am not willing to lose more blood or means in procuring it. If there are any in the country inclined to fight this question, I hope not to be included in that number. I shall not abuse them for their views & I hope that they will not deny me the right to withdraw from the contest.[9]

Faced with a collapsing Confederacy in 1864, Longstreet had shrewdly devised a military strategy to undermine Lincoln's reelection campaign. When in 1867 peace seemed on the verge of collapse, Longstreet was equally Machiavellian, proposing that the South's traditional white leaders join the Republican party and use it to their own ends. As in 1864, the crisis atmosphere and sense of desperation blinded Longstreet to the impracticality of his scheme.

Longstreet's desire for peace may have been in part a product of his war wound and the daily physical suffering he still experienced. Or perhaps he was more easily reconciled to the North's triumph than were his contemporaries because he did not identify narrowly with a particular ancestral place. He had fought for the whole South, not any individual state. Regardless, Longstreet failed to realize that the principles which had brought about secession had not all been swept away at Appomattox. He was therefore both angered and confused when his motives were misunderstood.

Longstreet's former comrades never seemed to appreciate that he was interested primarily in preserving the old order in the South, not in reconciliation with the North. One reason for the misunderstanding was his failure in public letters to express his commitment to white supremacy as strongly as he did in his private letter to Taliaferro. The implications of his proposal were not lost on the black populace of New Orleans, however. Shortly after Longstreet's involvement in political issues began, the *New Orleans Tribune* warned: "Look out, new enfranchised citizens. . . . We have by this time so many kinds of Republicans that General Longstreet is already nominated as your leader, and Jeff Davis himself will soon claim to be your best friend."[10]

Race was one of the most crucial factors in transforming Longstreet's image. The fact that Longstreet sought to *control* the black vote was lost on his fellow white Southerners, who saw only that Longstreet had dared to suggest collaboration with the party that had freed the slaves. Longstreet received several anonymous death threats in the mail following the publication of his letters. While he did not take them seriously, they disturbed him greatly.[11] Although he had anticipated some negative reaction, he was dismayed by the "extreme harshness" some persons expressed toward him. Many old friends turned away, and Longstreet's heart was heavy as he contemplated the consequences of his actions. In July he wrote his sister, "I now believe as General Hood says: 'They would crucify you!' but I think this number small and I am a little suspicious that he is one of them."[12]

Had Longstreet done no more than suggest cooperation with the Republicans, his reputation would probably not have suffered irreparable harm. But he exercised the courage of his convictions and eventually became a full-fledged Republican himself. The decision was not a sudden one but a slow process, occurring over a span of two years. In New Orleans he gradually formed acquaintances with James F. Casey, John M. G. Parker, J. G. Taliaferro, and Henry C. Warmoth—men destined to play crucial roles in governing Louisiana over the next decade.[13]

Why Longstreet found these men attractive is not known. Like many former soldiers he was exceedingly restless after the war and traveled constantly. He apparently found, as did many, that politics was the sole activity which could approach the military service in excitement. In this respect he differed from his fellow Southerners only in chosing a different political affiliation. He assumed that the bulk of the people in his native region would soon acknowledge the sincerity of his motives even if his actions did not meet with their approval.[14] In this assumption, he could not have been more wrong.

Appearances did not favor Longstreet and discouraged a dispassionate assessment of his actions. Democratic newspapers accused him of wanting to have his political disabilities removed so that he could run for office as a Republican. Such suspicions seemed confirmed when Longstreet received a Federal pardon on June 19, only a few days after his letter containing a de facto endorsement of Republican principles appeared in print.[15] The timing was coincidental. Longstreet had followed Lee's example, applying for a pardon in November 1865.[16] His application was initially rejected but was approved two years later. The fact that his pardon was championed by Grant and other Federal army officers, and by several senators and representatives, merely combined with the timing to create the erroneous impression that Longstreet had made some sort of deal with his former enemies.

Longstreet's subsequent actions heightened the belief that he had abandoned his Confederate comrades. For a period of over a year he widened his contacts with prominent Republicans and accepted their help in restoring his political rights. His supporters included Benjamin F. Butler, who as a Federal general ruling occupied New Orleans had become the man most hated by Southerners during the war. Even the slightest association with Butler would have tarnished Longstreet's reputation in the South, and Butler was a major supporter of a bill which passed Congress on June 24, 1868, removing the political disabilities of Longstreet and several other Southerners.[17]

Longstreet endorsed his kinsman Grant for the presidency in 1868, and less than a week after taking office Grant nominated Longstreet for the position of surveyor of the port of New Orleans, with a salary of $6,000 per year. The impression that Longstreet was now hand in glove with the conquerors was furthered not by the gift of the office itself (the spoils system being widely accepted) but by the fact that Grant was placing Longstreet in a position to work against Democrats in a crucial area.[18]

If Longstreet's contemporaries had been able to judge him in a vacuum, his pragmatic approach to Reconstruction might have been appreciated, if not endorsed. But Longstreet's actions occurred at a time of intense emotional turmoil throughout the South. To explain how a righteous cause, blessed by God, could fail, former Confederates devoted themselves to the memory of their acts. They cultivated what historians usually call the Lost Cause myth. This myth, and the mentality which produced it, profoundly affected the General's place in Southern history.

Seeds of the Lost Cause were present in the early histories of the war mentioned earlier in this book. The principles of total sacrifice and undying devotion which had made Jackson, Stuart, and Ashby such suitable wartime heroes made them also the first symbols of the Lost Cause. With such men to emulate, it was easy for veterans to conclude following Appomattox that they had been merely overwhelmed, not really beaten, and that Reconstruction was a continuation of the same struggle in a different manner. Now that the South faced the imagined threat of "Negro Rule" rather than Northern bayonets, the loyalty given to Jackson and others was easily transferred to the Democratic/Conservative parties during Reconstruction.

When Longstreet joined the Republicans instead of rallying to the Lost Cause, he exposed not only his present motives but his Confederate past to attack. For unlike the other veterans who returned home to face Federal occupation, Longstreet's loyalty appeared quite limited and conditional. When self-advancement seemed to be Longstreet's motive, his actual wartime sacrifices were forgotten, obscured by his scalawag image.

By making defeat seem honorable, the Lost Cause rationale heightened the South's already high concept of honor. Consequently, no group of men ever incurred greater dishonor in the eyes of their peers than the minority of white Southerners who supported the Republicans. "'Scalawags,'" wrote a contributor to the *Southern Magazine* in 1871, "are verminous, shabby, scabby, scrubby, scurvy cattle. Therefore there is a manifest fitness in calling the native southerner, of white complexion, who adopts the politics of the Radical party, a Scalawag."[19] Such men were seen as traitors not only to their region but to the white race as well. A popular definition ran: "A scalawag is a white man who thinks he is no better than a Negro and in so thinking makes a correct appraisal of himself."[20] For Southerners of Longstreet's generation and many generations to follow, any affiliation with the Radical Republicans meant to think the unthinkable, to confront squarely the great paradox which lay at the very heart of being a white Southerner: the presence of the black man.

The memory of the war lay at the core of the Lost Cause. Longstreet's political activities posed a threat to it because they seemed to question the legitimacy of the rebellion itself. From self-imposed exile in Canada, Jubal Early expressed the views of many Southerners when he wrote: "All the Confederates here have been much distressed at the course pursued by Longstreet. He has very much obscured the fame won by him during the war, and his letters are calculated to throw discredit on our course. It is for this reason that I regret his course more than any other."[21]

Relatives and friends expressed concern for Longstreet's military reputation after he began collaborating with the "enemy." "I would not have him tarnish his own laurels," remarked former subordinate Robert Toombs at a public meeting in Atlanta.[22] The General's kinsman L. Q. C. Lamar also lamented Longstreet's new alignment. Long-time friend D. H. Hill expressed the vain hope that Longstreet had meant his endorsement of Republican party principles as some sort of joke. If not, Hill concluded, then either Longstreet's "theology or his loyalty is at fault."[23]

Longstreet's family suffered severe social ostracism in consequence of his actions. Placing the wives and children of scalawags "under social ban" in an attempt to "freeze them out of white society" was a common tactic in Louisiana.[24] The degree to which Longstreet and his family suffered cannot be precisely determined but was doubtless great, as he implies in his memoirs. One lasting result of the ostracism was that Longstreet left the Episcopal church, the traditional church of American military men, North and South. He eventually became a Catholic.[25]

Fear that his now blackened name would damage the enterprise led Longstreet to sever his business connections with his good friends the Owens. Apparently for similar reasons he sold part of his insurance interests to Hood. During the summer of 1867, the Longstreets moved from New Orleans to Lynchburg, Virginia, probably from a combined desire to visit some of Louise's relatives, to be closer to Washington, and to escape the scorn of Louisiana residents. Longstreet's transformation from respected businessman to social outcast had been astonishingly swift. Louise Longstreet's reaction to these events is not known, but it could not have been easy for her, hearing Longstreet's now husky voice and watching him struggle to learn to write left handed, when her husband was branded a traitor to the South.[26]

Longstreet's reputation as a traitor was powerfully reinforced by the relationship between religion and the Lost Cause rationale for defeat. As a scalawag, he also came to be regarded as a Judas. The correspondence was obvious. Scalawags supposedly sold out the South for personal gain just as Judas Iscariot had betrayed Christ for silver. The comparison with Judas was not limited to Longstreet but was used widely with reference to scalawags in general or to specific individuals, such as Joseph Brown, former governor of Georgia.[27] The appellation as applied to Longstreet reflected the horror with which the most devoutly religious and puritanical section of the nation viewed his actions. When he continued to endorse the Republican party, discussing political issues openly and freely, his "heresy" made him appear to be something of an Antichrist. Longstreet inadvertently placed himself in stark contrast with the South's heroes at a time when the Lost Cause was transforming the Southern soldier, living and dead, into a veritable saint.

In order to accept the defeat without regarding it as tantamount to the loss of God's Grace, Southerners mentally transformed their recollections of the antebellum South. It became a superior civilization of great purity which God, in His mysterious wisdom, had sacrificed to the materialistic Yankees. The Confederate defeat and the ongoing ordeal of Reconstruction were frequently likened to Christ's sacrifice on the Cross and the Roman persecution of early Christians.[28] Traditionally disliking abstractions, Southerners tended to view both their religion and their history in terms of heroes, great men who embodied both Christian and historic truths and values. In the wake of defeat, the South's fallible soldiers, both living and dead, became saintly symbols of the Lost Cause.[29] Once the religious and secular strategies for coping with defeat had been combined, the contrast between these saintly figures and Longstreet—the Judas, the Antichrist—became even more obvious.

The disparities which so damaged Longstreet's image and adversely affected his place in Southern history abounded in Southern periodicals during the Reconstruction era. Interest in the war led to the rebirth of Southern magazines which gave special attention to its history. Journals such as *Southern Review* debated Reconstruction topics, adamantly defending the traditional conservative principles that Longstreet seemed willing to abandon. Longstreet's friend D. H. Hill published *Land We Love*, a magazine devoted to "Literature, Military History, and Agriculture." In 1869 Hill sold his interests to a Baltimore periodical, *New Eclectic*, which in that same year became the official organ of the Southern Historical Association. In 1871 its name changed to *Southern Magazine*. Together with a later periodical, *Southern Bivouac*, these magazines kept the memory of the war alive and fresh in the public mind. Filled with stories and poems by veterans who were loyal to the Lost Cause, they made Longstreet's continued affiliation with the Republicans seem selfish and self-serving.[30]

Land We Love provides an excellent example of how such periodicals affected Longstreet's image. Hill criticized Longstreet's postwar actions severely in one of his editorials,[31] but the real harm he did his friend lay in his own open and enthusiastic endorsement of the Lost Cause, replete with its saint figures and religious overtones.

Hill was Stonewall Jackson's brother-in-law. Although no love was lost between them, he filled his magazine with stories, anecdotes, and poems praising the Virginian. He emphasized the religious aspects of Jackson's character until Jackson seemed a man too good for this world. Other Confederate heroes received due attention as *Land We Love* readers contributed a flood of prose and poetry commemorating the Southern dead and explaining the defeat in religious terms. Wartime death was explicitly equated with Christian martyrdom, while present suffering under Reconstruction was perceived as a test of individual spiritual righteousness and fortitude—a test which Longstreet, by joining the South's oppressors, could not be said to have passed.

Lost Cause themes permeated virtually every genre of Southern literature during the 1870s and 1880s. The concepts of undying devotion and total sacrifice were particularly strong in Southern poetry during and after the war. This tendency combined with the romanticism already prevalent among Southern poets to enhance the image of the Confederate soldiers as cavaliers. The drab Longstreet suffered by contrast.[32]

The works of Henry Timrod, often called the poet laureate of the Confederacy, expressed the shock of defeat and the South's struggle to comprehend it. The young South Carolinian's famous poem "Ode," sung during a ceremony in 1866 to decorate the graves of Confederate soldiers in Charleston's Magnolia Cemetery, accurately foretold a future bright with memorials to Southern sacrifice and honor. The throng of mourners was assured that their husbands, sons, and brothers had perished in a sacred cause:

> Stoop, angels, hither from the skies!
>   There is no holier spot of ground,
> Than where defeated valor lies
>   By mourning beauty crowned.[33]

Reconstruction, the source of Longstreet's political "heresy," was also a common theme. Paul Hamilton Hayne was moved by the contrast between the present state of his native South Carolina and its proud past to write a lyrical lament entitled "Carolina." Hayne's more famous contemporary, Sidney Lanier, touched on Reconstruction in several poems written between 1868 and 1871. In "Raven Days" and "Laughter in the Senate" he bewailed the Confederate defeat and expressed disgust for carpetbaggers, scalawags, and freedmen.[34]

But nowhere was the connection between the war, Reconstruction, and religion made more explicitly than in the lyrics of Fanny Downing, a popular poet of the day and frequent contributor to Hill's magazine. Her poem "The Land We Love," which appeared in July 1866, read in part:

> Man did not conquer her, but God
> For some wise purpose of his own
> Withdrew his arm; she, left alone,
> Sank down resistless 'neath his rod.
>
> God chastens most who he loves best,
> And scourges whom he will receive.
> The land we love may cease to grieve,
> And on his gracious promise rest!
>
> Nestling her children to her side,
> She fought to make those children free;
> And when, by heaven's supreme decree,
> Her last fond hope of freedom died,
>
> She nobly yielded to its might,
> Gasping amid her fiercest pain:
> "God's way!—and he will make it plain—
> "His evening-time will bring us light!"
> . . . .
> Though howling waves around thee toss,
> Rest calm in thine exalted strength,
> Sublime though ruined, till at length,
> The crown of heaven replace thy cross![35]

The connection between such poetry and Longstreet's changing image was indirect, of course. Yet the type of poems that Mrs. Downing wrote remained fantastically popular for the rest of the nineteenth century. They reflected the continued bitterness of the general population toward the North and the almost universal refusal to come to terms with defeat in the sort of pragmatic fashion that Longstreet advocated.

The romantic strain in Southern prose also damaged Long-street's image. Sir Walter Scott's famous Waverly novels did more than popularize romanticism among Southern writers and readers. These chivalric tales greatly heightened the South's historical consciousness, instilling a greater awareness of present events as part of the grand saga of history.[36] This feeling was plainly reflected in the novels written by Southerners during and immediately after the war.

More than half the novels written in the South during the Civil War era were written by women. Preeminent among these was Augusta Jane Evans Wilson, a native of Columbus, Georgia, who by the time of her death in 1909 was one of the South's most popular novelists. She had been a tireless volunteer nurse during the war, and her acquaintances included many people well known to Longstreet: Beauregard, Toombs, Curry, and La Salle Pickett, George Pickett's wife. Her intense, almost religious fervor for the war effort was typical of that felt by thousands of Southern women. "I believe I loved our cause *as a Jesuit his order,*" she once confided.[37]

Mrs. Wilson expressed her sectional feelings openly and bitterly in *Macaria: Or Altars of Sacrifice,* which she completed in 1863. Although limited editions appeared in both the North and the South in 1864, the book's immense popularity arose from the 1868 edition, which, according to her biographer, contributed "to the romantic myth in which the North and the South have embalmed the War Between the States."[38]

Wartime passions were perpetuated in the subsequent decades by the works of Mrs. Wilson's professional and amateur contemporaries. In such novels as L. D. Whitson's *Gilbert St. Maurice,* Mary Tucker Magill's *Women: Or, Chronicles of the War,* and Mary Ann Cruse's *Cameron Hall: A Story of the Civil War,* the so-called gentler sex proved to be the staunchest defender of the Lost Cause, far less forgiving than the South's combat veterans. As one literary analyst noted, "The ladies fixed the pattern of tales in the 1860's and early 1870's with their admiration for Christian sacrifice and their uncritical and violently partisan pride in sectional virtues."[39]

Transforming the Confederate soldier into a saintly defender of righteousness, popular works such as *Raids and Romance of Morgan and His Men, Bertha the Beauty: A Story of the Southern Revolution,* and the extravagantly titled *Fitz-Hugh St. Claire: The South Carolina Rebel Boy: Or, It is No Crime to Be Born a Gentleman,* set a standard of conduct which Longstreet's activities seemed to besmirch.[40] "Disloyalty" was occasionally assailed openly, as in *Gilbert St. Maurice:*

> What shall we say to those who helped to bring darkness and death and defeat on the once proud and happy land of the South? To those who rushed frantically forward, as the first long line of Federal bayonets gleamed like silver in the sunlight, and *voluntarily* took the oath of allegiance to the United States Government, with the avowed intention to "save their property?" May the shadow of an avenging Nemesis pursue them relentless unto death.[41]

Female writers did not entirely dominate the literary scene. No author affected Longstreet's image more adversely than John Esten Cooke. Cooke enjoyed unrivaled popularity in the South until the mid-1880s, and his role in giving shape and substance to the Lost Cause would be difficult to exaggerate. He profoundly influenced succeeding generations of writers and helped to foster a collective false memory among Southerners, a memory which held no place for James Longstreet.

Born in what is now West Virginia, Cooke was related by birth or marriage to virtually every prominent family in the Old Dominion. His prewar novels such as *The Virginia Comedians* reflected his love of Sir Walter Scott and the myth that Virginians were descendants of English Cavaliers.[42]

Through his wartime biography of Jackson, expanded and republished in 1866, Cooke helped to enshrine the Confederate dead as righteous Christian martyrs. In a similar fashion his postwar works, whether fictional or reminiscences, converted men into symbols of the Lost Cause. He presented his characters as chivalric knights in the best tradition of Scott, often drawing parallels between Confederate heroes and Southern patriots of the Revolution.[43]

Cooke's immensely popular novels helped to raise Southern morale during Reconstruction and helped to foster the notion that Virginia had been the only important theater of the war. In *Surry of Eagle's-Nest* (1866), *Mohun* (1869), and *Hilt to Hilt* (1869), he extolled the superiority of Southern civilization in general with specific references to its gallant soldiers, virtuous women, and overall spiritual purity. Most important of all, his compelling prose transformed the stigma of defeat into a badge of merit that Southern veterans could wear proudly. As one historian noted, Cooke portrayed the war "not as a failure, but as a superb adventure, the very participation in which was a mark of honor."[44]

Cooke's impressive literary output injured Longstreet because it popularized perceptions of the war and its participants which made Longstreet appear disloyal and selfish. While Cooke's heroes remained steadfast, endorsing true conservative principles, Longstreet appeared to be working hand in glove with the enemy. The stress placed on breeding, cultural refinement, and proper ancestry in Cooke's fiction left Longstreet—a blunt soldier of backwoods origin and Dutch progenitors—a poor candidate for veneration. Longstreet, in short, did not fit the image of the Confederate veteran which Cooke popularized. Generations of Southerners who grew up reading the works of Cooke, Augusta Evans Wilson, and others thus had little inclination to include Longstreet in their list of Confederate idols.

At the same time that these diverse cultural, political, literary, and religious facets of the Lost Cause were producing a negative image of Longstreet, the General found his military reputation under attack. Significantly, the onslaught began only after the death of his friend Robert Lee.

When he died on October 12, 1870, Lee was only one of a large number of Confederate heroes and was still second to Stonewall Jackson in the eyes of most Virginians. Lee's status changed quickly, however, as a group of his former staff officers and subordinates made it their business to enshrine his memory. Unlike Jackson's admirers, who damaged Longstreet's image only by implying erroneously that Jackson was Lee's closest friend and second in command, Lee's defenders built up Lee's reputation by attacking Longstreet. Once the faults and failures for which Lee had been criticized during the war had been shifted to Longstreet's shoulders, Lee could emerge as the sort of pure and stainless hero that the Southern people, evolving the Lost Cause rationale, were beginning to expect.

Following Lee's death, a squabble arose over possession of his remains and the enshrinement of his memory. The Lee Memorial Association of Lexington and the Lee Monument Association of Richmond vied for public attention and support. Jubal Early, one of Lee's lieutenant generals, headed the Richmond forces, while the Lexington group was guided by Lee's former chief of artillery, the Reverend William Nelson Pendleton. Pendleton was assisted by another man of the cloth, the Reverend John William Jones.[45]

During the year 1872, Jones, Pendleton, and Early began to cooperate in efforts to bring the two factions together. Over the next two decades, in their excess devotion to Lee, these three men also carried out a carefully organized policy of character assassination against James Longstreet. In so doing they focused first Southern and then national attention on the battle of Gettysburg, creating the myth that it was *the* turning point of the war.

Early began the attack on January 19, 1872, when he delivered the second annual address to commemorate Lee's birthday at Washington College, which had recently been renamed Washington and Lee. He claimed that, during the night of July 1, in a conference with Ewell, Rodes, and Early, Lee had expressed his intention of attacking at dawn on July 2 with Longstreet's corps. Had Longstreet attacked at the hour Lee intended, Early claimed, Lee would have won the battle and the South would have been an independent nation.[46]

Early's motives deserve explanation, as he, more than any other man, convinced nineteenth-century Americans and twentieth-century historians that Longstreet's military career deserved censure. Early had been an outspoken critic of secession and had switched his loyalty to the South at the very last moment, a fact which some people remembered and held against him during the war. His military career was marked by controversy and failure. His hesitation on July 1, when Cemetery and Culp's hills were still vulnerable, was one of the major blunders of the Gettysburg campaign. Late in the war, while he led the badly outnumbered Second Corps in the Shenandoah Valley, he was so disastrously defeated that Lee, in response to public outcry, relieved him of command. Further humiliations followed as Early fled the country after the war, fearing Federal retaliation for his having ordered the burning of Chambersburg, Pennsylvania, during a raid. Living in Canada in acute poverty, he wrote a vitriolic defense of his last campaign only to have Lee politely but firmly withhold approval of either the book or his expatriation.[47] Yet with this book Early found himself. Writing Confederate history became his raison d'être, apparently satisfying some deep inner need to atone for his previous failures as a soldier. The reputation he had failed to win with the sword would be his with the pen.

Early returned to the United States in 1869. As previously mentioned, he headed the Lee Monument Association. In 1870 he became president of the Association of the Army of Northern Virginia, a benevolent society, and in the following year vice president for Virginia of the Southern Historical Association. In 1872 he accepted a similar post in the Nashville-based Confederate Burial and Memorial Association.[48]

Thus, after Lee's death, Early found himself in a position to wield great power and influence. Because of his outspoken defense of the South during Reconstruction, men who during the war had little reason to regard Early as anything but a failure began to look upon his opinions with respect.

When Early attacked Longstreet in his 1872 speech, he doubtless felt confident that most Southerners would automatically support him against Longstreet, whose name was linked in the popular mind with disloyalty and betrayal.[49] Because he was already seen as a Judas figure, Longstreet made a perfect scapegoat for the Confederate defeat. Longstreet's loyalty seemed limited and his actions an insult to the Confederate dead. Inasmuch as Lee was no longer alive to set the record straight, Longstreet's military record made an easy target. It was particularly vulnerable if the person casting aspersions appeared to be defending the record of a soldier such as Lee who had remained "true" to the cause.

Longstreet ignored Early's slander, even when Early's address was published in two widely circulated pamphlet editions. He may have assumed that no one would credit Early, given his mediocre war record and his wartime unpopularity. He could not anticipate the astonishing effect of the Virginian's remarks. Early's words took on great power and the ring of authority because he told Southerners exactly what they wanted to hear. His version of Gettysburg, which blamed Longstreet, provided an explanation for the Confederacy's defeat which neither entailed the loss of God's Grace nor questioned the superiority of Southern civilization. He chose as his scapegoat a man already intensely unpopular, who was not identified with any one state and who could therefore be attacked without insulting the memory of soldiers from any part of the South.

Longstreet's continued affiliation with the Republicans in Louisiana kept him in the public eye in a manner which increased the inclinations of Southerners to believe the worst about him, including Early's charges. As a supporter of the Radical governors Henry C. Warmoth and William P. Kellogg, Longstreet held positions which in Southern eyes appeared to reward his betrayal.

In 1870 Longstreet was appointed adjutant-general of the state. In January 1872, just days before Early's address at Washington and Lee, Longstreet was commissioned brigadier general in the state militia and was assigned responsibility for all the militia units and police forces in the city of New Orleans. During that year the Louisiana Republicans split into warring factions. Their in-fighting, which involved the Grant administration, continually attracted nationwide attention. As a result of these interparty conflicts, Longstreet resigned his post as state adjutant-general but kept his militia commission.[50]

Longstreet was fifty-one years old in 1872, and the auburn hair and beard which he now wore clipped rather short were streaked with gray. By combing his hair on the side rather than straight back, he covered his receding hairline and actually appeared less bald. Because of the wound he had received in the Wilderness, his health was never very good, but thanks to an income of some $15,000 from railway and insurance investments, he had no worries about providing for his family. The latter had grown steadily in number. In addition to Garland, now twenty-four, Robert Lee, age nine, and James, Jr., age seven, Longstreet had a new son and daughter. Fitz Randolph Longstreet was born in 1869, while Maria Louisa, the couple's tenth and last child, was born in July 1872. Although the Longstreets had lost five children during their years together, the five living in 1872 all lived to adulthood.[51]

The following year, 1873, was an active one for Longstreet. In March, the predominantly black police force of New Orleans was incorporated into the state militia. This event sparked several riots, and in helping to quell them Longstreet did not gain any popularity among conservative Southerners. In June he was given a lucrative four-year appointment to the Levee Commission of Engineers. This post initially involved much traveling and hard labor, although after two years it seems to have degenerated into a sinecure. Longstreet later claimed that he was not paid all the money owed him for this job.[52]

During the summer of 1873, Longstreet lived in Lynchburg, Virginia, where Louise and the younger children had gone to avoid the yellow fever season in New Orleans. As the town was quite small, it seems impossible that Longstreet and Early never met, yet such was apparently the case. By this time Early's slanderous remarks of the previous year were being repeated by others, attracting considerable attention and winning credence.

Foremost among those who joined Early in condemning Longstreet was William Nelson Pendleton. Despite his staff position, Pendleton had never been particularly intimate with Lee during the war. But as an Episcopal minister in Lexington while Lee headed Washington College, he had become a close friend of the entire Lee family. As chairman of the Lee Memorial Association, Pendleton devoted his life after 1870 to enshrining the "sacred memory" of his former commander. To raise money for a statue and mausoleum for the college campus, he and agents under his direction toured the South reciting eulogies of Lee, eulogies in which Lee's character began to seem so pure and stainless as to be Christ-like.[53]

The rivalry between Pendleton's organization and the Richmond group diminished after Early gave his address in 1872. The long-lasting friendship that Pendleton and Early developed united the two powerful organizations in spirit and purpose, particularly after Pendleton had altered his tour lectures to fit and to bolster Early's opposition to Longstreet.

Pendleton delivered his revised speech for the first time in January 1873 at the third annual celebration of Lee's birthday in Lexington. He stated that his reconnaissance on the morning of July 2 had been made because Lee expected Longstreet to attack at sunrise. Early's claim was thus supported by an apparently impeccable source, a minister of the gospel and intimate of Lee.[54]

The report that Pendleton submitted to Lee in 1863 concerning his reconnaissance on the morning of July 2 proves that his claim in 1873 was completely fabricated.[55] Pendleton did not stop here, however. His speech accused Longstreet of "culpable disobedience" and "treachery" in failing to attack at dawn and claimed that Lee's acceptance of responsibility for the disaster amounted to a magnanimous cover-up unparalleled in history.[56] As Christ assumed the burden of sin at Golgotha, Pendleton implied, so had Lee assumed the sins of Longstreet the Judas at Gettysburg.

Pendleton and his agents continued their fund-raising tour and lectures after 1873. The new speech denigrating Longstreet that they used removed Gettysburg as a major obstacle to the idealization of Lee. Delivered in town after town, the speech was a major factor contributing to Lee's emergence as the dominant Confederate hero of the war and served to blacken Longstreet's name at the grass-roots level.

The actions that Longstreet took to refute Early and Pendleton were ineffective. His initial response was dignified silence, reflecting either indifference or a belief that such blatant slander would never be credited. This reaction was unfortunate, for Longstreet's public reputation was no longer the sort which would allow him to rest on his wartime accomplishments. During his silence the Southern populace proved more than willing to believe the worst about him, and Lee's venerators gained a degree of acceptance for their fictitious version of the battle of Gettysburg which the General was never able to overcome.

By mid-August, Pendleton's lecture tour had reached Mississippi, and Longstreet was being entreated by friends and relatives to make a public reply. Longstreet was content, however, to publish a notice in several Virginia newspapers challenging Pendleton to present evidence to support his claims. He felt secure because two of his subordinates, Generals Lafayette McLaws and B. G. Humphreys, had published accounts of the battle which he believed sufficiently refuted Pendleton. A letter defending the General was also published in the *Vicksburg Herald* by Thomas Walton, his former aide.[57]

Henry B. Dawson of the New York–based *Historical Magazine* contacted Longstreet either late in 1873 or early in 1874 about the possibility of refuting Early and Pendleton through a full-length account of Gettysburg. Dawson was also in touch with Early concerning a rebuttal. The pugnacious Virginian was anxious to fight Longstreet with the pen, and Dawson apparently hoped the resulting controversy would boost circulation of his struggling journal. Longstreet declined Dawson's offer for lack of documents. He had sent all his wartime papers to Lee for Lee's book and was unable to supply Dawson with even a copy of his Gettysburg battle report.[58]

During this period Longstreet's public image plummeted still further, thanks to an outbreak of violence in Louisiana which sharply underscored his connections with the Radical Republicans. On September 14, 1874, the Crescent City White League attempted to overthrow Governor Kellogg's administration by force of arms. As head of the militia, Longstreet led the state's largely black troops against the insurgents, many of whom were Confederate veterans. In the ensuing street battle, the state militia broke and ran. One of the White League officers later wrote a friend, "It was with the greatest difficulty that I prevented the men from firing particularly at Longstreet."[59] Even so, Longstreet was wounded by a spent bullet and was captured by his foes, an experience which must have been the most humiliating of his life. Order was restored only at the intervention of federal troops.[60]

As Tom Goree had noted in 1861, silence, not debate, was Longstreet's characteristic response to situations or persons he disliked. But a severe six months' illness, not indifference, seemingly prevented Longstreet from confronting the Gettysburg issue after the New Orleans riots. By the spring of 1875, however, his health had recovered.[61]

Longstreet wrote Pendleton on April 4, challenging the Virginian to give a fuller account of his July 2 reconnaissance and the names of officers who according to Pendleton had witnessed Lee's anger when the alleged attack at dawn had failed to occur.[62] Pendleton replied on April 14, refusing to supply additional details or the names. He closed his letter with sarcastic references to the recent turmoil in New Orleans and suggested that Longstreet must be glad that the South had lost the war.[63]

When Longstreet replied on April 19, his letter revealed his own overconfidence and a naïve belief that the truth would somehow outweigh any assault upon his reputation. As a seer, Longstreet could not have been more wrong than when he wrote Pendleton:

> School-boys may be misled by you, but even with them I fancy that only the most credulous may be temporarily misled. It is my opinion that

your abuse, so far from impairing my interests or my reputation, will be more likely to enhance them in the estimation of honorable men. . . . The impertinent tone and language of your letter are in keeping with your disposition to propagate falsehood.[64]

During the rest of the year Longstreet collected information for an article on Gettysburg. He had an unexpected ally in Lafayette McLaws, the childhood friend whom he had relieved of command in 1864. Although McLaws still resented the incident, he was too honest a man to support Early's or Pendleton's false version of Gettysburg for the sake of revenge. In the account of the battle he sent Longstreet, he denied that any orders to attack at dawn had been given. Such orders, he noted, would have meant sending exhausted troops over unexplored ground against an enemy whose strength and position were unknown. McLaws believed that Pendleton's claims were actually a slur on Lee's generalship. He added that, once Longstreet had been ordered forward on July 2, his movements were as rapid as possible, delayed only by Lee's orders to follow a concealed route.[65]

Longstreet appreciated McLaws's sense of fair play, remarking in his letter of thanks that Bragg and Davis would enjoy seeing them renew their wartime quarrel. As for the alleged sunrise order, it was something Lee "probably never dreamed of."[66] Longstreet's position seemed secure against further slander because, in response to his inquiries, Lee's staff officers denied any knowledge of orders to attack at dawn on July 2.

Walter H. Taylor assured Longstreet that he had no knowledge of a sunrise attack plan and that he disapproved of Pendleton's actions. "I regard it as a great mistake on the part of those who, perhaps because of political differences, now undertake to criticize & attack your war record," he wrote. Charles Marshall denied knowledge of any dawn assault plan and noted that Lee's battle report gave no indication that the attack on July 2 had been made later than expected. A. L. Long wrote Longstreet that on the evening of July 1 and the morning of July 2 Lee had expressed a desire to attack Meade "as early as practicable," but he did not recall that the Confederate commander had planned a sunrise advance.[67]

The strongest denial came from Charles S. Venable, who attributed Pendleton's statement to the effects of an illness, probably catalepsy, which the Reverend suffered: "I cannot but attribute his statement about this order at Gettysburg to an absolute loss of memory said to be brought on by frequent attacks resembling paralysis. His whole statement with regard to Gettysburg is full of mistakes. . . . It is a sad pity it ever got into print."[68]

Longstreet tried to find a copy of his own Gettysburg report, together with those of Hill and Ewell. When he could not locate them in either Richmond or New Orleans, he journeyed to Washington to speak with the secretary of the treasury, the department that had taken charge of captured Confederate archives. He also solicited help from old friends. His contacts included Hood, Alexander, Seddon, and Goree.

Goree provided the most useful information, reminding the General that during the winter of 1864 he had carried dispatches from East Tennessee to Virginia. At that time, Northern newspapers had just published the official Federal reports of the battle of Gettysburg. Having just read them, Lee discussed the campaign with Goree. According to the Texan, Lee not only had no criticism of Longstreet but conceded in retrospect that he should have allowed Longstreet to make his flank attack on the morning of July 3. Goree dismissed Pendleton as "an old *granny*" whose figurehead status was "a notorious fact."[69]

Instead of waiting until his own piece on the Pennsylvania campaign was complete, Longstreet seized the first opportunity to refute Early and Pendleton. The February 1876 issue of *Scribner's Monthly* printed a letter from Lee to Davis dated August 8, 1863, in which Lee accepted full responsibility for Gettysburg and offered to resign. With the pretext of commenting on this letter, Longstreet wrote the *New Orleans Republican,* presenting some wartime correspondence of his own.

Longstreet's first letter was one he had written to his Uncle Augustus on July 24, 1863. In it he frankly expressed his belief that his plans, if adopted, would have won the battle. This was followed by a paragraph in which Longstreet seemed anxious to take responsibility for the defeat:

> As we failed of success I must take my part of the responsibility. . . . As Gen. Lee is our commander, he should have all the support and influ-

ence that we can give him. . . . I desire, therefore, that all the responsibility that can be put on me shall go there and remain there. The truth will be known in time, and I will leave that to show how much of the responsibility of the attack at Gettysburg rests upon myself.[70]

The attack to which Longstreet referred was the disastrous one of July 3. His letter was written in response to warnings from friends and relatives who feared that Lee would be cashiered for the defeat and that he might drag Longstreet down with him. Longstreet's "invariable reply" to any such suggestions was that "it was better that I should bear the responsibility, than to put it on our chief."[71] Although he had stated his objections to Lee's tactics in the strongest possible terms in his wartime report, Longstreet was apparently willing, for the good of the war effort, to share the public condemnation he expected to fall on the Virginia army after Gettysburg. But by failing to explain the context of this letter when he reprinted it in 1874, Longstreet gave his readers the erroneous impression that criticism of his actions at Gettysburg had begun during the war when in fact none had been voiced prior to Lee's death in 1870.

Longstreet followed his 1863 letter with an excerpt from one he claimed to have received from Lee in January 1864. He offered only a single sentence for public inspection, which read, "Had I taken your advice [at Gettysburg] instead of pursuing the course I did how different it all might have been."[72] Fitzhugh Lee, General Lee's nephew, immediately questioned the authenticity of Longstreet's letter from Lee and challenged Longstreet to produce the full text. Longstreet replied in an article in the *New Orleans Republican*. He defended the letter at length but produced no more of it, simply referring Fitzhugh Lee to Colonel Erasmus Taylor, former quartermaster of the First Corps. Taylor, Longstreet indicated, would vouch for its authenticity.[73]

Many historians have since concluded that Longstreet had invented the letter from Lee. Longstreet, however, had no need to manufacture evidence to prove his case against Early and Pendleton, as he had the replies from Lee's staff officers asserting that no order had been given to attack at sunrise. Furthermore, Wade Hampton, who despised Longstreet's politics, wrote Jubal Early on March 27, "I believe that the letters published by Longstreet [are] genuine for that he had told me soon after the war very much the same story."[74] More important, Erasmus Taylor was ready to back Longstreet's claim. In 1889, Taylor recalled the day the General had received the letter from Lee. "I was passing your room," he wrote, "when you called me in, and passing me the letter desired me to read it, saying that at some time it might be important for some other beside yourself to remember it."[75]

It might at first seem to surpass belief that Longstreet showed Taylor such a letter with instructions to remember it for the future. Yet the astonishingly blunt language of his Gettysburg official report attests to his strong determination to have it known eventually that the disaster of July 3 was none of his doing.

Longstreet was apparently referring in his article to a letter he had once received from Lee and had since lost. He decided unwisely to quote it from memory. His failure to ask Erasmus Taylor to make a public statement concerning its authenticity was another error, for his inability to produce the full text as Fitzhugh Lee demanded gave the public every reason to doubt his veracity. Why trust the word of someone disloyal to the Cause?

Jubal Early attacked Longstreet's article in the pages of the *Lynchburg Tri-Weekly Virginian*. Longstreet replied with yet another letter to the Louisiana press, stating that he had statements from Lee's former staff officers asserting that no order to attack at sunrise had been given. As further evidence he cited excerpts from the wartime diary of William Miller Owen of the Washington Artillery. With undisguised sarcasm he suggested that Early's record in the Shenandoah Valley disqualified him as a military critic.[76] Such remarks were counterproductive, however, for most Southerners could remember only that since the war Early had been an outspoken critic of Reconstruction, while Longstreet had joined the Republicans.

The greatest liability of Longstreet's last article lay in a single long sentence.

> As General Lee, upon assuming command of the Army of Northern Virginia, asked General Longstreet and other superior officers of that army their counsel as to the best plans to be pursued in our protection, and did General Longstreet the honor to adopt the plan that he suggested, to cross the river and turn General McClellan's right, it may

seem possible that General Longstreet had greater claims for respectful consideration than most of the young officers who volunteer[ed] suggestions.[77]

Lee's staff officers were aghast at this passage. Longstreet seemed to be setting himself up as the brains behind Lee, taking credit for Lee's victories. They had refuted the sunrise attack order because they knew it was not true, but in the wake of Longstreet's apparent egotism they enthusiastically joined Early's campaign to vilify Longstreet. Longstreet had inadvertently helped to bring about a coalition of powerful men who would radically affect his image and his place in Southern history.

8. The Anti-Longstreet Faction Emerges

MUCH OF LONGSTREET'S time and energy during the 1870s was devoted to a war of words, a war he lost very badly and which has profoundly affected his place in history. During this decade also, Early, Jones, and Pendleton set Robert E. Lee on the road to sainthood. Lee's devotees became so fanatical in their endeavors that they have rightly been described as a cult.[1] Longstreet was an integral part of this interesting phenomenon, through his role as scapegoat for Gettysburg.

In their efforts to enshrine Lee's memory, Early and Jones corresponded widely with former Confederates throughout the South, and thanks to their efforts a distinct anti-Longstreet faction emerged. It consisted of Early, Pendleton, Jones, Lee's nephew Fitzhugh Lee, and Lee's former staff officers Venable, Taylor, Long, and Marshall. They drew support from such men as Braxton Bragg, William Preston Johnston, C. M. Wilcox, Wade Hampton, and (eventually) Jefferson Davis. Their correspondence reveals an extreme prejudice against Longstreet for political reasons and a determination that the blame for Gettysburg, and thus the loss of the war, should be made to rest on his shoulders alone. They sought to discredit everything Longstreet wrote in defense of his good name as soon as it was published. A knowledge of their actions is necessary, among other reasons, to understand those of Longstreet.

Although they had denied the existence of any orders to attack at sunrise sent by Lee to Longstreet on July 2 at Gettysburg, Lee's former staff officers were desperately anxious to shift the blame for the Pennsylvania disaster from his shoulders to Longstreet's. Venable wrote Early in 1872, shortly after Early's Washington and Lee address. Despite the fact that Lee's own battle report proved it false, Venable claimed that Lee had expected Longstreet to send Hood's and McLaws's divisions forward with Pickett for the attack on July 3.[2] He maintained this claim despite massive evidence to the contrary for the rest of his life.

Long wrote to both Pendleton and Early. He now asserted that Lee had expected Longstreet's July 2 attack to begin earlier than it did and that he had expressed great annoyance when it did not get under way until 4:00 P.M. Marshall combed Lee's surviving papers for materials to use against Longstreet, reporting apologetically to Early when he could find no evidence that Lee had blamed Longstreet for anything. Taylor, who had been exuberant when Longstreet returned to Virginia from East Tennessee, now became an avid member of the group opposing Longstreet, praising Early for his criticisms of the General. "From the course pursued by Longstreet," he wrote, "I now feel that he should be handled with ungloved hands." Venable was likewise encouraging.[3]

Longstreet had proved to be his own worst enemy, turning Lee's staff officers against him by the letters and article that he had sent to the press. These men particularly resented the passage which implied that he was the brains behind Lee in McClellan's defeat. By claiming simply that Longstreet had been fatally late on July 2, without mentioning a specific hour, A. L. Long broadened the Gettysburg controversy in an important fashion. Venable's claim that Hood and McLaws were to have advanced on July 3 would also prove quite popular, despite ample evidence to the contrary. Their false accusations, which soon saw print, would dog Longstreet for the rest of his life and cloud his reputation to the present day.

John William Jones also eagerly supported Early and Pendleton in their tirade against Longstreet. A former chaplain of the Thirteenth Virginia Infantry, Baptist minister at Lexington, and postwar friend of the Lee family, he published in 1874 *Personal Reminiscences, Anecdotes and Letters of Robert E. Lee,* a standard source for most later writers on Lee and the war. The first fifty-five pages were a verbatim reprint of Early's speech against Longstreet at Washington and Lee.[4]

Jubal Early remained the key figure. He sent copies of his criticisms of Longstreet to influential people throughout the South, and the replies he received testify to the immediate, immense popularity of his derogatory attitude toward Longstreet. How easy it was to blame Gettysburg, the failure to win independence, and by implication all the woes of the Reconstruction on a scalawag! Fitzhugh Lee, Braxton Bragg, Wade Hampton, and other less prominent Southerners praised Early, Jones, and Pendleton for their campaign against Longstreet.[5] Thanks to his writings, which had actually been few and brief up to this time, Early rose quickly to a position of astonishing influence. "Believe me dear Genl.," an admirer wrote him in 1875, "the fear of your rebuke has held many a weak kneed Confederate to his duty."[6]

While Early was thus engaged, Longstreet was hard at work on an account of Gettysburg. This work, he remarked to McLaws, had been forced upon him by "Parson Jones, Parson Pendleton, and Generals Fitzhugh Lee and Early."[7] By March 1876 he had completed the rough draft of one article and was working on another. Nor did he have to look for a publisher. Alexander K. McClure, editor of the *Philadelphia Weekly Times,* shrewdly realized that a continuation of the Gettysburg controversy would sell papers. Having met Walter Taylor and noting his "romantic attachment for his great chief," McClure solicited from him an article on the Pennsylvania campaign. "I did not doubt," McClure later recalled, "that he would place the responsibility for the Gettysburg disaster upon Longstreet."[8]

Taylor did exactly as predicted. In "The Campaign in Pennsylvania" he accused Longstreet of deliberately delaying his attack on July 2 from the forenoon to the afternoon, with fatal results. He then claimed, as Venable had to Early in private, that Lee had meant for Hood's and McLaws's men to accompany Pickett in his July 3 charge.[9]

After Taylor's article went to press, the crafty McClure contacted Longstreet and discovered, not surprisingly, that the General was anxious to make a rebuttal. Because Longstreet's wound from the Wilderness made penmanship painful and difficult, Henry W. Grady, then a free-lance journalist in Atlanta, was hired to copy, edit, and polish Longstreet's rough drafts.[10] When Grady finished he mailed the manuscript directly to McClure, without giving Longstreet an opportunity to check it. Longstreet was greatly annoyed, as several embarrassing errors thus appeared in print. While Grady was at work,

Longstreet was approached by two additional parties interested in his writing on the battle. He intended to rest on his present work for some time, however, before writing a definitive account of his service record. He believed that by waiting he would be able to benefit from materials collected by other writers. Meanwhile, he doubted that "any mind of military judgment" would believe the version put forth by Early and his followers.[11]

Longstreet's articles appeared in McClure's paper on November 3, 1877, and February 28, 1878. They were also reprinted as "Lee in Pennsylvania" and "The Mistakes of Gettysburg" in 1879, forming part of the *Weekly Times* anthology *The Annals of the War Written by Leading Participants North and South.*[12] In both forms they enjoyed wide circulation and attracted much attention.

At first glance Longstreet's articles seemed irrefutable, and he received praise for them from many, including his old chief Joseph E. Johnston.[13] His lengthy quotations from the letters of Lee's staff completely destroyed the notion of a sunrise attack. While his account of the battle was not without errors, it was essentially accurate. Indeed, his writings might have won considerable approval had he taken into account, when composing them, that Lee had become a saint. Had he expressed profound reverence for Lee's memory and couched his actions in the most humble prose, he might yet have had a fair hearing despite his scalawag reputation and consequent unpopularity.

Longstreet was neither humble nor gentle, however. Stung by a decade of abuse for his political actions and resenting the deification of his friend Lee, the Old War Horse lashed out blindly, making excessive claims for himself. His portrayal of Lee as often narrow and provincial in his strategic thinking was historically accurate but hardly calculated to please. In recalling his talks with Lee before the battle about the propriety of using defensive tactics in the North, Longstreet egotistically left the impression that he had entered the campaign on some sort of contractual basis after negotiating with Lee as an equal. He charged Lee with gross overconfidence during the three-day struggle and overstated the odds against which the First Corps had fought. Through such needless exaggeration and a general tone of arrogance, Longstreet gave his readers reason to suspect that self-advancement, not self-defense, was the motive for his writings.

Longstreet's analysis of Lee's errors, executed in a clinical fashion with the implication that James Longstreet would never have made them, did his reputation no good. He had as much right to analyze Lee's generalship as anyone, of course. But because of his Republican affiliation, not one Southerner in a thousand was likely to concede Longstreet the right to criticize *any* soldier who had remained "true" to the cause, much less the saintly Lee.

As one would expect, Longstreet's articles for McClure were keenly examined by Jubal Early and his friends. They discussed the General endlessly in their correspondence, seeking ways to discredit him and to prevent anything he wrote about the war from being accepted as valid by future historians.[14] They soon had a magnificent opportunity to manipulate public opinion against him. In 1877 Louis Philippe Albert d'Orleans, Comte de Paris, a noted Civil War observer, wrote to the Southern Historical Society. He sought information for a multivolume history of the war. The president of the Society was Jubal Early, and the editor of its official journal, the *Southern Historical Society Papers,* was the Reverend Jones. The count sent Jones a list of questions, asking him to distribute them to prominent Confederates, so that he could obtain information on the Gettysburg campaign.[15]

Jones and Early quickly recognized that they now had an excellent excuse to collect information casting aspersions on Longstreet. It could be presented in the *Papers* in a seemingly objective fashion, as replies to the count, a neutral party. After careful consultation with Early, Jones sent out the questionnaires. Longstreet's views were not solicited, of course.[16] By July, Jones had collected a number of replies, four of which he printed in the August number of the *Papers.* He printed not the first four he received but the four that were most bitterly opposed to Longstreet, arranged so that they would have maximum impact.

Not surprisingly, the first article in reply to the count was that of Early, who repeated the now familiar charges that Longstreet had been late on July 2 and had failed to send in Hood's and McLaws's men on July 3. Jones followed the Virginian's statement with letters from Fitzhugh Lee, William Allan (a member of Ewell's staff), and Walter Taylor, all of whom backed Early's claims.[17]

The next two issues of the *Papers* contained replies from E. P.

Alexander, Cadmus Wilcox, John Bell Hood, A. L. Long, and Harry Heth, as well as a second letter from Walter Taylor—all of which Jones was sure his readers would view as confirmation of Early's claims in the first letter of the series. Wilcox, a North Carolinian who had commanded a brigade in the July 3 assault, blamed Longstreet for certain unflattering passages concerning the conduct of his brigade at the Wilderness which had appeared in William Swinton's *Campaigns of the Army of the Potomac.* Early recruited Wilcox late in 1875 with copies of his writings, and Wilcox remained in the anti-Longstreet camp thereafter.[18]

Jones was particularly pleased with Alexander's response. Never realizing the use to which it would be put, the artillerist had dashed off a quick reply to the Frenchman's inquiries.[19] Alexander dwelled on the time lost in the countermarch on July 2 without making it clear that this had not been Longstreet's fault. He also described Longstreet's extreme reluctance to send Pickett forward on the following day. By placing Alexander's letter among those that were solidly against Longstreet, Jones gave his readers the impression that Alexander supported the notions that Longstreet had been slow and uncooperative during the campaign. He made similar use of Hood's reply, which was actually a copy of a letter that Hood had sent Longstreet in 1875. Full of factual errors and particularly inaccurate as to the timing of events, Hood's letter, in Jones's estimation, was "a strong confirmation of Longstreet's tardiness and disobedience of orders."[20]

Lest there be any misunderstanding, however, Early contributed a forty-page article for the December number of the *Papers,* telling the journal's readers what they should conclude from the series to date. In answer to some of the count's questions, many of the writers had admitted that the absence of Stuart's cavalry and Ewell's failure to seize Cemetery Hill on July 1 were factors in the defeat. Early defended Ewell and Stuart at length, argued that the replies published proved that Longstreet was the sole culprit, and then boldly reaffirmed his original contention that Lee had expected Longstreet to attack at dawn on July 2.[21]

Early followed this statement with a twenty-one-page rebuttal of Longstreet's November 3 article in the *Philadelphia Weekly Times.* He cleverly forced his readers to make a direct choice between Longstreet the Judas and the all-forgiving, Christ-like Lee: "Either General Lee or General Longstreet was responsible for the remarkable delay that took place in making the [July 2] attack. I choose to believe that it was not General Lee."[22]

Early's next move was equally masterful. He persuaded a reluctant Jones to reprint Longstreet's first *Weekly Times* article in the *Papers*. Appearing in the January 1878 number, Longstreet's piece stood precondemned. Its tone and content could only further alienate readers who for five months had been so carefully coached in how to spot its "errors."[23]

In April, Jones published an additional rejoinder by Fitzhugh Lee. Written in close cooperation with Early, it included a statement by John Lee Carroll, former governor of Maryland, who claimed to have heard Lee blame Longstreet for losing Gettysburg.[24] In June, Jones reprinted Longstreet's second *Weekly Times* article, followed by the inevitable lengthy rebuttal by Early. The September issue of the *Papers* contained an article by Cadmus Wilcox accusing Longstreet of willfully disobeying Lee's orders on July 2. William C. Oates, commander of the Fifteenth Alabama at Gettysburg, made similar accusations in the October issue.[25]

With Oates's article the long series came to an end. Jones was confident that it had served its purpose. Gloating over their accomplishments, he wrote Pendleton, "I suspect that Longstreet is very sick of Gettysburg before this. Certainly there has not been left 'a grease spot' of him."[26]

It would be difficult to exaggerate the importance of the "Gettysburg series," as it came to be called. Early's defense of Stuart united the cavalryman's admirers with those of Lee. The large number of articles, the variety of authors, and the inclusion (without his permission) of Longstreet's own pieces, left the false impression that Longstreet had been judged responsible for losing Gettysburg but only after a fair and objective hearing. In fact the deck had been stacked against him in one of the cleverest orchestrations of innuendo and unsubstantiated accusations in American historiography. For many of Longstreet's contemporaries, and for many historians as well, the Gettysburg series proved Longstreet's guilt.

Longstreet remained blithely confident that his own writings de-

fended him adequately and that no one, least of all future generations, would credit the attacks on his military reputation. At a time
when, in retrospect, Longstreet should have been working feverishly
to clear his name, the General was primarily interested in Republican
party politics, activity that of course only tarnished his reputation still
further in the eyes of most Southerners.

9. A Georgia Republican Courting Clio

TO KEEP ABREAST OF new arrivals in the country, New York reporters often stationed themselves in the lobbies of the city's finest hotels. A *Tribune* journalist observing patrons at the prestigious Fifth Avenue Hotel in June 1881 was therefore able to interview General Longstreet the moment he returned from Europe, having just resigned his position as United States minister to Turkey in order to become Federal marshal for Georgia.

The reporter found Longstreet, then sixty years old, to be a fine-looking man whose auburn hair had turned almost completely white. Instead of the flowing beard he had worn during the war, Longstreet now sported luxuriant muttonchop sidewhiskers. In reply to the newsman's questions, he pronounced the climate of Constantinople delightful and said that it had been beneficial to his health. But he had missed his family greatly and looked forward to his new duties in Georgia.[1] Had he known how much abuse the marshal's job would bring him, he probably would have stayed abroad.

Longstreet had begun switching his political power base from Louisiana to Georgia six years earlier, in 1875. In that year the editor of the *Gainesville Southron* invited the General to settle with his family where he had spent his earliest years. Not all Georgians were pleased at the prospect. A letter to the *Southron* from an Augusta native who had served for four years as an officer in the First Corps revealed the degree to which Longstreet's Republican affiliation had alienated his former comrades. The Augustan suggested that the editor paint himself black and turn his womenfolk over to the tender mercies of Longstreet and "his Negroes." Any white man who would so much as speak to Longstreet, he declared, was not worthy to be called Georgian.[2]

Despite such sentiments, Longstreet purchased two properties in Gainesville. The first was the Piedmont Hotel, a white-columned, three-story structure which served as a winter home for the General and his family. His main residence, however, was a farm outside of town. There he built and "richly furnished" a large two-story home, filling it with books and his souvenirs of two wars. Situated on a hilltop, it overlooked a majestic unbroken expanse of ridges and streams. The General terraced his steeply sloping land carefully to prevent erosion, laying out an extensive orchard and vineyard.[3]

Politics, not farming, was Longstreet's real reason for moving to Georgia. He maintained his connections in Louisiana even after Reconstruction ended there in 1877, and he tried to get a new post there. But his primary interest was the Federal marshalship for Georgia, a position which paid well and entailed much political influence. Friends from both states sent high recommendations of him to the newly inaugurated president, Rutherford B. Hayes, but the only patronage the General was able to secure from the administration was an unimportant post as a deputy collector of internal revenue. In January 1879 he became postmaster of Gainesville, which he considered poor compensation for his sacrifices on behalf of the party to date. He was pleased with his nomination as minister to Turkey in May 1880 but accepted it with the understanding that the Georgia marshalship would be his as soon as it became vacant.[4]

Longstreet's diplomatic appointment was the sort of reward regularly dispensed in American politics. As all the serious work was handled by the legation's permanent staff, the position carried few duties and much prestige. It was not a sinecure, however, although the ambassador drew a salary of up to $10,000. The cost of living in Constantinople prevented the General from taking his family, and the elaborate entertainment that he was expected to provide was expensive. His tenure in the Middle East undoubtedly cost him more than he earned from it.[5]

Longstreet sailed for the Turkish capital on November 1, 1880, meeting with Sultan Abdul Hamid Khan II for the first time in early December. The General's only known accomplishment as minister was to secure permission for a group of American archeologists to work in Turkey. Although permission had previously been denied, Longstreet was able to sway the sultan, and in February 1881 the expedition was authorized.[6]

In April, Longstreet took an extended leave of absence, visiting Austria, Prussia, and France. He probably toured the battlefields of the Franco-Prussian War of 1870, a conflict he had followed with great interest through the newspapers. In May, Longstreet learned that the coveted Georgia post would at last be his. He had enjoyed his brief tenure as diplomat but confessed to a friend that the "position in Turkey was too far from home and home friends to be altogether agreeable, notwithstanding the great interest centered upon that once great empire."[7]

Unfortunately for Longstreet, his participation in Georgia politics served to heighten the negative image he had acquired as a Louisiana scalawag. He became embroiled in a much publicized struggle for control of the Republican party in the northern part of the state and was opposed, of course, by the Democrats as well. The ensuing tripartite turmoil won the General few friends and many enemies.

Georgia's Republicans were almost hopelessly divided, lacking unity in leadership, goals, and philosophy. Remaining true to the sentiments he had first expressed in 1867, Longstreet worked to build a party of native whites, men of property and standing who would represent the South's traditional interests. His chief opponents within the party, many of whom were Northerners, sought to exploit the black vote for short-term gains. The struggle between these two large factions, and between the subgroups within each, lasted twenty years.[8]

Unfortunately for Longstreet, President Chester Allan Arthur supported the General's political rivals, men who resented his intrusion into Georgia and coveted his lucrative and influential Federal job. A coincidental scandal in the marshal's department soon gave them an opportunity to oust Longstreet.[9]

The General's predecessor in the Atlanta office had been Marshal O. P. Fitzsimons. Both Fitzsimons and his deputies were corrupt, and the financial accounts they turned over to Longstreet were a shambles.

Unaware of this disarray, Longstreet retained most of Fitzsimon's deputies, and the corruption continued. Their fraudulent conduct came to light early in 1884 when the Justice Department undertook a nationwide investigation of the Federal marshalships.

While Longstreet was never accused of dishonesty, he incurred severe public censure for having allowed the unscrupulous deputies to remain in office. Some investigators believed that the real problem lay with thirty-six-year-old Garland Longstreet, who as his aged father's chief deputy had virtually taken control of the office. One witness told Justice Department investigators that Garland was "entirely incompetent to manage the office, on account of dissolute habits and want of ability." Another claimed he had "deceived his father time and time again," acting in collusion with Fitzsimons's men to falsify expense accounts.[10]

Believing the allegations to be politically motivated, Longstreet stood behind not only Garland, whose wrongdoing was far from proven, but all his deputies, some of whom were unquestionably corrupt. Far from defrauding the government, Longstreet proclaimed, he and his men had failed to receive their full salaries. The issue seemed tailor-made for the General's political rivals, who induced President Arthur to remove Longstreet from office. Arthur claimed that he was responding to a request from the Attorney General's office; actually he was punishing Longstreet for having failed to support his reelection bid. The office promptly went to John E. Bryant, one of Arthur's chief Georgia supporters.[11]

Longstreet's difficulties received widespread attention in the press. Many newspaper reports acknowledged that he had been removed as part of a political payoff, not because of incompetence, but the fact remained that the General's name had been repeatedly linked in public with fraud and corruption.[12] Like his friend Grant, whose administration had been scandal ridden, Longstreet was judged by the company he kept. When Longstreet complained publicly that the Government still owed him $2,000 of his generous $6,000 salary, it could only have added to his popular image as Judas, a man who had sold out his Confederate friends for personal gain.

Longstreet's participation in Georgia politics also earned him powerful enemies among the state's Democratic leaders, who feared that Longstreet was attempting "to radicalize the State."[13] Chief among the General's opponents was former acquaintance John B. Gordon, who had commanded one-half of Lee's rapidly dissolving army during the retreat to Appomattox. An officer of skill and ability, Gordon nevertheless owed his advancement largely to the near collapse of Lee's command structure late in the war, when so many of the Confederate commander's lieutenants were tried and found wanting. After the war, Gordon became part of a triumvirate of Georgia Democrats who dominated the state politically for over two decades.[14]

Gordon owed his political success in no small part to Jubal Early and the Lee cult. Longstreet's status as a pariah and the deaths of Jackson, Ewell, Stuart, and A. P. Hill left the tall, handsome Georgian with a claim to intimacy with Lee rivaled only by that of Early himself. Gordon shrewdly exploited his slight relationship with Lee, linking his name with Lee's whenever possible and promoting himself as the "Hero of Appomattox." These actions plus his firm stance against Reconstruction allowed him to win two terms in the United States Senate and two consecutive terms as governor of Georgia.[15]

Gordon did not take part in the machinations which led to the Gettysburg series, but he joined the anti-Longstreet faction the moment Longstreet offered a political challenge to his power in northern Georgia. When the controversy over Longstreet's war record reached a new peak in the mid-1880s, Gordon joined Longstreet's detractors with enthusiasm.

The controversy over Gettysburg had never really ended. Despite his intention of resting on his two articles to the *Philadelphia Weekly Times*, Longstreet discussed Gettysburg at length in a July 1879 newspaper interview. The famous battle had been lost, he argued, when Lee became overly excited and took the offensive. Referring to the July 3 assault, he claimed that Lee had later bemoaned, "Why didn't you stop all that thing that day!"[16] Discussing the second day's fight, Longstreet was shamelessly boastful, distorting and exaggerating the accomplishments of the First Corps. He stated that Lee all too often lost his "admirable equipoise" whenever "a crisis or disaster threatened." Although he loved Lee "like a brother," Longstreet said, Joseph E. Johnston had been the better general.[17]

Over the next two years Longstreet sent several letters on Civil

War topics to various newspapers, commenting on the writings of others, but he did not consider writing full-length articles of his own. "I don't much think I shall write except to expose the wickedness of those who seek to do me injustice," he informed a friend.[18] Yet he had ever-increasing reasons to be concerned for his reputation. The anti-Longstreet views expressed in the *Southern Historical Society Papers* proved to have a profound impact on the accounts being written about the war.

In 1879 former lieutenant general Richard Taylor published *Destruction and Reconstruction: Personal Experiences of the Late War*. A native of Kentucky, Taylor had served under Lee and Jackson but had transferred west in 1862. His knowledge of Gettysburg was thus limited to what he had read about it. In a passage which sharply illustrates the success of Early and his supporters in enshrining Lee's memory, together with the manner in which Longstreet's writings damaged his own case, Taylor wrote:

> A recent article in the public press, signed by General Longstreet, as-cribes the failure at Gettysburg to Lee's mistakes, which he (Longstreet) in vain pointed out and remonstrated against. That any subject involv-ing the possession and exercise of intellect should be clear to Longstreet and concealed from Lee, is a startling proposition to those having knowledge of the two men. We have Biblical authority for the story that the angel in the path was visible to the ass, though unseen by the seer his master; but suppose, instead of smiting the honest, stupid animal, Bal-aam had caressed him and then been kicked by him, how would the story read? And thus much concerning Gettysburg.[19]

That a general essentially from the western arena should in-clude such a passage in his memoirs indicates the degree to which the Gettysburg issue had absorbed the interest of all Confederate vet-erans, regardless of the theater in which they had served. Taylor's "knowledge of the two men" was not based on personal intimacy, as he implied. His anger at Longstreet the Judas for attempting to steal credit from the Christ-like Lee further illustrates the manner in which Longstreet's negative image was accepted and spread by persons not directly related to the factors which had originally produced it.

Two other books demonstrate the way in which Longstreet's rep-utation had been tarnished. John William Jones's *Army of Northern Vir-ginia Memorial Volume*, published in 1880, was a collection of speeches from the annual meetings of the Association of the Army of Northern Virginia, an organization dominated by the Lee cult. The majority of this book was devoted to eulogies of Lee; Longstreet's name was conspicuous by its virtual absence. One speech by John W. Daniel of Early's staff provided strong reinforcement of the opposition to Longstreet recently expressed in Jones's journal. Alluding to Longstreet's alleged failure to attack on July 2 at dawn at Gettysburg, Daniel neatly damned Longstreet in a backhanded manner, eloquently combining the images of Lee as Christ and Longstreet as Judas:

> "It is all my fault," said he [Lee]; but not such will be the verdict of the just historian who with a clear eye and steady hand shall trace, through the tumultuous and sanguinary incidents of that day, the course of him who, after exposing his person to all the dangers of the fray, would crucify, on self-erected cross, his own illustrious name, and make that reputation, more precious than life itself, vicarious sacrifice for his lieutenants and his men.[20]

When Lee assumed the blame, Daniel continued, "the Divinity in his bosom shone translucent through the man, and his spirit rose up to the Godlike."[21]

Far more important in terms of Longstreet's place in history was the impression created in 1881 by Jefferson Davis's *The Rise and Fall of the Confederate Government*. Early, Jones, and Pendleton had all gone to extraordinary lengths to ingratiate themselves with the former Confederate president and assisted him in his research. They were doubtless pleased when Davis's book reprinted part of Pendleton's 1873 speech at Washington and Lee damning Longstreet. Lest Pendleton's statements be questioned, Davis reminded his readers that the responsibility for the Gettysburg defeat "has been so fully discussed in the *Southern Historical Society Papers* as to relieve me from the necessity of entering into it."[22]

The aspersions cast on his military record were probably a major reason why, in 1884, Longstreet decided to take up his pen once more. Even while not writing himself he had remained keenly interested in what his fellow Confederate veterans were publishing. He discussed what was in print with many of his former comrades and continued to collect information on his own campaigns for future use.[23]

D. H. Hill, who had been blamed by many for the famous "lost dispatch" incident in the 1862 Maryland campaign, occasionally expressed to Longstreet his anger at the manner in which Early and his friends were building Lee's reputation at the expense of others. He told Longstreet: "The vanity of the Virginians has made them glorify their own prowess & to deify Lee. They made me the scapegoat for Maryland and you for Pennsylvania. I told old granny Pendleton to his face in Charlotte that his charges against you were foolish."[24]

Hill was anxious to restore a historically accurate awareness of the close personal relationship between Longstreet and Lee: "You were his [Lee's] confidential friend, more intimate with him than anyone else. I know that he would be grieved at such talks as Pendleton & Jones have made. I am willing for you to use anything written by me in regard to Lee's implicit trust in you or anything to your own credit that does not disparage others."[25]

Fate provided Longstreet with an excellent platform to defend his war record. During the summer of 1883, Robert Underwood Johnson and Clarence C. Buel, two editors for the *Century,* a magazine, initiated a plan to solicit articles from as many of the war's surviving leaders as possible.[26] The project was an enormous success from the magazine's point of view. Running from November 1884 to November 1887, the "Battles and Leaders of the Civil War" articles boosted circulation by 100,000 and eventually earned the firm over $1,000,000. Most of the articles were collected in the four-volume anthology *Battles and Leaders of the Civil War,* providing a wealth of material for future historians. But far from elucidating disputed points in history, the so-called war series generated new ones. On the Confederate side, for example, Joseph E. Johnston and P. G. T. Beauregard argued about the battle of Manassas; Johnston and G. W. Smith disputed events at Seven Pines; and Beauregard and William Preston Johnston disagreed about Shiloh. The pages virtually trembled with the blows of aging warriors more interested in present argument with former comrades than in past strife with erstwhile enemies.[27]

The editorial team of the *Century* first contacted Longstreet in April 1884, asking him for an article on Fredericksburg. Longstreet initially declined, despite urgings from his old chief Joseph E. Johnston that he accept. But he relented several months later and eventually became one of the most prolific contributors to the war series.[28]

As he had when writing for McClure, Longstreet arranged to have the services of a copyist and editor, at the magazine's expense. Joel Chandler Harris, the author of the Uncle Remus stories, and Josiah Carter of the *Atlanta Constitution* were selected for the task. By September 16, Longstreet had placed a rough draft of his Fredericksburg article in Harris's hands. He also met with Harris in December. Yet the role played by Harris remains unclear. The work on most of Longstreet's pieces seems to have been done exclusively by Carter.[29]

Longstreet ultimately wrote five articles for the *Century,* covering the Fredericksburg, Peninsula, Second Manassas, Maryland, and Pennsylvania campaigns. He was paid the considerable sum of $2,200 for them, while Carter earned $515 for his work. The procedure was thorough. Longstreet would write a very rough draft for Carter. Having read it, Carter would either discuss it with the General in person or submit a list of questions about it to him in writing. Carter would then edit and rewrite the manuscript as he saw fit, returning it to Longstreet. Longstreet made such corrections in this draft as he desired before returning it to Carter. After final polishing, Carter would send the article to Johnson and Buel, who edited it once more.

Although Longstreet approved and was fully responsible for the contents of each article, he granted Carter a free hand with the prose. For instance, he instructed Carter to "touch up" the manuscript on Antietam "with as much pathos as you may be pleased to apply." He also urged Carter to be sure the common soldiers received their "hard earned honor."[30]

Pathos notwithstanding, Longstreet's contributions to the war series served only to blacken his already tarnished reputation still further. His task would not have been easy under any circumstances. In merely setting the record straight he was certain to appear critical of Lee and Jackson; their reputations as faultless generals had been built in no small part at his expense. Unfortunately, Longstreet was arrogantly critical of each man in many instances.

Longstreet's first *Century* article, "The Seven Days Fighting Around Richmond," appeared in July 1885. It contained criticisms of Jackson's sluggish performance during the campaign which were quite justified. These, however, were couched in language bound to alienate not only veterans but the whole generation of Southerners who had grown up since Jackson had been martyred. Some of Longstreet's remarks seemed childish and petty, as when he wrote: "Jackson should have done more for me than he did. When he wanted me at Second Manassas, I marched two columns by night to clear the way at Thoroughfare Gap, and joined him in due season."[31] As in his articles for the *Philadelphia Weekly Times*, Longstreet left the conceited impression that he had fought the war on some sort of contractual basis and that he alone had held to the bargains struck.

It should be remembered that Jackson had given way to Lee as the dominant Southern hero only in the preceding decade. Longstreet's comments were prompted by jealousy and frustration caused by twenty-two years of public mourning over Stonewall. In a private letter he expressed his irritation at the Jackson legend: "That Jackson was clever there is no doubt, but that he was superhuman as Virginians who have written about him would have the world believe there is room for grave doubts. . . . I failed to discover in him perfection as a Field Marshall or in patterns of character."[32]

Jealousy of Jackson and belittlement of Lee's strategic ability pervaded Longstreet's next two articles for the *Century*. "Our March Against Pope," published in February 1886, warmly praised Ewell, Stuart, and Toombs but contained little to please admirers of Jackson. Longstreet accused the Virginian of not supporting him during some points of the campaign. He gave Jackson scant credit for his brilliant maneuvers against Pope and none at all for his stalwart defense during the battle of Second Manassas. In "The Invasion of Maryland," which appeared in June of that same year, Longstreet slighted Jackson's capture of Harpers Ferry, arguing that McLaws had faced the greater danger but that "the Virginia newspapers" had crowned Jackson a hero once more.[33]

For anyone already prejudiced against Longstreet, much of what he wrote about Lee for the *Century* must have confirmed suspicions that he was stubborn and argumentative by nature and sought to force his will on Lee. Hindsight thoroughly warped the General's narrative. No plan of Lee's was so good that Longstreet did not claim to have offered a better one, nor did Lee's strategy ever prove weak without Longstreet's having predicted that it would. Often Longstreet's prose seemed deliberately disparaging of his commander and nothing of their warm friendship and complete mutual trust was evident. Longstreet's portrayal of their relationship was often as distorted as anything his detractors invented. Readers in the 1880s, as well as future historians, would fail to appreciate how thoroughly Longstreet's *Century* articles were a product of frustration, a reaction to years during which he suffered abuse while Lee and Jackson were deified.

Longstreet's article "The Battle of Fredericksburg" appeared in the *Century* in August 1866. Its tone was markedly different from that of previous pieces. While it was not without a few passages that might have given offense, it did not describe Jackson's reputation as inflated or criticize Lee's strategic ability. Indeed, Longstreet defended Lee's decision not to counterattack following the battle. Had all of Longstreet's pieces in the war series resembled this one, his reputation would have suffered no further harm.

Although it appeared fourth, the Fredericksburg article was actually the first one written by Longstreet and the only one definitely known to have been edited by Joel Chandler Harris. Was Harris responsible for its moderation? Conversely, could Carter, acting perhaps on instructions from the *Century*, have deliberately worded the other articles to provoke controversy and thereby to increase sales? Possibly, but it should be remembered that Longstreet was pleased with both Harris and Carter and approved all of the articles.[34]

Longstreet's final article, which appeared in February 1887, was on Gettysburg. In "Lee's Invasion of Pennsylvania," he devoted mercifully little space to defending himself against the now fifteen-year-old charge that Lee had expected him to attack at dawn on July 2. Indeed, he largely refrained from ascribing a specific time to events throughout the article, thus skirting controversy. But he criticized Lee at length. He accused Lee of assigning A. P. Hill to the Third Corps rather than McLaws or D. H. Hill simply because he was a Virginian and claimed that morale suffered as a consequence. As in previous writings, he left the egotistical impression that he had fought the battle on some sort of contractual basis, Lee having virtually promised to remain on the defensive. When Lee attacked, Longstreet implied, he broke his word. Longstreet argued that his own plans "would and could have saved every man lost at Gettysburg," yet the public blamed *him* for the defeat.[35]

D. H. Hill, who had a low opinion of Lee, praised Longstreet's contributions to the *Century*, but he cautioned Longstreet that he could expect to be "savagely assaulted by the Virginians."[36] Lafayette McLaws, who labeled Early the "Confederate Falstaff," noted the dangers of writing Confederate history: "As for Malvern Hill, who is going to tell the truth about it. The whole truth. If I was to write what I saw concerning the total want of plan in the attack . . . , I would be denounced by our own people as a calumniator. . . . we attacked in the most desultory, harum scarum way. The same thing occurred at Gettysburg."[37]

The general reaction to Longstreet's articles was indeed quite negative. The *Century* printed some direct rebuttals, and he was sharply criticized in some of the articles that other Confederates wrote for the series.[38] That he was not more thoroughly attacked was no fault of the *Century*'s editors. Buel and Johnson sought articles from Early, Fitzhugh Lee, and Charles Marshall to juxtapose with Longstreet's. Marshall refused, Early merely granted permission to reprint some of his existing works, and Fitzhugh Lee, who was initially anxious to attack Longstreet in print, never produced anything.[39]

Jefferson Davis included a reply to Longstreet's *Century* pieces in an article for the *North American Review.* Published in January 1890, a month after Davis's death, it blamed Longstreet for losing Gettysburg and denied that Lee had meant to exonerate Longstreet when he said that the disaster had been "all my fault."[40] Early attacked the General in the pages of the *State,* a Richmond newspaper. He labeled Longstreet a "renegade" and "viper" and repeated Richard Taylor's comparison of Longstreet with an ass.[41]

Throughout the 1880s and 1890s members of the anti-Longstreet faction published books and articles making Longstreet the scapegoat for the Southern defeat and belittling his military record. The most notable included A. L. Long's *Memoirs of Robert E. Lee* and Fitzhugh Lee's *General Lee,* each of which won a wide audience.[42] The almost universal acceptance by late nineteenth-century Southerners of Longstreet's responsibility for the Gettysburg debacle was sharply illuminated by a series of articles in the *North American Review* by Garnett Wolseley. Wolseley was a respected military critic and one of Britain's most distinguished soldiers. Because his articles critiqued not only the *Century*'s Civil War publications but books outside the war series as well, they provide an opportunity to judge the state of Longstreet's image as seen by a neutral outsider.

Wolseley accepted the *Southern Historical Society Papers'* Gettysburg series and other writings of the anti-Longstreet faction as proof that the various alleged failures by Longstreet lost the famous battle for the South. He thought Longstreet's criticisms of Lee and Jackson in the *Century* inappropriate and unseemly, concluding from them that Longstreet had fought the war in a mood of consuming jealousy and with delusions of grandeur.[43]

In Wolseley's opinion Lee's "all my fault" statement did more than testify to his Christ-like spirit; it marked Lee's superior devotion to the South and explained why Lee never charged Longstreet with any failures at Gettysburg:

> Nothing is more characteristic of the man than that, when quietly reviewing the situation, he should realize how all-important it was to the cause of the Confederacy that no personal difference should arise between him and Longstreet, and that he should consequently have taken all the blame upon himself. Most soldiers will think that General Longstreet has not served his own cause well by appealing so much to the generous silence of his chief. He has, at least so far as all future histories of the war are concerned, deprived himself of the benefit of that silence by the way in which he has laid himself out to make charges against the chief who refrained, under the most dire provocation, from one word of reproach against him.[44]

With this argument the anti-Longstreet thesis in Southern history reached its fullest development. The fact that Lee never criticized Longstreet became acceptable proof of Longstreet's guilt. The repeated assaults made by Early and his supporters and Longstreet's own embarrassing, exaggerated counterclaims were both necessary for such twisted logic to be embraced by military scholars. Longstreet was his own worst enemy, fleshing out and lending credence to a picture of himself that the Lee partisans had created. Persons such as Wolseley, who knew neither

Lee nor Longstreet, proved quite willing to believe that the postwar images of both men were historical reality, and all facts concerning the war were either consciously or unconsciously interpreted so that they would conform to these images.

Longstreet's efforts to defend his military reputation had been futile. The consequences after his death, when twentieth-century historians turned to the writings of Confederate veterans for information on the war, would be profound. This outcome was of course not apparent to Longstreet at the time. Far from being worried about his image, present or future, the General was entering into one of the most active periods of his long and varied life. Strangely enough, some of the happy times he enjoyed late in his life were linked with the anti-Longstreet faction's success in promoting the Lost Cause.

10. A Procrustean Ending

To DISCOURAGE PILFERING in his extensive vineyard, Longstreet kept a musket on hand. The aged general
was rumored to be a crack shot, and few youngsters wished to test his
marksmanship.[1] In the spring and summer Longstreet spent many
hours on the farm that his neighbors called Gettysburg behind his
back. Wearing a broad-brimmed straw hat and a linen duster as white
as his own snowy hair and sidewhiskers, he tended his vines and
pruned his orchard with loving care. He raised turkeys as well, selling
these and his homemade wine to local residents and visitors.[2]

There was much happiness in Longstreet's autumn years. In
1889 he was sixty-eight years old and probably still supported his son
Fitz Randolph, who was twenty, and daughter Maria Louisa, seventeen. Some of his five living children resided with him until 1894,
possibly longer. His financial resources were moderate but comfortable. The *Century* had paid him handsomely for his articles, but his
political eclipse after his removal as marshal meant the loss of a major
source of income. His farm was not profitable, and his second home,
the Piedmont Hotel, was only marginally so.

Longstreet gave the Piedmont his personal attention each winter, as a correspondent for the *New York Times* discovered. The reporter wrote of Longstreet: "He is the very embodiment of good humor.
He tries to make everyone comfortable, and as his hotel commands
the best breeze from the Blue Ridge, he usually succeeds. He will
mount three flights of steps to carry an apple to some little fellow who

learns to know and love the bronzed face and white hair of this Southern veteran."[3]

Thanks to federal laws benefiting Mexican War veterans and a Georgia state law for disabled Confederates, Longstreet collected approximately sixty dollars per month in pensions. He tried to supplement his income by investing in a goldmine just outside Gainesville, but nothing came of this venture, and he was very frustrated at having been defrauded out of railway stock worth $250,000 by New Orleans businessmen. He never lacked money, however, and was greatly embarrassed by an 1888 report in the *Atlanta Constitution* that he was poverty stricken.[4]

Yet Longstreet was not without times of trial and sorrow. His longtime friend and benefactor Grant died in 1885 after a heroic struggle against throat cancer. Longstreet joined in the public tributes to the Northern hero but expressed his intimate sentiments in a private letter to organizers of a memorial meeting for Grant in Atlanta: "He was my lifetime personal friend, kindest when I was most fiercely assailed. May his soul, through the mercy of God, rest in peace. Amen."[5]

In 1889 Longstreet's beautiful country home burned to the ground. He lost all his war souvenirs, including his Confederate uniform and sword, a sash Jeb Stuart had given him, and a pair of Mexican spurs he had worn in both the Mexican War and the Civil War. The dwelling had not been insured, and the General could not afford to rebuild. He moved into a simple frame cottage which had been built earlier as an outbuilding.[6]

An infinitely greater tragedy occurred in January 1890 when Longstreet's wife Louise died at the age of sixty-two. A family acquaintance writing for the *Atlanta Constitution* recalled the loving relationship of the "venerable couple." Despite his flowery prose, the journalist was doubtless accurate when he reported: "Fear though he knew not, yet over the grave of his dead wife his strong frame quivered, and the stern soldier of other days stood unmanned in the presence of death."[7]

The writer erred, however, in describing Longstreet as still possessing a strong frame. His wound from the Wilderness continued to trouble him, forcing him to write left handed most of the time and reducing his voice almost to a whisper. From the 1870s until his death he also suffered frequently from what he simply described as attacks of illness, which sometimes incapacitated him for months.[8] The cumulative effect of tragedy and infirmity was, not surprisingly, mental depression. In 1890 Longstreet's former staff officer Osmun Latrobe wrote:

> I received a letter from him [Longstreet] a few days ago; in it he said: "My arm is paralyzed; my voice that once could be heard all along the lines, is gone; I can scarcely speak above a whisper; my hearing is very much impaired, and sometimes I feel as if I wish the end would come; but I have some misrepresentations of my battles that I wish to correct, so as to have my record correct before I die." What a change![9]

Despite such adversity Longstreet remained remarkably active. He spent much of his time working on his memoirs, particularly in the winter months when cold weather confined him to the Piedmont Hotel. The project was not an easy one. Official papers were difficult to obtain and the 1889 home fire destroyed much of the material he had collected and all the manuscript he had written to that point, forcing him to begin again.[10] He distrusted his own memory, and books written by others on the basis of recollections, and sought to base his work on official documents as much as possible.[11]

As the letter to Latrobe quoted above indicates, the General knew that this would be his last opportunity to defend himself against the Virginia "third rates," as he called Early and his followers. In addition to clearing his name he hoped to testify to the valor, intelligence, and endurance which the common soldiers on both sides had displayed during the war.[12] The memoirs would also provide an opportunity to settle old scores. "I do not expect to handle facts with gloves in my account but let chips fall where they may," he informed Lafayette McLaws.[13]

Longstreet received assistance from all the staff officers in his inner circle: Goree, Sorrel, Latrobe, Fairfax, Alexander, and Erasmus Taylor. As with previous literary ventures he engaged a copyist and editor, in this case Pascal J. Moran of the *Atlanta Constitution*. Analysts have since noted significant discrepancies in style in the General's memoirs, as well as numerous errors he simply should not have made.

It would seem that he gave Moran a much freer hand than his previous assistants, but there is no reason to doubt that he reviewed the entire finished manuscript and fully approved it.[14]

By 1894 Longstreet had essentially completed his work, yet delays of a nature not now known plagued him. This, in his opinion, turned out to be fortunate, for it allowed him to reply directly in his text to Fitzhugh Lee's *General Lee,* which appeared that year. The Virginian had criticized Longstreet's performance at Seven Pines and the Wilderness as well as at Gettysburg, and Longstreet quickly revised his manuscript to meet these accusations. In April 1885 he wrote a friend:

> It seems providential that I did not publish last year for the attacks by Fitzhugh Lee and others not only justify but call for stronger demonstrations than I had made, and I have gone over my work and put it in clear light, and not to my disadvantage. The records speak volumes that Fitzhugh and his coterie cannot gainsay, and discredit all of their scandalous efforts.[15]

Longstreet soon signed a contract with J. B. Lippincott of Philadelphia, and his memoirs were published in December 1895 (bearing the date 1896) as *From Manassas to Appomattox.*[16] In 697 pages of entertaining, if occasionally labored, prose, the General presented his views on a war which had occurred almost half his lifetime ago.

Longstreet's prejudices were evident in the way he treated the war's major personalities. Grant received nothing but praise, as did old friends George Pickett and Harvey Hill. Longstreet defended Pickett's questionable record at the battle of Five Forks and argued that Hill was not responsible for the famous "lost dispatch" of the Antietam campaign. He also expressed admiration for Richard Ewell, Richard Anderson, A. P. Hill, and Rooney Lee, Robert E. Lee's son, whom he described as "the noble son of a noble sire." Jeb Stuart he described on several occasions as the almost perfect cavalryman, a man whose death had been a grievous blow to the Confederacy.[17]

Longstreet praised his protégé Micah Jenkins, who had died at his side in the Wilderness, but he had even more praise for Lafayette McLaws, who had been so wonderfully supportive during the postwar years. He could not, of course, avoid giving an account of Fort Sanders and his preferment of charges against the Georgian. But noting that President Davis had dismissed the proceedings against McLaws, Longstreet wrote that this resolution of the affair was

> very gratifying to me, who could have taken several reprimands to relieve a personal friend of embarrassing position. General McLaws was a classmate, and had been a warm personal friend from childhood. I had no desire to put charges against him, and should have failed to do so even under the direction of the authorities. I am happy to say that our personal relations are as close and interesting as they have ever been, and that his heart was big enough to separate official duties and personal relations.[18]

As previously explained, Longstreet's court-martial of McLaws was entirely justified. But the confused passage quoted above is deliberately misleading. It is a measure of the man that, in his desire to mend fences, Longstreet would distort the truth in such a self-serving way rather than openly apologize. The General could be terribly petty.

Longstreet's portrayal of his critics was equally calculated. For example, he blamed Fitzhugh Lee for the decline in the quality of the cavalry corps in the Army of Northern Virginia after Stuart's death.[19] He criticized the Virginian's conduct during the Second Manassas campaign, singling out an incident in which one of Robert E. Lee's orders had been captured by Pope. As a result, he claimed, Fitzhugh Lee had "lost the fruits of our summer's work, and lost the Southern cause. Proud Troy was laid in ashes."[20] This passage was probably one Longstreet changed after reading Fitzhugh Lee's *General Lee*. Thirty years of abuse had reduced Longstreet to the level of his accusers. Old and bitter, unable to escape his popular image as architect of the Southern defeat, he finally sought a counterscapegoat. The real wonder is that he had not done so years earlier.

Jubal Early, of course, did not fare well at the General's hands. Describing the battle of Williamsburg, Longstreet remarked that Early's brigade had not been in "safe hands." Concerning the events of July 2 at Gettysburg he wrote:

> There was a man on the left of the line who did not care to make the battle win. He knew where it was, had viewed it from its earliest formation, had orders for his part in it, but so withheld part of his command from it as to make co-operative concert of action impossible. He had a

pruriency for the honors of the field of Mars, was eloquent, before the
fires of bivouac and his chief, of the glory of war's gory shield; but when
its envied laurels were dipping to the grasp, when the heavy field called
for bloody work, he found the placid horizon, far and away beyond the
cavalry, more lovely and inviting. He wanted command of the Second
Corps, and, succeeding to it, held the honored position until General
Lee found, at last, that he must dismiss him from field service.[21]

In another passage he stated simply that Early had been "the weakest
general officer of the Army of Northern Virginia."[22]

As in previous writings, Longstreet displayed a distinct jealousy
of the reputations of Jackson and Lee. This reached the extreme
when in a footnote he claimed absurdly that Jackson had left the battle of Antietam "for refreshments."[23] While he wrote of Lee with affection, Longstreet was unsparing in his criticism of his former commander's strategy. As a detached analysis with the admitted benefit of
hindsight, much of the General's criticism was quite valid. But all too
often Longstreet presented his postwar reflections as insights with
which he had been blessed at the time.

As in so many other writings, Longstreet sounded arrogant and
conceited. His criticisms of Lee merely made Lee seem all the more
Christ-like and forgiving, and himself petty by contrast. Longstreet's
prose was a reflection of his postwar sufferings and frustrations, but
many historians would accept it at face value and consequently portray him as a scheming recalcitrant subordinate.

Longstreet did not completely lose touch with reality in his
memoirs, however. While he refuted some of the postbellum writings
of Lee's staff officers, he also paid high tribute to them as "intelligent,
active, zealous young men" during the war.[24]

Shortly after the publication of *From Manassas to Appomattox*, Moxley Sorrel wrote Tom Goree that the book was selling well, but press
reviews of it were mixed. The most perceptive ones cautioned readers
that the old soldier was having his last say and sometimes lost his
objectivity.[25] The important point is that nothing in Longstreet's
memoirs changed his image or favorably affected his place in Southern
history. On the contrary, the book seemed to confirm that Longstreet
was the stubborn, jealous subordinate his detractors had claimed.

Had Jubal Early been living, he would doubtless have written a major response to Longstreet's book, but he died in 1894. Since then, Fitzhugh Lee and John B. Gordon had shared leadership of the anti-Longstreet faction, but neither produced a rebuttal. Walter Taylor published a highly critical review of Longstreet's memoirs in the *Richmond Times,* but the main response came from the Reverend Jones. His article "The Longstreet-Gettysburg Controversy" was published in the *Richmond Dispatch* and was reprinted in the *Southern Historical Society Papers.* Jones was able to exploit to great advantage the vanity, pettiness, and egotism Longstreet displayed in much of his prose.[26] But without the leadership of Early or Pendleton (who had died in 1883), the group of men who had done so much to discredit Longstreet showed minimal interest in the book. *From Manassas to Appomattox* failed to improve Longstreet's reputation because of the book's internal faults and the manner in which the anti-Longstreet faction had prepared the public to view all his writings. The hostile reaction it evoked from some Southerners was really rather slight compared with that which greeted the General's previous efforts with the pen.

By the late 1890s there seemed little enough chance that Longstreet would ever join the ranks of Confederate heroes. By that time the South, and increasingly the nation as a whole, had developed a romanticized stereotype of the Confederate soldier which effectively disqualified the blunt, pragmatic Longstreet. More was involved than the Lee cult. Veneration of the Lost Cause affected literature as well, in a manner adverse to Longstreet.

Benefiting from postwar mass marketing techniques, Southern writers such as Thomas Nelson Page, George Cary Eggleston, Constance Cary Harrison, George W. Cable, and Joel Chandler Harris produced books which sold hundreds of thousands of copies. While literary analysts would not consider them a unified group, they shared a fascination with the Confederacy. Writing in a period when perhaps one-half of the American population had either been born after 1865 or had immigrated after that date, they profoundly affected Longstreet's place in history. Even authors usually described as "realists" rather than "romantics" perpetuated a view of the war which represented not the real past but the past of the Lost Cause, replete with its many anti-Longstreet facets.

While the impact of fiction on Longstreet's place in history was diverse, its effect was cumulative. In the hands of Southern authors, the antebellum period became Edenic, a time before the Fall. Southern civilization was portrayed as superior, uniquely blessed. Works such as Page's "Unc' Edinburg's Drowndin'" and his many other short stories combined with Harris's *Free Joe and Other Georgian Sketches* and the famous Uncle Remus tales to popularize the "happy darky" stereotype. They also raised the plantation myth to its zenith in romantic literature. Against this idealized background, Longstreet's Reconstruction activities must have seemed like the betrayal of an entire culture and his role similar to that of the Snake in the Garden.

Novels and short stories by such authors as James Lane Allen, Grace King, George Cary Eggleston, and Virginia Boyle drew sharp comparisons between the mythical prewar South and the harsh realities of the postwar present. Reconstruction itself was a popular topic for novelization. *Red Rock,* by Page, *Gabriel Tolliver,* by Harris, and the immensely popular *The Clansman* (source of the ultraracist 1915 movie *Birth of a Nation*), by Thomas Dixon, contributed to the idea that all loyal Confederates should have resisted Yankee occupation to the utmost. Longstreet's scalawag activities thus linked him with the villains, not the heroes, of generations of readers.

The war itself was a perennially popular topic. In addition to the authors mentioned above, Mary Noailles Murfree, John Fox, Jr., Mary Johnston, and Ellen Glasgow were widely read Civil War novelists. Their works varied from rather conventional romances, such as Johnston's *The Long Roll* and *Cease Firing* to more realistic treatments, as in Cable's *Kincaid's Battery* or Glasgow's trilogy, *The Voice of the People, The Battle-Ground,* and *The Deliverance.* For children, Page's *Among the Camps* and *Two Little Confederates* held center stage until the Civil War centennial some seventy-five years later.

Caught up in the Lost Cause, Southern authors gave prominence to cavalier aristocrats or martyrs such as Lee, Jackson, Stuart, or Turner Ashby. References to Longstreet were scant but could be subtly and effectively derogatory, as in Mary Johnston's *The Long Roll:*

> Three men were in the room. One [Longstreet] having a large frame and a somewhat heavy face kept the chair beside the table with a kind of granite and stubborn air. He rested like a boulder on a mountain slope; marked with old scars, only waiting to be set in motion again to grind matters small.

[Longstreet] got ponderously to his feet.

Longstreet spoke in his heavy voice.

> In Lee's tent . . . was held a council of war—Lee, Stonewall Jackson, Longstreet, Jeb Stuart. Lee sat beside the table, Jackson faced him, sabre across knees, Longstreet had his place a little to one side.[27]

The novel did not hint that Longstreet was Lee's principal adviser and second in command; indeed, just the opposite was implied. In this and many other novels, the man Lee considered his indispensable aide and the best general in the world was presented to postwar readers as a stolid, stationary officer, merely a dependable blunt instrument that stood at Lee's beck and call. Thus fiction helped to lock Longstreet out of the pantheon of Confederate heroes. It linked him strongly with the South's Reconstruction villains and created an image of the Confederate soldier that did not fit him.

Longstreet was apparently unaware of how his image was faring in fiction. Apart from his memoirs, he had three main interests during his autumn years: reunions, remarriage, and a reentry into politics. Reunions and related veterans' activities were of long-standing interest to him. The Republican press had made much of Longstreet throughout the 1870s as a prototype of the properly reconstructed rebel. Not until the 1880s, however, was he truly popular with the Northern people as a whole. In 1883 he was a guest speaker at the Chicago World's Fair. Because of his wound his voice did not carry well, and he lost his place during his address and became visibly confused. Yet the effort was well received, for he had chosen as his topic the story of his application for amnesty and U. S. Grant's role in helping him secure it.[28] Longstreet had accidentally hit upon a formula which would soon make him one of the most avidly sought-after Southern speakers for Northern audiences in the late nineteenth century. His friendship with Grant was the key.

Grant's highly publicized battle against cancer and desperate struggle to finish his memoirs largely erased the memory of his scandal-ridden presidency and postwar business ventures. When he died in 1885, Northern reporters discovered that Longstreet was the sole major Southern figure of the war who would not only testify to Grant's personal greatness but also endorse his military genius without reservation. Longstreet admired his kinsman's military skills and did not hesitate to praise them. While other former Confederates were writing books and articles to "prove" that the South had never really been beaten, merely overwhelmed by superior numbers, Longstreet gave Grant and the men he had led their full due. This, and not his Republican affiliations, made Longstreet the darling of Union veterans everywhere. From 1885 until his death Longstreet was welcome at any gathering of former Federal soldiers, for he told them exactly what they wanted to hear: that they had fought well under a hero worthy of every man's respect.

Only a few months after Grant's death Longstreet was offered $1,000 to speak in Boston. He declined this astonishingly generous proposal, explaining to a friend, "I have feared to trust my voice since the bullet passed through my throat at the Wilderness."[29] In 1888, however, he agreed to participate in the reunion and ceremonies marking the twenty-fifth anniversary of Gettysburg. He was the only officer among the few Confederate veterans who arrived on July 1. Lost in a sea of thousands of former Federal soldiers, the erstwhile rebels were lionized in grand fashion. Longstreet's speech that afternoon was greeted with thunderous applause as the memories of the fateful battle moved him almost to tears. Although Longstreet's political enemy John B. Gordon was a speaker on the following day, they did not make their differences public but shook hands cordially on the podium.[30]

In 1892 Longstreet was a guest at a Saint Patrick's Day dinner hosted by the Irish Societies of Atlanta. Sharing the honors with him was Daniel E. Sickles, the Federal general who had opposed him at Gettysburg. Both men consumed a quantity of Irish whiskey during the evening. That soon neither felt any pain was evidenced by Sickle's success in inducing Longstreet to sing "The Star Spangled Banner" in lieu of a speech. Both men had a keen sense of humor. After leaving the gathering, they took turns repeatedly escorting one another to their respective lodging, two aging soldiers, tramping back and forth along the dark Atlanta streets, unwilling to end the evening's pleasure.[31]

Perhaps it is not surprising that Longstreet and Sickles became fast friends. Sickles, who had lost a leg at Gettysburg, was blamed by many Northerners for preventing a greater Union victory, as he had realigned his troops without orders on July 2. They shared the status of pariah, although Sickles's plight was never as extreme as Longstreet's in this regard. They met again in Philadelphia in 1893 to commemorate the seventy-first anniversary of Grant's birthday. They were joined by other Union veterans as well as by Osmun Latrobe, E. P. Alexander, and William Mahone, a Virginian who had served with the First Corps during the retreat to Appomattox. On impulse, the party took a train to Gettysburg the next day, touring the field and exchanging reminiscences and jests. Their park tour guide, upon learning that Longstreet was almost completely deaf (he used a hearing trumpet), politely delivered his talk directly into the General's right ear. Despite severe heat and dust, Longstreet also returned to Gettysburg that July for the thirtieth anniversary observances. Well over 10,000 veterans attended. On his way home, Longstreet joined Latrobe at Antietam, where they assisted government authorities in marking the battlefield.[32]

Longstreet sustained activities at a quick pace for a man of his years. In June 1895 he attended a reunion in Chicago; that September he spoke at the ceremonies opening the Chickamauga National Battlefield Park. In 1896 he spoke in Boston and was forced to turn down a similar invitation from New York the following year. Requests for photographs, writings, speeches, and copies of his book came to him from across the nation. "There is hardly a mail which does not bring me one or more such letters," he wrote in 1897.[33]

Longstreet was not too busy, however, to fall in love again at age seventy-six. He first met attractive, vivacious Helen Dortch sometime in the 1880s. A native of Franklin County, Georgia, she had attended Brenau College in Gainesville with the General's daughter. On September 8, 1897, Longstreet and Helen were married at the governor's mansion in Atlanta, with Judge J. B. Gaston, mayor of Gainesville, acting as best man. Although newspapers reported the bride's age as twenty-two, she was probably thirty-four. Like her husband, Helen was a devout Catholic. They honeymooned briefly near Atlanta and later took a trip to Mexico, revisiting some of the battlefields where Longstreet had fought before his second wife was born.

Exceptionally strong-willed, Helen did not always get along with the General's children, but her devotion to Longstreet, whom she outlived for fifty-eight years, was deep and sincere. Much of her time and fortune in widowhood was devoted to a futile attempt to re-establish her husband's military reputation.[34]

As the old century gave way to the new, Longstreet's popularity among Northern audiences showed no signs of abating. J. H. Stine, an Illinois acquaintance, wrote him in 1900, "We are preparing for an old fashioned 4th of July celebration, and everyone asks me can you get General Longstreet." Stine promised "a sea of people to greet you as far as you can see."[35] Whether Longstreet accepted this invitation is not known, but despite poor health he did journey to West Point in 1902 for the centennial of the United States Military Academy. E. P. Alexander joined him there, and both were treated grandly.[36] In August of that same year he enthusiastically agreed to join veterans of the Army of the Potomac for a September reunion at Gettysburg, but a foot injury later prevented him from attending.[37]

At no time did Longstreet let his popularity in the North go to his head. Helen recalled two anecdotes "that the General was fond of telling on himself":

> He was invited to the unveiling of a Confederate monument in Chicago. Arriving in the early morning of the day of the unveiling, he was escorted by a committee to the Palmer House and installed in a magnificent suite. The Palmer House was at that time the most famous hotel in Chicago. The General happened to notice a placard on the parlor door, announcing that the rate for the suite was $50 per day. He felt unable to pay such a price and immediately after the unveiling, which occurred in the late afternoon, he packed for the journey south on a midnight train, although he had expected to remain in Chicago several days. When he called at the Cashier's desk for his bill, the clerk said, deferentially,
>
> "General, Mr. Palmer cabled from Paris that you were to be the guest of the hotel, as long as you honored Chicago with your presence."
>
> The porter had already brought down the General's luggage, and in dignity, he felt obliged to make his regretful journey a few days earlier than planned.
>
> Another experience he always told with a chuckle. He was a guest at a banquet in New York in celebration of Grant's birthday. He was very deaf after the war. . . . There were numerous speakers at the banquet and although he couldn't hear a word, he cheered in politeness. One of the speakers drew forth long continued applause in which the General joined most enthusiastically; and to be extra polite he cheered a little

longer than anyone else; then turning to General Sickles . . . inquired: "What were they cheering?" Sickles spoke into his ear trumpet: "They were cheering you, General; the speaker had paid you a grand tribute."[38]

Longstreet's participation in strictly Southern activities was an- other matter entirely, for these were almost completely controlled by his avowed enemies. Confederate veterans had begun banding to- gether as early as 1866, to ensure proper burial of the dead and care for widows and orphans. A host of fraternal organizations arose from such beginnings. The largest and most powerful of these prior to 1889 was the Association of the Army of Northern Virginia, which had branches in every former Confederate state. Founded by Jubal Early in 1870, its active members and officers included many of Lee's staff officers, together with Pendleton, Jones, and Fitzhugh Lee. At annual banquets the Association promoted Lost Cause themes gener- ally, including the deification of Lee and the vilification of Long- street.[39]

In 1889 almost all veterans' activities in the South fell under the control of John B. Gordon, founding president of the United Con- federate Veterans (UCV). During the next fourteen years, Gordon achieved a degree of influence over Southern veterans exceeded only by Jubal Early. By 1898 there were 1,084 local chapters of the organi- zation. Called "camps," each was named after a Confederate hero. Lee, Jackson, Stuart, and Davis were frequently honored in this man- ner, but only two camps were named after Longstreet—one in Gainesville, Georgia, and another in Macon, Mississippi, where one of the General's sisters lived. At its zenith in 1903, the UCV had over 80,000 members, one-third of all living Southern veterans. Its in- terests were promoted by an unofficial journal, *Confederate Veteran* magazine, and a parallel organization, the United Daughters of the Confederacy (UDC), was established in 1893.[40]

The UCV, UDC, and the *Confederate Veteran* each had as one of its announced goals the presentation of a "correct" view of the history of the war to future generations.[41] By the late nineteenth century, this view was understood to entail the worship of Lee and the use of Long- street as scapegoat for Gettysburg and by extension for the loss of the war. The implication would seemingly be that Longstreet neither attended nor was welcome at Southern veterans' activities, but such was not the case. Early and his followers had been so successful in promoting the Lost Cause that all things Confederate, even the pariah Longstreet, became fascinating to the public as well as to the old soldiers. Although never forgiven for his political heresy nor absolved of guilt for his alleged failures at Gettysburg, Longstreet was a living link with the past and as such simply could not be ignored. His prominence among Southern veterans increased yearly as, one by one, almost every high-ranking Confederate preceded him to the grave.

When Longstreet did attend Southern veterans' events, the common soldiers invariably welcomed him with enthusiasm. The unveiling of the Ben Hill monument in Atlanta in 1886 was a case in point, and as it has been heretofore inaccurately reported, some detail is merited.

To promote the gubernatorial candidacy of John B. Gordon, newspaperman Henry W. Grady arranged for the former general to accompany Jefferson Davis on his appearances in Alabama and Georgia. This tour became a triumphal procession for Davis. Although he had not been overly popular during the war, Southerners were positively frantic at the chance to see the one and only president of their would-be nation. When Davis and Gordon arrived in Atlanta to dedicate a monument to the late Ben Hill, a prominent senator, a crowd of almost 100,000 greeted them. Following the ceremonies Gordon announced his candidacy. He soon found himself governor of Georgia.[42]

According to some contemporary accounts and subsequent histories, Longstreet burst in on the ceremonies uninvited. Wearing his Confederate uniform, he slowly rode to the speaker's platform amid thunderous cheers. Joining the dignitaries, he and Davis embraced warmly, a spontaneous reconciliation of reconstructed and unreconstructed rebels.[43]

The enthusiasm which greeted Longstreet was real, and so was his hearty greeting of Davis, but the circumstances were different from those recorded. Longstreet and his entire staff had been invited to the ceremonies by Grady, although on such short notice that only Erasmus Taylor was able to join the General. The following day Grady, ever the publicity man, apparently fabricated the story that Longstreet had come to Atlanta on his own initiative.[44]

An even greater display of Southern affection for Longstreet occurred in Richmond in May 1890, when he attended the ceremonies at the unveiling of a statue of Lee. Dr. Cullen, the former chief surgeon of the First Corps, asked Longstreet to attend this event with him. The General declined, as he had received no invitation from its sponsors and did not wish to intrude. Meanwhile, the Washington Artillery of New Orleans, in reply to their invitation, asked to be designated Longstreet's escort during the ceremonies. Learning that their old leader had not been invited, they notified the Richmond authorities that they had voted not to attend unless Longstreet was at least asked to come. Perhaps on the impression that he would never dare show his face when Early, Jones, Gordon, and Fitzhugh Lee were present, the sponsors dispatched an invitation to Gainesville.[45]

Longstreet promptly accepted the invitation. He was anxious to see old friends in the Washington Artillery who had written him urging him to attend. His health, which had been "very feeble for some months past," improved at the prospect. He asked his New Orleans comrades quietly to arrange for him to sit with their unit, for he wanted no special position during the ceremonies nor any fuss made over his presence.[46]

The event proved to be one of the most enjoyable in Longstreet's life. In a letter to Tom Goree he recalled:

> My carriage attracted more attention I suppose than was expected and we were sidetracked, but that only made it more unpleasant for the managers. Generals Fitz Hugh Lee, Gordon, and other grandees rode along, but little noticed by the troops in line, but as they passed our carriage they broke and crowded about us and hurried around in such crowds as to block the street, which threatened to break up the procession, and when urged on tried to take the horses from the carriage, and pull it along with them, and it was all that Latrobe and Cullen could do to urge them on, and preserve their line of order.[47]

Pressure from the prestigious Washington Artillery was sufficiently strong in 1892 to force Gordon to invite his bitter enemy to the third annual UCV meeting in New Orleans. Longstreet described this event to Goree as well: "It was especially unpleasant to General Gordon for me to be of [at] the reunion, even as a guest. The old soldiers when they see me forget their new leader in peace, and it tries his patience."[48] Longstreet's presence at one night meeting made the scheduled activities impossible: "Right soon the business was interrupted by calls for opportunity to come up and shake my hand, and ended by hurrying Gordon and others of the managers from the stand in order to make room for the soldiers to come up and meet me."[49]

Longstreet assumed that this upstaging of Gordon would prevent him from ever receiving another UCV invitation, but he was not concerned. He preferred Northern reunions; in the North he met no prejudices. "Everywhere except in the South," he wrote in 1894, "soldiers are accepted as comrades upon equal terms without regards to their political affiliations. So I have come to regard it a high compliment to be excluded from the U.C.V."[50]

If, however, Longstreet concluded from the cheering Southern veterans and the discomfiture his presence caused his enemies that his military record had been vindicated, he was sadly mistaken. The General's paradoxical popularity in the late nineteenth century came despite, not because of, his prolific writings in self-defense. The aging veterans who fawned over him were attracted not so much to James Longstreet as to Lee's lieutenant. For despite his political heresy and alleged military failures, Longstreet was a link with the Lost Cause and the mythic past which critics like Early, novelists like Cooke, poets like Timrod, and churchmen like Jones had taught whole generations of Southerners to revere. Nothing was forgiven Longstreet, but much could be overlooked in the frenzy to venerate everyone who had worn the gray alongside Lee. The *Atlanta Constitution* had expressed this attitude in an 1888 article which erroneously reported that Longstreet was poverty stricken:

> Lee's lieutenant-general at Appomattox! Could man hold worthier title to the affection and veneration of the southern people than to wear that title . . . ?
>
> Many of us who admired Longstreet as a fighter have not liked his course as a civilian since the war. But he has been more sinned against than sinning. . . .
>
> But Longstreet criticized Lee! Well, so have others—notably President Davis.
>
> But, but, but!

> Away with your buts! . . . remember how Longstreet suffered with us, and let us share with him our abundance or our pittance, and not let "Lee's Old War-Horse" want, whilst wounds and years are hurrying him to his grave.[51]

Despite such appeals, the stigma of Longstreet's political affiliations remained strong, in great part because he remained active in the Republican party. He supported Benjamin Harrison's candidacy in 1888 and met with the president-elect in Indianapolis that December. There was speculation that Longstreet would be offered a cabinet position, but he was never seriously considered for so exalted a post. He campaigned even harder for William McKinley in 1896, touring Georgia and delivering a pro–gold standard speech. He hoped to be appointed ambassador to Mexico for his pains, but the coveted post went to someone else.[52]

Longstreet did not go unrewarded, however. One of the choicest plums at the president's disposal was the office of United States Commissioner of Railroads. This was a blatant sinecure, involving minimal inspection duties and paying a generous salary. Under Grover Cleveland's Democratic administrations, Joseph E. Johnston and Wade Hampton had held the office. When Longstreet was nominated in 1897, Hampton fought to retain the post, enlisting the support of Senator John W. Daniel, a former member of Early's staff. At the confirmation hearings, Senator Daniel included among his objections to Longstreet as a federal office holder the General's recent criticisms of Lee in his autobiography! When the vote went in favor of Longstreet, Hampton refused to speak to him or to facilitate the transition in any manner.[53]

Longstreet enjoyed his position but disliked Washington. "This climate don't suit me," he wrote one of his sons, "and I am happy to find some way to escape from it." He used his inspection duties and the free passes he received from almost every railway company to indulge his love of travel. He probably took his duties more seriously than anyone expected, issuing a formal report ten months after taking office. In this he recommended increasing the transcontinental track to accommodate the increased flow of trade that was expected to result from the United States occupation of Hawaii and the Philippines during the Spanish-American War. Throughout his travels the

General was well received. In San Diego, for instance, he was feted at a dinner given by U. S. Grant, Jr. He used the occasion to pay splendid tributes to his late friend.[54]

Longstreet was doubtless gratified that the Republican party had rewarded his loyalty. His life was not entirely pleasant, however. In 1903 his political enemy John B. Gordon published *Reminiscences of the Civil War.* The book's chapter on Gettysburg was printed as an excerpt in the July issue of the highly popular *Scribner's Monthly* magazine. Gordon not only raised the familiar charge that Longstreet had been fatally tardy on July 2 at Gettysburg, he claimed that "had Lee's orders been promptly and cordially executed, Meade's centre on the third day would have been penetrated and the Union army overwhelmingly defeated."[55]

To bolster this conveniently vague assertion Gordon offered not facts but Lee's failure to blame Longstreet. "To those who knew General Lee well," wrote Gordon (who had not known Lee well at all), "the assumption by him of entire responsibility for the failure at Gettysburg means nothing except an additional and overwhelming proof of his almost marvelous magnanimity."[56] Once again Lee's supposedly Christ-like nature was used to liken Longstreet to Judas, the betrayer.

Longstreet was too ill to reply to Gordon, but his young wife took up her pen with a vengeance. Helen's rebuttal of Gordon was published under several titles in newspapers across the country in January 1904, but by the time it appeared in print both Longstreet and Gordon were dead. Longstreet had suffered severely from rheumatism for at least a year, probably longer. His weight dropped from its usual 200 pounds to a mere 135 pounds. By September 1903 he could no longer ride a horse. He had also developed cancer in his right eye, which was treated in Chicago that December with x-rays.[57]

Despite pain and discomfort, Longstreet seemed healthier on New Year's Day 1904 than he had in some time. But on the following morning, Saturday, January 2, he contracted pneumonia and sank quickly. Large quantities of blood began to flow from his mouth, and he hemorrhaged so badly that the throat wound he had received forty-nine years earlier was reopened. Delirious for some time, he eventually lost consciousness and died shortly thereafter. In his last moments, Longstreet's mind wandered back to those pleasant times on the Texas frontier, and he confused his second wife Helen with Louise. The General's final words were: "Helen, we shall be happier in this post."[58]

"Lieutenant-General James Longstreet, the 'war-horse' of the Confederacy, has at last again joined his old command." Thus wrote the *Atlanta Constitution* of the elaborate funeral for Longstreet in Gainesville. The mayor declared a period of public mourning, and the General's body lay in state at the courthouse for two days. Thousands came to file past the bier and view the casket, draped in flags of both the United States and the Confederate States of America and surrounded by flowers. Georgia's Governor Joseph M. Terrell arrived in time for the Catholic funeral service on January 6, and his official troop of horse guards escorted the body to Alta Vista Cemetery. Longstreet was laid to rest with full military honors. Atop his casket lay the tattered gray jacket of an anonymous Confederate veteran who requested it be interred with his old chief.[59]

A flood of tributes to Longstreet were published over the next few days, many from previously hostile sources. Helen Longstreet collected articles from the *Washington Post, St. Louis Globe-Democrat, Atlanta Journal, New Orleans Picayune,* and a host of other papers praising her late husband. Many of the General's old friends contacted her, and none was more open and sincere in his expression of grief than Osmun Latrobe, who wrote: "He was so much to me. For four years I had ridden at his side, and shared his confidence, and had learned to love him well. No unkind word or look stands between us, and my sorrow is that of one of his sons."[60]

All was not forgiven, however. Fewer than 5 percent of the UVC's chapters passed resolutions honoring Longstreet. The Savannah chapter of the UDC refused to send flowers to the funeral, as they blamed him for losing the South's independence. This behavior angered some veterans of Longstreet's corps, and the whole unpleasant business was reported in the national press.[61]

If Longstreet had been his own worst enemy, alienating people through his embittered writings, he had also been a living presence too great to be ignored. He had even enjoyed a paradoxical popularity during his last years because of the South's continuing commitment to the Lost Cause and all things Confederate. His wartime accomplishments were too much a part of the memories of living men for him to be completely obscured, his place in history completely ruined by those who had worked to discredit him. But with Longstreet's death, and as the number of Confederate veterans diminished yearly, the situation would change. The next sixty years would show just how thoroughly the anti-Longstreet faction had done its work.

11. Longstreet Postmortem

DEATH BROUGHT NO MORATORIUM on criticism of James Longstreet. This fact is crucial for an understanding of his place in Southern history. The early years of the twentieth century saw the publication of a final spate of works by key members of the anti-Longstreet faction. In 1906 the seventy-year-old Reverend Jones produced *Life and Letters of Robert Edward Lee, Soldier and Man,* which included a twenty-page refutation of Longstreet's memoirs and a totally unsupported claim that Lee "did not hesitate to say in the intimacy of private friendship that he lost the battle of Gettysburg mainly because of *Longstreet's disobedience of orders.*"[1] Walter Taylor's *General Lee: His Campaigns in Virginia with Personal Reminiscences,* published the same year, contained specific criticism of almost all of Longstreet's writings and repeated the old charges about tardiness at Gettysburg.[2] Jubal Early's memoirs, edited by his niece and published posthumously in 1912 made the same allegations.[3] Charles Marshall's memoirs were not published until 1927, twenty-five years after his death. In *An Aide-de-Camp of Lee* he contended that, in addition to being late on July 2, Longstreet had failed to inform Lee of a critical shortage of artillery ammunition on July 3, an oversight which doomed the famous charge and cost the battle. Marshall's writings were edited by Sir Frederick Maurice, a distinguished British soldier, who added to the text numerous remarks of his own against Longstreet.[4]

The *Southern Historical Society Papers* continued to print bitterly anti-Longstreet articles up to the eve of the First World War,[5] while the United Daughters of the Confederacy labored to ensure that a "correct" version of Southern history reached future generations. During the 1920s the UDC chapters undertook an intense study of the war, month by month. When suggesting studies of Gettysburg, the organization's historical department reminded its readers, "General Lee's character reached the sublime in taking upon himself the faults and failures of others."[6]

Many of the school textbooks used across the nation prior to the 1930s also presented an unfavorable view of Longstreet. *Makers of American History* (New York, 1904) lauded Lee for not blaming the Pennsylvania reverse on his subordinates. *Half-Hours in Southern History* (Richmond, 1907) blamed Longstreet for not attacking earlier on July 2 at Gettysburg, for not properly supporting Pickett on the following day, and for arguing unnecessarily with Lee throughout the entire campaign. *An American History* (Boston, 1913) ascribed Lee's failure in Pennsylvania to "a disastrous misunderstanding with General Longstreet," whom Lee had wanted to attack at dawn. The famous Philadelphia publishing house J. B. Lippincott published a series of history texts between 1914 and 1921, all of which blamed Longstreet by name for the Southern defeat. The list could easily be lengthened.[7]

Many other textbooks either omitted Longstreet entirely from their narrative of the war or focused on Lee and Jackson at his expense. The General received scant credit for his wartime efforts, and his position as Lee's second in command and most trusted adviser was almost never recognized.[8]

Many of the memoirs published by Confederate veterans during the twentieth century reinforced the negative view of Longstreet found in textbooks. William C. Oates scathingly denounced him in *The War Between the Union and the Confederacy and Its Lost Opportunities* (1905). From this reading of the postbellum publications of Longstreet, Early, Pendleton, and Fitzhugh Lee, Oates concluded that "Longstreet deserved to have been arrested and dismissed from the service as the least penalty his conduct merited."[9] Alexander Hunter's *Johnny Reb and Billy Yank* (1905) quoted extensively from Gordon's

1903 article blaming Longstreet for errors at Gettysburg. William L. Royall also argued that Longstreet was responsible for losing the battle in *Some Reminiscences* (1909), as did William H. Morgan in *Personal Recollections of the War of 1861–5* (1911). And in *Reminiscences of a Rebel* (1913), Wayland F. Dunaway drew his readers' attention to Lee's saintly qualities when he supposedly accepted responsibility for the defeat to cover the errors of his subordinates.[10]

Longstreet was not of course condemned in every book published by a Confederate veteran. Robert Stiles's *Four Years Under Marse Robert* (1904) contained a poignant, moving account of the General's accidental wounding in the Wilderness. Two of Longstreet's staff produced works destined to become classics of the genre, *Military Memoirs of a Confederate* (1907), by E. P. Alexander, and *Recollections of a Confederate Staff Officer* (1905), by G. Moxley Sorrel. Both of these sought to free Longstreet from the scapegoat role the Lee partisans had thrust upon him.[11] Even so, it is clear that through their textbooks and the memoirs of their fathers' generation, the Southern children of the early twentieth century absorbed a strongly negative view of Longstreet.

Increasingly, Civil War history was passing from the hands of participants to popular and professional historians who depended on the printed word rather than on memory for their information. Biography was the most popular form of history, and the biographies written of Lee served to anchor Longstreet in his unfavorable place in Southern history. He was usually portrayed as recalcitrant, argumentative, and anxious to obtain independent command. In *Robert E. Lee the Southerner* (1909), Thomas Nelson Page charged that at Gettysburg Longstreet's "slowness and surliness . . . probably cost Lee this battle and possibly cost the South, if not its independence, at least the offer of honorable terms."[12] In *Lee the American* (1912), Gamaliel Bradford claimed that Lee "always himself remained with Longstreet and left Jackson to operate independently, as if the former were more in need of personal supervision."[13] Longstreet's position as second in command was thus twisted into an allegation that Lee lacked confidence in him. Bradford blamed Longstreet for the Gettysburg defeat, as did almost all of his contemporaries who wrote of Lee: Wayne Whipple

(*The Heart of Lee*, 1918); Frederick Maurice (*Robert E. Lee the Soldier*, 1925); James Young (*Marse Robert*, 1929); William E. Brooks (*Lee of Virginia*, 1932); and Robert Winston (*Robert E. Lee*, 1934).[14]

Dependent upon biased sources, historians of the early twentieth century blamed Longstreet not only for losing Gettysburg but for fatal errors on other fields as well. By 1934, Longstreet was more of a scapegoat for the South's loss of the war than ever before. The extreme vanity, jealousy, egotism, and obstinacy observable in his own postwar writings were incorrectly assumed to be characteristic of his wartime conduct as well. Nor did there seem to be any reason to question the accounts of men such as Early, Long, Marshall, or Pendleton, whose only motive seemed to be defense of the saintly Lee.

When Douglas Southall Freeman's four-volume *R. E. Lee* was published in 1934–1935, Longstreet's reputation reached its nadir in the twentieth century. The author had received a Ph.D. from Johns Hopkins University in 1908. Born in Lynchburg, raised in Richmond, the son of a former private in the Army of Northern Virginia, he belonged to the last generation of Americans for whom the Civil War veteran was a common sight and a frequent acquaintance.

In *R. E. Lee*, Freeman portrayed the war in the eastern theater as much in terms of a contest between Lee and Longstreet as between rebel and Federal soldiers. This contest was said to have begun at Second Manassas, when Longstreet suggested that Lee not attack on August 29. "The seeds of much of the disaster at Gettysburg," he wrote, "were sown in that instant—when Lee yielded to Longstreet and Longstreet discovered that he would." Longstreet concluded from this incident that "he could dominate Lee."[15]

In the Suffolk campaign, Freeman saw evidence of Longstreet's "vanity," "cocksureness," and weakness for alcohol, his allegedly stubborn behavior driving Lee almost to despair.[16] He believed that Jackson's death paved the way for a contest of wills between Lee and Longstreet at Gettysburg:

> Longstreet's service in Southside Virginia . . . had given him a taste of independent command, and had greatly increased his opinion of himself as a strategist. . . . Now that Jackson was no more, Longstreet seemed to feel that it was his prerogative to devise as well as to execute, to dictate the strategy as well as to direct the tactics, to be the com-

mander's commander and to guide his errant faculties by his superior military judgement.[17]

Freeman took pains throughout his work to reduce the status of Stonewall Jackson, apparently from fear that his reputation detracted from that of Lee. But he fully endorsed the myth that Jackson, not Longstreet, had been Lee's principal and most trusted lieutenant. He dismissed obvious evidence of the strong relationship between Lee and Longstreet with a statement that Lee "usually camped near Longstreet in order to hasten the movements of that leisurely general."[18] This misinterpretation allowed the author to explain an apparent paradox, Lee's failure to spend much time with Jackson, his supposedly primary subordinate.

Freeman's case against Longstreet at Gettysburg encompassed four chapters and had a monumental impact on future historians' view of the battle. His research was based entirely on works by members of the anti-Longstreet faction or others reflecting a similarly negative view of the General. He cited Longstreet's own writings largely to suggest that the commander of the First Corps suffered from boundless egotism and vanity. The great battle was actually lost, according to Freeman, on the evening of July 1, "in the mind of Longstreet, who at his camp, a few miles away, was eating his heart away in sullen resentment that Lee had rejected his long-cherished plan of a strategic offensive and a tactical defensive."[19]

Although he rejected the sunrise attack thesis, Freeman cited A. L. Long as proof that Longstreet's July 2 attack was fatally late. He claimed that Longstreet's conduct was so stubbornly slow that had Jackson been in Lee's place he would have relieved Longstreet of command. Freeman realized that Lee's battle report proved that Hood and McLaws were never intended to advance with Pickett, but his description of Longstreet following the famous July 3 assault was a masterpiece of innuendo:

> If he [Lee] saw Longstreet again, after encountering him while he was attempting to rally Pickett's survivors, there was not the slightest touch of crimination. Longstreet, in fact, having fortified himself with rum, was somewhat confused in mind. Although there is not the slightest suggestion that he was drunk, he was doubtful whether or not he had ordered McLaws to leave his exposed position.[20]

Having cited the anti-Longstreet faction's works as "proof" that Longstreet had been both tardy and insubordinate, Freeman interpreted the strongest evidence to the contrary—Lee's silence—as confirmation and a reflection of Lee's high moral character. He supplemented this with a totally erroneous claim that Longstreet had been confused and a meaningless (but in this context, devastating) reminder that, while Lee was a teetotaler, Longstreet was not.

R. E. Lee was one of the top ten nonfiction best-sellers of 1935. Over the next decade it sold thousands of copies, exceeding the publisher's sales projection by more than 900 percent. Freeman won the Pulitzer Prize and was catapulted to the forefront of Civil War historiography, where he remained until his death in 1953.[21]

Hard on the heels of *R. E. Lee* came the first biography of Longstreet, Hamilton J. Eckenrode and Bryan Conrad's *James Longstreet: Lee's War Horse* (1936). Eckenrode was a friend of Freeman, a fellow Johns Hopkins graduate, and an officer in the Southern Historical Society. The book he wrote with Conrad, however, contained many passages that Freeman probably disputed. And Early and his followers would have been shocked at the authors' claim that "Lee and Jackson were both popular with the soldiers who served under them, but it is doubtful if either of them commanded the measure of devotion that was Longstreet's."[22]

While Eckenrode and Conrad criticized Longstreet as tardy and insubordinate at Gettysburg, they also faulted Lee severely for his slack control of his forces and unncessary aggressiveness. They believed that postwar criticisms of Longstreet were motivated in part by his career as a Radical Republican.[23]

Even so, this first biography adversely affected Longstreet's place in history. Eckenrode and Conrad strongly endorsed Freeman's view of the war as a contest of wills between Lee and Longstreet and claimed that the war had been lost primarily because of Longstreet's supposedly overriding ambition:

> [Longstreet] was beside himself with thirst and hunger for fame and high position. . . . Always he sought to push himself forward, not over-careful as to the means; ever he was discontented at being under Lee, thinking himself to be the better man, seeing in his mind's eye movements that would demonstrate his superiority. That itching of his colored all his generalship.[24]

They charged Longstreet with causing defeats or rendering victories incomplete at Seven Pines, Malvern Hill, Antietam, Chancellorsville, Missionary Ridge, and the Wilderness.[25] In the thirty years since his death, the General's role as scapegoat for the Confederate defeat had grown to astonishing proportions!

Historians such as J. C. F. Fuller and James G. Randall published works during the 1930s and 1940s that contained negative references to Longstreet.[26] These were supplemented by posthumous publication of Confederate memoirs, some of which also accused Longstreet of various errors and shortcomings.[27] The strongest reinforcement of the anti-Longstreet view, however, appeared in another monumental work by Douglas Southall Freeman.

Freeman's three-volume *Lee's Lieutenants,* published in 1943, is rightfully considered a masterpiece of scholarship and prose, but the author's bias against Longstreet is clear. In his second analysis of Gettysburg Freeman emphasized that no one person was responsible for Lee's defeat, but his narrative of the battle nevertheless clearly depicted Longstreet as a scapegoat and a Judas. As portrayed, Longstreet was not so much trying to force his will on Lee as being stubborn by nature—so much so that, when his own tactical proposals were rejected, he was unable to follow Lee's orders with the speed and enthusiasm necessary to ensure victory. The Pennsylvania campaign became a tragedy of Shakespearean proportions. Through defect of character rather than willful intent, Longstreet betrayed Lee at his hour of greatest need, thus contributing mightily to the loss of the battle and the war.[28]

Lee's Lieutenants also damaged Longstreet's place in history by failing to describe the command structure of the Army of Northern Virginia accurately. A disproportionate amount of the study focused on Jackson. Little of this was complimentary, for as in *R. E. Lee,* Freeman seemed to regard Jackson as jeopardizing Lee's reputation, and he took pains to emphasize Jackson's subordinate role. Even so, Freeman consistently presented Jackson, not Longstreet, as Lee's foremost lieutenant and most trusted adviser. He saw Longstreet as a figurehead second in command whom Lee, with keen insight into Longstreet's supposed lethargy, used to follow up the swift masterstrokes he delivered through the faster, more intelligent Jackson. Thanks to its enormous, long-lasting popularity, *Lee's Lieutenants* cemented the misconception that Jackson had been Lee's primary subordinate and that the study of the Civil War was synonymous with the study of the Virginia theater and the Lee-Jackson team.[29]

As in the previous century, Longstreet's image and his place in history were also shaped by literature. Novels by authors of the Southern Renaissance—Robert Penn Warren, Allen Tate, John Crowe Ransom, William Faulkner, Andrew Nelson Lytle, and others—demonstrated the region's continued fascination with its Confederate heritage. In *Intruder in the Dust* (1948) Faulkner referred specifically to the lasting place of the might-have-beens of Gettysburg in the Southern psyche.[30] None of these famous authors wrote directly of Longstreet, however, and one must turn to popular but less known writers to understand how the General was perceived.

Civil War novels were enormously popular during the first half of the twentieth century. These damaged Longstreet because the South of popular fiction was the South of the Lost Cause. Disproportionate emphasis was placed on Lee and Virginia, but little attention was paid to Longstreet. Authors such as Thomas Dixon, Irvins Cobb, James Boyd, Thomasine McGhee, and Gerald Johnson helped to make Lee a national, not just sectional, hero.[31] But they ignored the Lee-Longstreet friendship and did not number the General among their heroes.

National veneration of the Lost Cause affected Longstreet's image significantly. During the 1930s Stark Young's *So Red the Rose* and Margaret Mitchell's *Gone with the Wind* reached number three and number one, respectively, on the list of best-selling fiction. By the end of the Civil War centennial, its popularity boosted by the 1939 movie adaptation, *Gone with the Wind* had sold just under 7,000,000 copies.[32] The genteel, cultured settings which figured so prominently in these novels were a part of the world of the Lost Cause, not reality. The mind excited by such fiction turned to romantic, cavalier figures such as Lee and Stuart, not to the brusque, uncolorful Longstreet.

Longstreet was sometimes overtly condemned in fiction. Allen Dwight portrayed the General as inherently slow in his 1934 novel for juveniles, *Linn Dickson, Confederate*, repeating the old Early-Pendleton charge that he was late at Gettysburg.[33] In *A Sea Island Lady* (1939), by Francis Griswold, a Confederate veteran blames Longstreet not only for losing Gettysburg but also for all the evils of Reconstruction as well. Observing a young black lad handling a portrait of Lee, the old soldier remarks: "Careful there! Do you know whose portrait that is? . . . That great man, upon whose noble countenance you have the honor of gazing, is the man who would have *saved you from yourself*, but for the damnable insubordination of—of a trusted general at Gettysburg!"[34] Similarly, characters in Clifford Dowdey's 1937 novel *Bugles Blow No More* express the opinion that the South's one chance for independence was lost when "cold-eyed, burly" Longstreet "betrayed" Lee in Pennsylvania.[35]

The greatest damage to Longstreet by far, ironically, was perpetrated by Ben Ames Williams, the grandson of Longstreet's sister Sarah. Williams made his controversial ancestor the central historical figure in his novel *House Divided* (1947), a best-seller more than 1,400 pages long. To learn something of the General's private and social life, Williams contacted Longstreet's widow, Helen, his son Fitz Randolph, and several nieces and nephews. On the basis of this research, he portrayed Longstreet as polite and good humored, a loving husband, and an exceptionally devoted family man.[36]

For the military side of Longstreet, and for the General's deepest personality traits, however, Williams relied on Longstreet's critics. Like Eckenrode and Conrad, he depicted Longstreet as strong tempered and overbearing; like Freeman, he presented the General as willful and insubordinate. "I can never do, wholeheartedly, what someone else tells me to do when I'm sure he's wrong," declares Williams's fictional Longstreet. "A wise superior will never insist that I do something I think is a mistake."

At the time of Jackson's death in 1863, the author has Longstreet privately acknowledge Jackson's superiority. "I'm slow, ponderous. I can hit just as hard, but not as quickly," he reflects. In Pennsylvania, the fictional Longstreet angers Lee by failing to attack as early as expected on July 2. Aware that he is acting "as unreasonable as a sulking small boy," Williams's Longstreet is tragically unable to give Lee the instant obedience and celerity of movement that the situation demands.[37]

Williams was also highly critical of Longstreet in *The Unconquered*, the best-selling 1953 sequel to *House Divided*. Although Williams admires Longstreet's moral courage during Reconstruction in the novel, his sympathy is clearly with the Conservatives. He credits much of Longstreet's resolute political stance to the same sort of stubborn obstinacy he had shown at Gettysburg, a refusal to admit he was wrong rather than sincere conviction.[38]

Although his historical fiction presented the warmest and most human view of Longstreet to date, nothing in Williams's novels suggested that the perspective of the anti-Longstreet faction or that of later historians was inaccurate to any significant degree. Williams's work formed part of a great body of literature which, taking its cue from inherited prejudices and scholastic bias, gave weight to the prevailing negative view of Longstreet.

The centennial of the Civil War sparked a publishing boom which began in the early 1950s and lasted for two decades. The books ranged in quality from excellent to ghastly. The best of them tended to explore neglected figures and to question the axioms of previous generations of historians. Thanks to this trend, Longstreet's image enjoyed slight but significant revision.

James Longstreet: Soldier, Politician, Officeholder, and Writer, by Donald Bridgman Sanger and Thomas Robson Hay, was published in 1952. The bulk of it had been written by Sanger, a colonel in the United States Army, in 1933. From it he published an article in *Infantry Journal* in 1936 entitled "Was Longstreet a Scapegoat?" refuting the popularly accepted version of Gettysburg and absolving Longstreet of any errors. After Sanger's death in 1947, his friend Thomas Hay extended the book manuscript to cover the postwar period.[39] The resulting two-part biography possessed both great merit and serious shortcomings.

Sanger considered Longstreet "the best fighting general in the armies of the Confederacy and the best corps commander, North or South." While admitting that Longstreet had erred badly at Seven Pines, he defended the General against charges that his advice at Second Manassas had prevented a more decisive victory or that, being dilatory at Suffolk, he had denied Lee the use of two divisions at Chancellorsville.[40] The author's main interest, however, lay in the controversial Gettysburg campaign.

A sunrise attack order on July 2, Sanger noted, would have meant marching the First Corps to exhaustion and hurling it against an enemy whose strength and position were almost entirely unknown.

His careful study of troop positions, marching times, terrain conditions, and the physical space required by two divisions marching in column revealed that the men under Hood and McLaws had actually attacked on July 2 as soon as humanly possible.

Sanger criticized Longstreet for not handling his troops better once the attack had begun and agreed with earlier historians that the General's repeated protests against the assault on July 3 were insubordinate. But he found no fault in Longstreet's conduct of the famous charge, blaming its repulse on Lee's failure to support it with the remaining elements of Hill's corps.[41]

Convincing though it was as an analysis of Longstreet's battles, Sanger's study had limitations with respect to the General in a larger sense. The author was overly concerned to defend Longstreet during his troubles in East Tennessee, an episode which had revealed a strong streak of pettiness in the General. And he never recognized Longstreet's strong desire to return to service under Johnston.

Hay's study of Longstreet's postwar years was brief, focusing on politics in Lousiana and Georgia with no attempt to explore the General's private life or inner feelings. His analysis of the Gettysburg controversy failed to convey the extent to which Early and his followers had worked together against Longstreet. Indeed, despite Sanger's overwhelming evidence, Hay accepted the anti-Longstreet faction's claim that the General was tardy on July 2! He also credited an erroneous statement by John William Jones to the effect that Longstreet was responsible for starting and continuing the entire controversy.[42]

The obviously conflicting statements in the book by Sanger and Hay probably robbed it of the potential to change Longstreet's place in Southern history radically. North Carolina journalist Glenn Tucker ignored it almost completely when he wrote *High Tide at Gettysburg*. Published in 1958, this was the first major separate study of the battle since 1873 which did not treat Longstreet as a scapegoat. Although Tucker accepted the notion that Longstreet was inherently slow and stubborn, he rejected the theory of a sunrise attack order for July 2 and did not charge Longstreet with any tardiness. He portrayed Longstreet not as a sulking, insubordinate egotist but as a loyal officer doing his best to assist Lee.[43]

In 1962 Tucker published an article entitled "Longstreet: Culprit or Scapegoat?" which identified Early's 1872 Washington and Lee slander as the "initial salvo in the long Longstreet-Early feud." Giving a brief history of the war of words between Longstreet and his detractors, Tucker suggested that Early and Pendleton had been motivated in their attacks not only by their hatred of Longstreet's Republican politics but by a desire to distract attention from their own mistakes during the Pennsylvania campaign.[44]

Still fascinated by the battle and its controversies, Tucker produced *Lee and Longstreet at Gettysburg* in 1968. The author relied heavily on the published and unpublished writings of Lafayette McLaws to refute the claims of Early and Pendleton. Like Sanger, he concluded that Longstreet was the finest corps commander the war produced.[45]

Favorable views of Longstreet appeared in a few other instances. George R. Stewart's *Pickett's Charge* (1959), Ernest and Trevor Dupuy's *The Compact History of the Civil War* (1960), and Nash K. Burger and John K. Buttersworth's *South of Appomattox* (1959) all defended his conduct at Gettysburg.[46] This was the limit of the revisionist trend, however. Tucker planned to do a biography of Longstreet but could not find a publisher interested. During this same period Abbott M. Gibney, a friend of the General's grandson William Longstreet, wrote a biography of Longstreet for young readers. This excellent study, *War Horse of the Confederacy*, absolved the First Corps commander of any blame for Gettysburg. Like Tucker, Gibney found publishers unreceptive, and the work never saw print.[47]

Works critical of Longstreet meanwhile appeared in great numbers, overwhelming the few that cast him in a favorable light. Two of the best-selling authors of the Centennial period were journalists: Bruce Catton and Clifford Dowdey. Catton, a Michigan native, was for many years editor of *American Heritage* magazine. During the 1950s and 1960s he wrote a three-volume history of the war, a trilogy on the Army of the Potomac, and a host of newspaper and magazine articles. In 1954 he won the Pulitzer Prize for *A Stillness at Appomattox*. By the time of his death in 1978 his readers numbered in the millions. Because he relied on previously published sources, Catton's view of Longstreet conformed to that of the anti-Longstreet faction. In *Terrible Swift Sword* (1963) he depicted the First Corps commander as "dogged . . . and opinionated," marveling at Lee's strange reluctance to impose his will on his stubborn second in command. In a 1957 article he wrote that, at Gettysburg, Longstreet's "sulks and delays" gave Meade time to concentrate and were a major factor in the South's loss of the battle.[48]

The Virginia-born Dowdey has already been mentioned as a novelist. He also wrote a number of popular histories, all critical of Longstreet in the extreme: *The Land They Fought For* (1955); *Death of a Nation: The Story of Lee and His Men at Gettysburg* (1958); *Lee's Last Campaign* (1960); and *Seven Days: The Emergence of Lee* (1964). He also edited a collection of Lee's papers, which he filled with footnotes and editorial comments hostile to the General.[49]

In one book Dowdey compared Longstreet's refusal to allow Hood to flank the Little Round Top at Gettysburg with Peter's denial of Christ.[50] His study of Lee's Seven Days campaign included the revealing chapter title "The God Emerges." No author was more bitterly critical of Longstreet than Dowdey, and none made better use of the religious imagery with which the Lost Cause myth had enshrouded Lee. For Dowdey the Civil War was a passion play, with Lee as Christ and Longstreet as not merely Judas but the Antichrist.

Longstreet's reputation also suffered from the cumulative effects of many lesser assaults. Biographies of Civil War figures were enormously popular during the 1950s and 1960s. Preoccupied with their own subject, biographers all too often accepted and repeated without question the prevailing derogatory view of Longstreet.[51] As it had since 1872, Gettysburg remained crucial to Longstreet's place in history. Works which accepted and perpetuated the anti-Longstreet faction's version of the battle included Joseph Mitchell's *Decisive Battles of the Civil War* (1955), G. F. R. Henderson's *The Civil War: A Soldier's View* (1958), and Shelby Foote's three-volume *The Civil War: A Narrative* (1958–1974).[52] Books which used all or part of the standard accusations against Longstreet ranged in quality from monographs by professional historians, such as Clement Eaton's *A History of the Southern Confederacy* (1959) to poorly researched works by writers cashing in on the burgeoning popular interest in the war. Examples of the latter included *Rebel Boast* (1956), by Manly Wade Wellman; *They Met at Gettysburg* (1956), by Edward Stackpole; and *The Guns of Gettysburg* (1958), by Fairfax Downey.[53]

The celebration of the Centennial itself also affected Longstreet's reputation adversely, for the South which captured the imagination of the American public was the South of the Lost Cause, complete with its many myths detrimental to the General. The Confederate cavalryman, for example, became a national obsession. A weekly television series, *The Gray Ghost,* traced the supposed exploits of John S. Mosby, while Jeb Stuart, Turner Ashby, Bedford Forrest, and John Hunt Morgan were immortalized on bubblegum cards, paper placemats, and packets of Dixie Crystal sugar. There was no room in this company of cavaliers for Longstreet. While veneration of the Army of Northern Virginia reached an all-time high, the commander of the stalwart First Corps was completely overshadowed by the legends of the saintly Lee and the martyred Jackson.

Only Abraham Lincoln rivaled Lee as the preeminent symbol of the Centennial, and in the South there was no contest. This intense focus on Lee—or rather, on the artificial Lee of the Lost Cause— reinforced the importance of Longstreet's role as scapegoat for Gettysburg. The short-lived revisionism by Tucker, Sanger, and others was buried beneath the popular assumption that Longstreet had lost Gettysburg and consequently the war.

Finally, Longstreet's reputation suffered during the centennial because of his statelessness, his lack of identification in the popular mind with any specific geographic area within the South. If Longstreet had had readily discernible roots in any state, its residents might have seized upon the revisionist works concerning the General and might have promoted him as a state hero to attract tourists, if for no other reason.

But Alabama, Georgia, and South Carolina all failed to launch a campaign to reestablish Longstreet's good name and to claim him as their own. Gainesville residents showed an appreciation of the General, but Georgians as a whole ignored him. So did South Carolinians. The guide manual published by South Carolina for its citizens made no mention of Longstreet but instead encouraged its citizens by repeatedly referring to Lee. State teachers learned nothing of Edgefield's famous son from the pamphlet but were admonished to cite Lee and Jackson in their classrooms as examples of iron will and high moral character.[54]

Lacking partisans associated with his place of birth or residence, and lacking the cavalier, aristocratic image which so lent itself to commercialization, Longstreet was largely omitted from the centennial. The process begun by Early and his followers in the 1870s was complete. With his role as scapegoat for the Confederate defeat firmly entrenched as an integral part of the Lost Cause, James Longstreet, a man during the war acknowledged to be one of the South's foremost combat commanders, emerged from the centennial a figure of pity and scorn.

Epilogue

THE VANITY, JEALOUSY, AND overt desire for self-advancement which marked Longstreet's postwar prose were a product of his controversies with Early and his supporters and did not characterize Longstreet during the war. The assumption that they were lifelong characteristics has been a major historical error. But no single person or factor created Longstreet's negative image. It resulted from a complex combination of personalities and circumstances.

Contributing factors included Jubal Early's guilt for having fled the South in 1865 and his obsession with Confederate history as a means of assuaging that guilt and compensating for the disgrace in which his career had ended. They included the desires of William Nelson Pendleton and John William Jones to bask in the reflected glory of Robert E. Lee and to win among Confederate veterans in peacetime a status that they had not enjoyed as soldiers. Also implicated was the sensitivity of Lee's staff to their chief's reputation and the assumption that to suspect him of any error was to do a disservice to his memory. It involved officers such as John B. Gordon and Fitzhugh Lee, who endorsed the Lost Cause and exploited Lee's name to further their postwar political careers. And it involved the entire Southern reaction to the defeat and Reconstruction, which made Longstreet's Republican affiliation appear to be an abomination and made his role of scapegoat believeable.

Finally, and most important of all, it included Longstreet's reaction to his accusers. Although the Lost Cause maintained a firm grip on historians for generations, Longstreet's image would probably not have emerged from the centennial so little changed since the 1870s had not historians and the reading public been able to see in the General's writings apparent confirmation of his alleged wartime nature and behavior. In the final analysis the anti-Longstreet faction had no greater ally than Longstreet himself.

James Longstreet's negative image is not likely to change. His role in Southern culture has been that of villain, not hero, and cultural roles cannot be overturned by scholarship. The most laudatory biography imaginable could not give Longstreet anything to compare with the hundred years of adoration accorded Lee and Jackson. The artificiality of the stereotypical Confederate hero is not the issue. Longstreet's picture did not hang in schoolrooms for generation after generation. His birthplace did not become a shrine nor his grave a place of pilgrimage, and his birthday was not made a state holiday. As long as Southern history remains something that is lived and felt as much as read, Longstreet will be remembered primarily as Lee's tarnished lieutenant.

Abbreviations

Annals of the War / *The Annals of the War Written by Leading Participants North and South, originally published in the Philadelphia Weekly Times.* Philadelphia: Times Publishing, 1879.

B&L / Johnson, Robert Underwood, and Buel, Clarence C., eds. *Battles and Leaders of the Civil War.* 4 vols. New York: Century, 1887–1888.

N.C. Regts. / Clark, Walter, ed. *Histories of the Several Regiments and Battalions from North Carolina in the Great War, 1861–'65.* 5 vols. Goldsboro: Nash Brothers, 1901.

O.R. / *The War of the Rebellion: A Compilation of the Official Records of the Union and Confederate Armies,* 128 vols. Washington, D.C.: Government Printing Office, 1880–1901. All references are to series 1 unless otherwise noted.

SHSP / *Southern Historical Society Papers*

VMHB / *Virginia Magazine of History and Biography*

Notes

All notations use a shortened form. For full publication data, see the bibliography.

Preface

1. Dufour, *The Night the War Was Lost,* 9–10.

Prologue: Longstreet Antebellum

1. Sanger and Hay, *James Longstreet,* 6.
2. Ibid., 6–7.
3. Wade, *Augustus Baldwin Longstreet,* 85, 89, 117–18, 246; Longstreet, *From Manassas to Appomattox,* 15.
4. Wade, *Augustus Baldwin Longstreet,* 34–36, 121–23, 143–44, 153–56, 219–22, 297.
5. Ibid., 118–24, 132–38, 219–22, 230–31.
6. Sanger and Hay, *James Longstreet,* 9, 12.
7. Ibid., 14n; see also the prefaces of Williams's novels.
8. McMaster, *Musket, Saber, and Missile,* 18–20; Sanger, *Story of Old Fort Bliss,* 20.
9. James Longstreet to I. M. McDowell, Mar. 29, 1858, Longstreet Papers, Historical Soc. of Pa.
10. Sanger and Hay, *James Longstreet,* 7–8.
11. Winton, "Ante-Bellum Instruction of West Point Officers," 17–18, 28–29, 56.
12. Wilhelm, *Eighth U.S. Infantry,* 30–32.
13. Ibid., 155–56; Utley, *Frontiersmen in Blue,* 70–73.
14. Sanger and Hay, *James Longstreet,* 11–13; Wilhelm, *Eighth U.S. Infantry,* 35–38.

15.   McMaster, *Musket, Saber, and Missile,* 18–19; Wilhelm, *Eighth U.S. Infantry,* 50–51.

16.   Most recently this debate has involved McWhiney and Jamieson's *Attack and Die: Civil War Tactics and the Southern Heritage* and Hattaway and Jones's *How the North Won: A Military History of the Civil War.* McWhiney and Jamieson argue that many Civil War leaders, particularly Southerners, learned from their West Point training, Mexican War experiences, and current military manuals that offensive tactics held the key to victory. Hattaway and Jones, however, emphasize the engineering orientation of West Point education and the stress that their instructor Dennis Hart Mahan placed on the use of field fortifications. This, they believed, allowed most Civil War leaders to grasp relatively early the tremendous power of the defensive.

17.   Wilhelm, *Eighth U.S. Infantry,* 35–38; Rodenbough and Haskins, *Army of the United States,* 517–18; Kirby Smith, *To Mexico with Scott,* 202–203; Scott, *Memoirs* 2: 487–91; Justin H. Smith, *War with Mexico* 2:145–46.

18.   Wilhelm, *Eighth U.S. Infantry,* 28–29, 36–38.

1: From Manassas to Antietam

1.   Longstreet, *From Manassas to Appomattox,* 29–30; Curry, *Civil History,* 161; *O.R.,* series 4, vol. 1: 181, 400, 420. Longstreet had practical reasons for waiting until spring to resign. The weather would be better for traveling, and his daughter Mary Anne, born Jan. 1, 1860, would be in better condition to make the trip. Once he had left Albuquerque, however, he grew impatient and deposited his family with friends at Fort Bliss so that they could continue the journey at a more comfortable pace.

2.   T. J. Goree to Sarah W. Goree, June 23, 1861, Goree Papers, LSU. This letter indicates that Longstreet arrived in Richmond on June 21, not June 29, as he states in his memoirs; it also indicates that he intended to form a group of mounted infantrymen, not join the paymaster's department, as his memoirs indicate.

3.   Ibid.; Longstreet, *From Manassas to Appomattox,* 32–33.

4.   Beauregard, "The First Bull Run," *B&L* 1: 196–98.

5.   Longstreet, *From Manassas to Appomattox,* 33–34; Sanger and Hay, *James Longstreet,* 22–25.

6.   Sanger and Hay, *James Longstreet,* 23–25.

7.   *O.R.* 2: 461–62.

8.   Hunter, *Johnny Reb and Billy Yank,* 52.

9.   T. J. Goree to P. W. Kittrell, Aug. 2, 1861, Goree Papers, LSU.

10.   *O.R.* 2: 461–62.

11.   Ibid. 2: 461–65; Morgan, *Personal Reminiscences,* 60; T. J. Goree to P. W. Kittrell, Aug. 2, 1861, Goree Papers, LSU.

12. Beauregard, "The First Bull Run," *B&L* 1: 201–202; Roman, *Military Operations* 1: 94.

13. Quoted in Hunter, *Johnny Reb and Billy Yank*, 64; Longstreet, *From Manassas to Appomattox*, 45–53; *O.R.* 2: 543–44; Sorrel, *Recollections*, 26.

14. Sorrel, *Recollections*, 14–15, 25, 31–32, 35–36; *O.R.* 2: 544.

15. Sorrel, *Recollections*, 23–24.

16. T. J. Goree to S. W. Goree, Aug. 27, 1861, Goree Papers, LSU.; punctuation and spelling corrected.

17. *O.R.* 2: 896–97, 913–14; 51, pt. 2: 229; R. H. Chilton to P. G. T. Beauregard, Aug. 14, 1861, Longstreet Papers, Historical Soc. of Pa.; Williams, *P. G. T. Beauregard*, 101–102.

18. Luvaas, "Joseph E. Johnston," 5–6; Govan and Livingood, *A Different Valor*, 19, 21.

19. Joseph E. Johnston to James Longstreet, Feb. 3, 1879, Longstreet Papers, Georgia Archives; Johnston, *Narrative of Military Operations*, 73–74.

20. Sanger and Hay, *James Longstreet*, 35.

21. T. J. Goree to S. W. Goree, Sept. 27, 1861, Goree Papers, LSU; italics are in the original.

22. Cate, *Lucius Q. C. Lamar*, 85.

23. Quoted in Mayes, *Lucius Q. C. Lamar*, 7.

24. Murphy, *L. Q. C. Lamar*, 66; Haskell, *Haskell Memoirs*, 13.

25. T. J. Goree to S. W. Goree, Dec. 14, 1861, Goree Papers, LSU; Stiles, *Four Years Under Marse Robert*, 59.

26. "Longstreet on the War," *New York Times*, July 19, 1879.

27. La Salle Pickett, "The Wartime Story of General Pickett," 37.

28. Haskell, "Reminiscences of the Confederate War," 26, Southern Historical Collection, Univ. of N.C.

29. T. J. Goree to S. W. Goree, Dec. 14, 1861, Goree Papers, LSU.

30. Sanger and Hay, *James Longstreet*, 36–37; Sorrel, *Recollections*, 37–38.

31. *O.R.* 11, pt. 1: 275–76, 564–68; Sanger and Hay, *James Longstreet*, 41–45.

32. *O.R.* 11, pt. 1: 275–76, 565.

33. Sanger and Hay, *James Longstreet*, 51–54.

34. Ibid., 53–55; *O.R.* 11, pt. 3: 580.

35. Alexander, *Military Memoirs*, 77.

36. Freeman, *Lee's Lieutenants* 1: 242–43, 246–47, 250, 262–63.

37. Connelly, *Marble Man*, 16–17; Rowland, *Jefferson Davis* 11: 269–70.

38. Quoted in Reid, *History of the Fourth Regiment*, 91; Connelly, *Marble Man*, 17; Alexander, *Military Memoirs*, 109–10.

39. Hattaway and Jones, *How the North Won*, 193–201.

40. Connelly, *Marble Man*, 17–20.

41. Connelly and Jones, *Politics of Command*, 33.

42. Quoted in Lane, *Dear Mother*, 173.

43. Quoted in Phillips, "Correspondence of Robert Toombs" 2: 601.
44. Ibid. 2: 601; Morgan, *Personal Reminiscences,* 136; Cumming, *Kate,* 54; Lane, *Dear Mother,* 171.
45. Freeman, *Lee's Dispatches,* 11.
46. T. J. Goree to S. W. Goree, July 21, 1862, Goree Papers, LSU.
47. Ibid.; Robert E. Lee to Jefferson Davis, Aug. 17, 1862, Davis Collection, Tulane Univ.; Freeman, *Lee's Lieutenants,* 1: 601–11, 613, 620–32, 663, 671–73; 2: 247.
48. Owen, *In Camp and Battle,* 134; Moses, "Autobiography," 54, Moses Papers, Southern Historical Collection, Univ. of N.C.
49. Connelly, *Marble Man,* 165–70, 172–73, 176, 180–82.
50. Sanger and Hay, *James Longstreet,* 77–85.
51. Freeman, *Lee's Lieutenants* 2: 120.
52. Sanger and Hay, *James Longstreet,* 87.
53. Ibid.; Longstreet, *From Manassas to Appomattox,* 181–82; Longstreet, "Our March Against Pope," *B&L* 2: 519–20.
54. Sanger and Hay, *James Longstreet,* 86–87.
55. Ibid., 88–89; Sorrel, *Recollections,* 98; Longstreet, "Our March Against Pope," *B&L* 2: 519–20.
56. Sorrel, *Recollections,* 113; Moses, "Autobiography," 54, 56, Moses Papers, Southern Historical Collection, Univ. of N.C.; Owen, *In Camp and Battle,* 113.
57. Sorrel, *Recollections,* 113.
58. Murfin, *Gleam of Bayonets,* 113–14, 399–400; Hattaway and Jones, *How the North Won,* 232–33.
59. Longstreet, "Invasion of Maryland," *B&L* 2: 663; Jackson, quoted in Murfin, *Gleam of Bayonets,* 115–16; Longstreet, *From Manassas to Appomattox,* 207.
60. Murfin, *Gleam of Bayonets,* 281.
61. Ibid.; *O.R.* 19, pt. 1: 145, 839–40, 954–55.
62. Sorrel, *Recollections,* 103, 115; Owen, *In Camp and Battle,* 146.
63. Quoted in Pryor, *Reminiscences of War and Peace,* 194.
64. James Longstreet to Thomas B. O'Bryan, Jan. 10, 1889, Assoc. of Army of Northern Va. Papers, Tulane Univ.; Squires, "'Boy Officer' of the Washington Artillery," 12, 16; Longstreet, "Invasion of Maryland," *B&L* 2: 669; Owen, *In Camp and Battle,* 85; Long, *Memoirs of Robert E. Lee,* 219.
65. *O.R.* 19, pt. 1: 840–41.
66. Quoted in Owen, *In Camp and Battle,* 157.
67. *O.R.* 11, pt. 3: 580.
68. James Longstreet to Joseph E. Johnston, Oct. 5, 1862, Longstreet Papers, Duke Univ.
69. Ibid.
70. *Southern Literary Messenger* 24 (Sept.–Oct. 1862): 582.
71. Freeman, *Lee's Lieutenants* 2: 149–52.

72. *O.R.* 19, pt. 1: 143.
73. Ibid. and 19, pt. 2: 629–30.
74. Pollard, *Lee and His Lieutenants,* 412; Freeman, *Lee's Lieutenants* 2: 136; Alexander, "Confederate Chieftains," 34–37.
75. James Longstreet to Louis T. Wigfall, Nov. 7, 1862, Wigfall Papers, Library of Congress; King, *Louis T. Wigfall,* 140–41; Connelly and Jones, *Politics of Command,* 58; *O.R.* 11, pt. 2: 760.
76. James Longstreet to R. H. Chilton, Sept. 28, 1862, Longstreet Papers, Chicago Historical Soc.; Thompson, *Robert Toombs,* 160–61, 164, 174, 198–99; Longstreet, *From Manassas to Appomattox,* 161, 166, 189; Sorrel, *Recollections,* 100–101.
77. Phillips, "Correspondence of Robert Toombs" 2: 601; Stovall, *Robert Toombs,* 260; Abele, *Alexander H. Stephens,* 207.
78. *O.R.,* ser. 4, vol. 1: 400, 420; Rice, *J. M. L. Curry,* 38, 43, 46; Curry, *Civil History of the Government of the Confederate States,* 161.
79. "A Quarrel and Its Ending: Why Jefferson Davis and General Longstreet Fell Out," *New York Times,* June 4, 1893.
80. Eggleston, *Rebel's Recollections,* 153; *O.R.* 19, pt. 2: 643; Freeman, *Lee's Lieutenants* 2: 247; Vandiver, *Mighty Stonewall,* 406.
81. Jones, *Roster of Confederate Officers,* 9–10.

2: From Fredericksburg to Gettysburg

1. Catton, *Glory Road,* 19–23.
2. *O.R.* 21: 568–69; Longstreet, "Battle of Fredericksburg," *B&L* 3: 72–73; Owen, "A Hot Day on Mayre's Heights," *B&L* 3: 97.
3. *O.R.* 21: 569, 578, 592–93, 595; 51, pt. 2: 662. Walter H. Taylor refers to Longstreet's "earthworks" in *General Lee,* 143. See also Sanger's discussion of entrenchments in Sanger and Hay, *James Longstreet,* 110n. His "five trenches" is apparently a misprint for "fire trenches."
4. *O.R.* 51, pt. 2: 662.
5. Longstreet, "Battle of Fredericksburg," *B&L* 3: 81; Alexander, quoted in Hattaway and Jones, *How the North Won,* 306–307.
6. William B. Pettit to Wife, Dec. 16, 1862, Pettit Papers, Southern Historical Collection, Univ. of N.C.; punctuation added.
7. Ibid.
8. *O.R.* 21: 568–72.
9. Hattaway and Jones, *How the North Won,* 306–308.
10. Quoted in Catton, *Never Call Retreat,* 23.
11. *O.R.* 21: 572–73, 632–35. Longstreet may not have entrenched more thoroughly than he did because of Lee's suspicions throughout early December that Burnside might shift his army elsewhere. See ibid., 1048–50.
12. Longstreet, *From Manassas to Appomattox,* 323–24.

13. Sanger and Hay, *James Longstreet*, 117.
14. Ibid.
15. *O.R.* 18: 896; Sorrel, *Recollections*, 126, 180–81; Dawson, *Reminiscences*, 56, 63; Moses, "Autobiography," 51, Moses Papers, Southern Historical Collection, Univ. of N.C.
16. Klein, *Edward Porter Alexander*, 3, 9, 14–15, 32–33, 71; Wise, *Long Arm of Lee*, 93–94, 143, 704, 756–57; Alexander, *Military Memoirs*, 52, 58, 71–72, 280.
17. Freeman, *Lee's Lieutenants* 2: 438.
18. Eckenrode and Conrad, *James Longstreet*, 364.
19. Alexander, "Confederate Chieftains," 35–38.
20. Sanger and Hay, *James Longstreet*, 123.
21. Ibid.; *O.R.* 18: 895–96; Freeman, *Lee's Lieutenants* 2: 469.
22. G. M. Sorrel to Henry L. Benning, Apr. 3, 1863; James Longstreet to Henry L. Benning, Apr. 18, 1863, Benning Papers, Southern Historical Collection, Univ. of N.C.; *O.R.* 18: 977, 998–99, 1002, 1007, 1025.
23. *O.R.* 18: 924–27, 933–34, 942–44, 950–51, 954, 958–60, 976–99; Sanger and Hay, *James Longstreet*, 142, 145–46.
24. *O.R.* 18: 924–27, 933–34, 966–67, 969–70, 1024–25.
25. Ibid., 898–99, 906–907, 911–12, 921–22, 927, 933–34, 966–67, 1018, 1024–25.
26. Ibid., 903, 923–27, 933, 944, 950, 955–60.
27. Ibid., 926.
28. Longstreet, *From Manassas to Appomattox*, 158–59.
29. *O.R.* 18: 1049.
30. Sanger and Hay, *James Longstreet*, 151.
31. James Longstreet to Lafayette McLaws, June 3, 1863, McLaws Papers, Southern Historical Collection, Univ. of N.C.
32. Lafayette McLaws to Wife, July 7, 1863, in ibid.
33. Roman, *Military Operations* 2: 2, 81–83; James Longstreet to Louis T. Wigfall, Feb. 4, 1863, Wigfall Papers, Library of Congress.
34. Longstreet, "Lee's Invasion of Pennsylvania," *B&L* 3: 245n.
35. Longstreet, *From Manassas to Appomattox*, 332. Longstreet's postwar dislike of certain Virginia officers makes it difficult to ascertain his wartime opinion of Virginians.
36. Wise, *Long Arm of Lee*, 146.
37. Hassler, "Civil War Letters of General William Dorsey Pender," 70. Lee in fact considered Pender "most gallant" and recommended him for promotion. See Freeman, *Lee's Dispatches*, 91–92; Rowland, *Jefferson Davis* 5: 229–30.
38. Connelly, "Robert E. Lee and the Western Confederacy," 131; "Opposing Forces at Gettysburg," *B&L* 3: 437–39. Wade Hampton to Louis T. Wigfall, May 17, 1863, Wigfall Papers, Library of Congress.
39. Quoted in Hamlin, *Old Bald Head*, 133.
40. Ibid.

41. Hattaway and Jones, *How the North Won,* 362–64, 373n, 384–85; Connelly, *Marble Man,* 202–203.

42. Connelly, *Autumn of Glory,* 68, 73–74.

43. Ibid., 32–33.

44. Connelly and Jones, *Politics of Command,* 52–54.

45. *O.R.* 18: 959.

46. James Longstreet to Louis T. Wigfall, Feb. 4, 1863, Wigfall Papers, Library of Congress.

47. Connelly and Jones, *Politics of Command,* 121–23; James A. Seddon to James Longstreet, May 3, 1875, Longstreet Papers, Emory Univ.

48. James A. Seddon to James Longstreet, May 3, 1875, Longstreet Papers, Emory Univ.; James Longstreet to Lafayette McLaws, July 25, 1873, McLaws Papers, Southern Historical Collection, Univ. of N.C.; Longstreet, "Lee in Pennsylvania," *Annals of the War,* 415–16; Longstreet, *From Manassas to Appomattox,* 327–28; Connelly, *Autumn of Glory,* 104–105.

49. Connelly and Jones, *Politics of Command,* 59.

50. Hattaway and Jones, *How the North Won,* 384–85, 397–98.

51. James Longstreet to Louis T. Wigfall, May 13, 1863, Wigfall Papers, Library of Congress.

52. Jackson's death eliminated Longstreet's chief rival for fame under Lee's command, but it is not likely that this in any way caused him temporarily to shelve his ideas for a western concentration. His best opportunities for fame and independent command lay in the West. If Longstreet had had an inordinate desire for glory, he would hardly have argued on behalf of Lee's plan in speaking to Wigfall, a leading advocate of western concentration.

53. James Longstreet to Lafayette McLaws, July 25, 1873, McLaws Papers, Southern Historical Collection, Univ. of N.C.; Longstreet, *From Manassas to Appotomax,* 334.

54. *O.R.* 17, pt. 2: 318; Girard, *Visit to the Confederate States,* 78; McCabe, *Life and Campaigns of Robert E. Lee,* 393; Maurice, *Aide-de-Camp of Lee,* 231; Hattaway and Jones, *How the North Won,* 397–98, 414.

55. Compare the letter from Longstreet to Lafayette McLaws, July 25, 1873, McLaws Papers, Southern Historical Collection, Univ. of N.C., with Longstreet's *From Manassas to Appomattox,* 331, and "Lee in Pennsylvania," *Annals of the War,* 417. In his letter to McLaws, written when his role as a scapegoat was just forming, Longstreet does not state that Lee promised to remain on the defensive, only that he was distressed when Lee did not do so.

3: "The Best Fighter in the Whole Army"

1. *O.R.* 27, pt. 2: 313–16, 357–58, 442–43.

2. Ibid., 306–307, 316, 687, 692.

3. Ibid., 307, 316–17; Longstreet, *From Manassas to Appomattox*, 346–47; Sorrel, *Recollections*, 156–57, 164; Hall, "The Spy Harrison," 21–24.

4. Robert E. Lee to William C. Rives, May 21, 1863, Davis Collection, Tulane Univ.

5. *O.R.* 27, pt. 3: 943; Lane, *Dear Mother*, 246, 251; first quotation in Caldwell, *History of a Brigade*, 99; second quotation in Trundle, "Gettysburg Described in Two Letters from a Maryland Confederate," 212; Simpson, *Hood's Texas Brigade*, 259–61. Simpson provides a graphic picture of the results of the Texans' enthusiasm, which went far beyond military necessity or Lee's intentions. Only food, however, was taken, not property.

6. Fremantle, *Three Months in the Confederate States*, 237, 246–47.

7. Francis C. Lawley to James Longstreet, July 28, 1896, Longstreet Papers, Emory Univ.; Lonn, *Foreigners in the Confederacy*, 181, 360; Luvaas, "Prussian Observer with Lee," 105–106; Ross, *Cities and Camps of the Confederate States*, 37, 44.

8. *O.R.* 27, pt. 2: 317, 444–45, 468–69; Reed, "Gettysburg Campaign," 188; Hunt, "First Day at Gettysburg," *B&L* 3: 274, 281–83; Hamlin, *Old Bald Head*, 145–46.

9. Tucker, *High Tide at Gettysburg*, 171, 174; Freeman, *Lee's Lieutenants* 3: 90–91; Hamlin, *Old Bald Head*, 145–47.

10. *O.R.* 27, pt. 2: 469–70; Bushong, *Old Jube*, 146–47; Tucker, *High Tide at Gettysburg*, 211–12.

11. *O.R.* 27, pt. 2: 444; Freeman, *Lee's Lieutenants* 3: 92–96, 100; Trimble, "Campaign and Battle of Gettysburg," 211–12.

12. *O.R.* 27, pt. 2: 318; Taylor, "Campaign in Pennsylvania," *Annals of the War*, 308; Bushong, *Old Jube*, 146–47.

13. Hunton, *Autobiography*, 98.

14. Walter H. Taylor to Jubal A. Early, Nov. 9, 1877, Early Papers, Library of Congress. Taylor states that he cannot recall the hour that Lee reached the field on July 1.

15. Diary of Osmun Latrobe, entry for July 1, 1863, Virginia Historical Soc.; Lafayette McLaws to James Longstreet, June 12, 1873, McLaws Papers, Southern Historical Collection, Univ. of N.C.; *O.R.* 27, pt. 2: 358.

16. Fremantle, *Three Months in the Confederate States*, 252.

17. Ibid., 252–53.

18. Ibid., 254; Longstreet, "Lee's Right Wing at Gettysburg," *B&L* 3: 329.

19. Sanger and Hay, *James Longstreet*, 167–68.

20. James Longstreet to Lafayette McLaws, July 25, 1873, McLaws Papers, Southern Historical Collection, Univ. of N.C. Longstreet published three versions of his conversation with Lee, varying the details. For a discussion of them, see Tucker, *Lee and Longstreet at Gettysburg*, 50–52 passim.

21. *O.R.* 27, pt. 2: 318.
22. Longstreet, *From Manassas to Appomattox,* 359; Longstreet, "Lee in Pennsylvania," *Annals of the War,* 421; Lafayette McLaws to James Longstreet, June 12, 1873, McLaws Papers, Southern Historical Collection, Univ. of N.C.
23. Fremantle, *Three Months in the Confederate States,* 255–56; Longstreet, "Lee in Pennsylvania," *Annals of the War,* 439.
24. Charles Marshall to Jubal A. Early, May 13, 1878, Early Papers, Library of Congress.
25. *O.R.* 27, pt. 2: 446; Tucker, *High Tide at Gettysburg,* 212–14, 217; Bushong, *Old Jube,* 147; Charles Marshall to Jubal A. Early, May 13, 1878, Early Papers, Library of Congress.
26. Lafayette McLaws to James Longstreet, June 12, 1873, McLaws Papers, Southern Historical Collection, Univ. of N.C.; McLaws, "Gettysburg," 67–68; Hood, *Advance and Retreat,* 56; Polley, *Hood's Texas Brigade,* 154.
27. Longstreet, "Lee in Pennsylvania," *Annals of the War,* 439; Fremantle, *Three Months in the Confederate States,* 256–57; Ross, *Cities and Camps of the Confederate States,* 48.
28. Scheibert, "Letter from Maj. Scheibert," 92.
29. Riley, "Robert E. Lee's Battle with Disease," 222.
30. *O.R.* 27, pt. 2: 350; Freeman, *Lee's Lieutenants* 3:111; Coddington, *Gettysburg Campaign,* 372–74.
31. Longstreet, "Lee in Pennsylvania," *Annals of the War,* 422; Maurice, *Aide-de-Camp of Lee,* 233.
32. McLaws, "Gettysburg," 68; James Longstreet to Lafayette McLaws, July 25, 1873, McLaws Papers, Southern Historical Collection, Univ. of N.C.; "Longstreet at Gettysburg," 1 (unidentified newspaper clipping dated Feb. 20, 1888, in ibid.).
33. McLaws, "Gettysburg," 68; James Longstreet to Lafayette McLaws, July 15, 1873, McLaws Papers, Southern Historical Collection, Univ. of N.C.; "Longstreet at Gettysburg," 1 (unidentified newspaper clipping dated Feb. 20, 1888, in ibid.).
34. Trimble, "Campaign and Battle of Gettysburg," 212; Hamlin, *Old Bald Head,* 149.
35. *O.R.* 27, pt. 2: 318–19; Longstreet, "Lee's Right Wing at Gettysburg," *B&L* 3: 340–41.
36. Freeman, *Lee's Lieutenants* 3: 129.
37. *O.R.* 27, pt. 2: 358; Longstreet, "Lee in Pennsylvania," *Annals of the War,* 422; Freeman, *Lee's Lieutenants* 2: 546, 548, 559; Sanger and Hay, *James Longstreet,* 176; Alexander, *Military Memoirs,* 391–92.
38. Ross, *Cities and Camps of the Confederate States,* 49.
39. Ibid., 51–52.
40. Freeman, *Lee's Lieutenants* 3: 116; Longstreet, *From Manassas to Appomattox,* 365–66.

41. T. J. Goree to James Longstreet, May 17, 1875, Goree Papers, LSU; *O.R.* 27, pt. 2: 350–51, 358; Ross, *Cities and Camps of the Confederate States,* 52; Alexander, *Military Memoirs,* 392; Sorrel, *Recollections,* 168; McLaws, "Gettysburg," 1–2, 4; Longstreet, "Lee's Right Wing at Gettysburg," *B&L* 3: 240–41. Johnston denied that he had been assigned to be Longstreet's guide but stated in a postwar letter that he understood his orders "to mean that I was to be with General Longstreet to aid him in any way that I could." See S. R. Johnston to Lafayette McLaws, June 27, 1892, Johnston Papers, Library of Congress; Fitzhugh Lee, "A Review of the First Two Days' Operations at Gettysburg," 183–84.

42. James Longstreet to Lafayette McLaws, July 25, 1873, McLaws Papers, Southern Historical Collection, Univ. of N.C.; Longstreet, "Lee's Right Wing at Gettysburg," *B&L* 3: 1–4; Walter H. Taylor to E. P. Alexander, June 28, 1904, Taylor Papers, microfilm, Virginia State Library.

43. Quoted in William Youngblood to James Longstreet, Sept. 5, 1892, Longstreet Papers, Emory Univ.; Youngblood, "Unwritten History of the Gettysburg Campaign," 312–15.

44. Quoted in Owen, *In Camp and Battle,* 246; Ross, *Cities and Camps of the Confederate States,* 52; Fremantle, *Three Months in the Confederate States,* 261; Sorrel, *Recollections,* 168; Coddington, *Gettysburg Campaign,* 405–406; Dickert, *History of Kershaw's Brigade,* 236–39; Moore, *A Life for the Confederacy,* 153.

45. *O.R.* 27, pt. 2: 316–20, 358–59, 447, 607–608; Morrison, "Memoirs of Henry Heth," 306; Coddington, *Gettysburg Campaign,* 444–45; Hassler, "'Fighting Dick' Anderson," 10, 40; Bushong, *Old Jube,* 150–52.

46. Fremantle, *Three Months in the Confederate States,* 259–60.

47. *O.R.* 27, pt. 2: 320; Alexander, *Military Memoirs,* 415; James Longstreet to Lafayette McLaws, July 25, 1873, McLaws Papers, Southern Historical Collection, Univ. of N.C.; Longstreet, "Lee in Pennsylvania," *Annals of the War,* 342–43; Longstreet, *From Manassas to Appomattox,* 355–56. Longstreet is the only source for the details of his meeting with Lee that morning, but there are so many discrepancies between his accounts that one is forced to draw inferences from his and Lee's battle reports, as does Coddington, *Gettysburg Campaign,* 455–59.

48. *O.R.* 27, pt. 2: 320; Wilson, "James B. Pettigrew," 22.

49. *O.R.* 18: 926.

50. Longstreet, "Lee in Pennsylvania," *Annals of the War,* 343; Longstreet, *From Manassas to Appomattox,* 386–87.

51. James Longstreet to James B. Walton, July 3, 1863, Walton Papers, Tulane Univ.; Alexander, *Military Memoirs,* 422–23; Klein, *Edward Porter Alexander,* 88–89; *O.R.* 27, pt. 2: 360.

52. Longstreet, "Lee's Right Wing at Gettysberg," *B&L* 3: 345.

53. Alexander, *Military Memoirs,* 421–24; Klein, *Edward Porter Alexander,* 89–90.

54. Haskell, *Haskell Memoirs,* 50.

55. *O.R.* 27, pt. 2: 360.

56. Sorrel, *Recollections,* 173.

57. James L. Kemper to E. P. Alexander, Sept. 20, 1869, Longstreet Papers, Harvard Univ.

58. La Salle Pickett, "Wartime Story of General Pickett," 619; Longstreet, *From Manassas to Appomattox,* 397.

59. Longstreet, *From Manassas to Appomattox,* 386–87; Isaac R. Trimble to John W. Daniel, Nov. 24, 1875; Hunton, "Answers of Eppa Hunton to Questions Proposed by Hon. John W. Daniel," dated Feb. 15, 1904, both in Daniel Papers, Duke Univ.; James L. Kemper to E. P. Alexander, Sept. 20, 1869, Longstreet Papers, Harvard Univ.; C. H. C. Brown to J. B. Walton, n.d., Walton Papers, Tulane Univ.; William Alexander Gordon, untitled typescript memoirs, 114, Gordon Papers, Washington and Lee Univ.; Wilson, "James B. Pettigrew," 22–23; Bright, "Pickett's Charge," 228–34.

60. Fremantle, *Three Months in the Confederate States,* 266.

61. Ibid., 267–69; *O.R.* 27, pt. 2: 338–46.

4: The Bull of the Woods at Chickamauga

1. W. G. Coyle to William Miller Owen, July 14, 1885, Louisiana Historical Soc. Collection, Tulane Univ.; Moore, *A Life for the Confederacy,* 153.

2. Quoted in Fremantle, *Three Months in the Confederate States,* 267.

3. Youngblood, "Unwritten History of the Gettysburg Campaign," 317; quoted in Dawson, *Reminiscences,* 97; Inman, *Soldier of the South,* 61–72.

4. La Salle Pickett, "Wartime Story of General Pickett," 622; Blackford, *Memoirs of Life In and Out of the Army* 2: 85.

5. Mosby, "Personal Recollections of General Lee," 69.

6. Quoted in Tucker, *High Tide at Gettysburg,* 332–33.

7. Alexander, *Military Memoirs,* 423.

8. Quoted in Alexander, "Letter from E. P. Alexander," 102.

9. Wade Hampton to Louis T. Wigfall, July 15, 1863, Wigfall Papers, Library of Congress.

10. Berkley, *Four Years in the Confederate Artillery,* 52; Gaillard, *Franklin Gaillard's Civil War Letters,* 37.

11. Quoted in Freeman, *Lee's Lieutenants* 3: 168.

12. William H. Ker to Sister, July 18, 1863, Ker Letters, LSU.

13. Thomas L. Rosser To Wife, July 7, 1863, Freeman Papers, Library of Congress; Gordon typescript memoirs, 116, quoting wartime letter, Gordon Papers, Duke Univ.

14. Quoted in West, *Texan in Search of a Fight,* 98.

15. Owen, *In Camp and Battle,* 256–57.

16. Robert E. Lee to Jefferson Davis, July 4, 7, 8, 16, 24, 29, 1863, Davis

Collection, Tulane Univ.; Lee, *Recollections and Letters of Robert E. Lee,* 101; Dowdey, *Wartime Papers of R. E. Lee,* 551.

17. Robert E. Lee to Jefferson Davis, July 29, 1863, Davis Collection, Tulane Univ.

18. *O.R.* 27, pt. 3: 1040–41.

19. Daniel, *Richmond Examiner During the War,* 97–99; Andrews, *South Reports the War,* 315–18; *Charleston Mercury,* quoted in Herman Leonard, "Gettysburg Invasion—Who Was Responsible?" 4 (copy of unpublished typescript provided by Wilbur Thomas, Washington, D.C.).

20. D. H. Hill to James Longstreet, June 5, 1885, Longstreet Papers, Duke Univ.; D. H. Hill to R. L. Dabney, July 21, 1864, Hill-Dabney Letters, Virginia State Library; Connelly and Jones, *Politics of Command,* 182–83.

21. William Preston Johnston to Wife, July 16, 1863; ibid. to Uncle, July 17, 1863, Barrett Collection, Tulane Univ.; Kean, *Inside the Confederate Government,* 91.

22. Longstreet, "Lee in Pennsylvania," *Annals of the War,* 414–15. The authenticity of this letter was debated during Longstreet's lifetime. Wade Hampton, who disliked Longstreet intensely, believed it genuine, as it matched views Longstreet expressed to him immediately following the war, before Gettysburg had become a matter of controversy. See Wade Hampton to Jubal A. Early, Mar. 27, 1876, Early Family Papers, Virginia Historical Soc.

23. James Longstreet to Louis T. Wigfall, Aug. 2, 1863, Wigfall Papers, Library of Congress.

24. Wade Hampton to Louis T. Wigfall, July 15, 1863, in ibid.

25. Louis T. Wigfall to Halsey Wigfall, Aug. 16, 1863, in ibid.

26. *O.R.* 51, pt. 2: 752–53; Freeman, *Lee's Dispatches,* 108–109.

27. Louis T. Wigfall to C. C. Clay, Aug. 13, 1863, Clay Papers, Duke Univ.

28. James Longstreet to Louis T. Wigfall, Aug. 18, 1863, Wigfall Papers, Library of Congress.

29. James Longstreet to Louis T. Wigfall, Feb. 4, May 13, 1863, and Joseph E. Johnston to Louis T. Wigfall, Mar. 4, 1863, in ibid.; Louis T. Wigfall to Joseph E. Johnston, Aug. 9, 1863, Johnston Papers, College of William and Mary.

30. James Longstreet to Robert E. Lee, Sept. 2, 1863, Longstreet Papers, Georgia Archives.

31. *O.R.* 29, pt. 2: 699.

32. Ibid.

33. Longstreet, *From Manassas to Appomattox,* 434.

34. James Longstreet to Robert E. Lee, Sept. 2, 1863, Longstreet Papers, Georgia Archives.

35. Quoted in Longstreet, *From Manassas to Appomattox,* 435.

36. James Longstreet to Louis T. Wigfall, Aug. 18, 1863, Wigfall Papers, Library of Congress.

37. Johnston, *Narrative of Military Operations*, 242.
38. Longstreet, quoted in *O.R.* 29, pt. 2: 713–14; Hattaway and Jones, *How the North Won*, 442–44.
39. Alexander, *Military Memoirs*, 449; Sanger and Hay, *James Longstreet*, 199.
40. James Longstreet to Louis T. Wigfall, Sept. 12, 1863, Wigfall Papers, Library of Congress.
41. *O.R.* 30, pt. 2: 287; Connelly, *Autumn of Glory*, 211.
42. Connelly, *Autumn of Glory*, 199; Heartsill, *Fourteen Hundred and 91 Days*, 152; Alexander, *Military Memoirs*, 450–51; Hood, *Advance and Retreat*, 61–63.
43. *O.R.* 30, pt. 2: 287–88; Sorrel, *Recollections*, 193.
44. *O.R.* 30, pt. 2: 288, 290–92; Polk, *Leonidas Polk* 2: 255; Hill, "Chickamauga—The Great Battle in the West," *B&L* 3: 652.
45. Connelly, *Autumn of Glory*, 210.
46. Ibid., 222–23; Dickert, *History of Kershaw's Brigade*, 268–69; Lane, *Dear Mother*, 272.
47. *O.R.* 30, pt. 2: 288–89; Connelly, *Autumn of Glory*, 223–24; Lane, *Dear Mother*, 273–75; Polley, "Reminiscences of Chickamauga," 11; Gaillard, *Franklin Gaillard's Civil War Letters*, 48–50.
48. Owen, *In Camp and Battle*, 281, 288; Haskell, *Haskell Memoirs*, 133; Anderson, "Campaign and Battle of Chickamauga," 415.
49. Connelly, *Autumn of Glory*, 224–28.
50. *O.R.* 30, pt. 2: 290; Ross, *Cities and Camps of the Confederate States*, 125; Goggin, "Chickamauga," 222–23; Kean, *Inside the Confederate Government*, 115–16.
51. Ross, *Cities and Camps of the Confederate States*, 125; Goggin, "Chickamauga," 222–23; Kean, *Inside the Confederate Government*, 115–16.

5: From East Tennessee to Appomattox

1. Connelly and Jones, *Politics of Command*, 69.
2. Longstreet, *From Manassas to Appomattox*, 466–67; Polk, *Leonidas Polk* 2: 288–89; *O.R.* 30, pt. 2: 54–55.
3. Lee, quoted in *O.R.* 52, pt. 2: 549–50; 30, pt. 4: 750–56; Polk, *Leonidas Polk* 2: 288–89.
4. D. H. Hill to Lafayette McLaws, Aug. 29, 1864, McLaws Papers, Southern Historical Collection, Univ. of N.C.; Polk, *Leonidas Polk* 2: 291; Mackall, *A Son's Recollections of His Father*, 182–85; Ross, *Cities and Camps of the Confederate States*, 136; Eliot, *West Point and the Confederacy*, 190, 207; Kean, *Inside the Confederate Government*, 115–16; Eaton, *Jefferson Davis*, 185.
5. Connelly, *Autumn of Glory*, 239, 243, 245–56.
6. Longstreet, *From Manassas to Appomattox*, 466.
7. W. W. Halderman to William Preston Johnston, Sept. 26, Oct. 3, 1863,

Barrett Collection, Tulane Univ.; Blackford, *Memoirs* 2: 161, 163; *O.R.* 31, pt. 3: 656, 644–65; Connelly, *Autumn of Glory,* 246, 249, 252.

8. James Longstreet to Benjamin F. Cheatham, Oct. 21, 1863, Cheatham Papers, Southern Historical Collection, Univ. of N.C.; Micah Jenkins to G. M. Sorrel, Oct. 31, 1863, Jenkins Papers, Duke Univ.; James Longstreet to Lafayette McLaws, Oct. 7, 1863, McLaws Papers, Southern Historical Collection, Univ. of N.C.; *O.R.* 52, pt. 2: 547–48, 550–58; Connelly, *Autumn of Glory,* 256–61.

9. Jefferson Davis to Braxton Bragg, Oct. 29, 1863, Davis Papers, Tulane Univ.; *O.R.* 31, pt. 3: 634–37; Dowdey, *Wartime Papers of R. E. Lee,* 602–603; Connelly, *Autumn of Glory,* 262–65.

10. *O.R.* 31, pt. 3: 635, 637, 671–72, 679–81, 686–87, 703, 707.

11. Sanger and Hay, *James Longstreet,* 230–34.

12. Quoted in Longstreet, *From Manassas to Appomattox,* 518–19; *O.R.* 31, pt. 1: 497–98; G. M. Sorrel to Lafayette McLaws, Dec. 17, 1863, Benning Papers, Southern Historical Collection, Univ. of N.C.

13. Sanger and Hay, *James Longstreet,* 233; Klein, "Knoxville Campaign," 41–47.

14. Lafayette McLaws to Wife, July 7, 1863, McLaws Papers, Southern Historical Collection, Univ. of N.C.

15. Dawson, *Reminiscences,* 101–102; Sorrel, *Recollections,* 135; Ross, *Cities and Camps of the Confederate States,* 124; James Longstreet to Braxton Bragg, Oct. 16, 1863, Longstreet Papers, Harvard Univ.; *O.R.* 31, pt. 3: 757–58.

16. Sorrel, *Recollections,* 212; Polley, "Reminiscences of Chickamauga," 11; *O.R.* 5: 1001–1002; Dickert, *History of Kershaw's Brigade,* 295, 302–303.

17. Swanson and Johnson, "Conflict in Tennessee," 103–106. Although they repeat some old myths about Longstreet, the authors' analysis of the controversy is very good.

18. *O.R.* 31, pt. 3: 859, 866–67.

19. Ibid., pt. 2: 518.

20. Ibid., pt. 1: 467, 470; J. B. Robertson to Henry L. Benning, Nov. 4, 1863, Benning Papers, Southern Historical Collection, Univ. of N.C.

21. *O.R.* 31, pt. 1: 467–68.

22. Lafayette McLaws, Special Order No. 168, Dec. 18, 1863; Lafayette McLaws to Henry L. Benning, Dec. [?], 18, 1863, all three in Benning Papers, Southern Historical Collection, Univ. of N.C.; Lafayette McLaws to Braxton Bragg, Feb. 25, 1864, Bragg Papers, Western Reserve Historical Soc.; Braxton Bragg to Lafayette McLaws, Mar. 4, 1864, McLaws Papers, Southern Historical Collection, Univ. of N.C.; *O.R.* 52: 633–34.

23. *O.R.* 31, pt. 1: 471; Oates, *War Between the Union and the Confederacy,* 338–39.

24. *O.R.* 31, pt. 1: 471–72.

25. E. M. Law to Lafayette McLaws, Apr. 29, 1864, McLaws Papers, Southern Historical Collection, Univ. of N.C.

26. *O.R.* 31, pt. 1: 474–75.

27. Ibid., 473–74, 505–506.

28. E. M. Law to Lafayette McLaws, Apr. 29, 1864, McLaws Papers, Southern Historical Collection, Univ. of N.C.

29. *O.R.* 31, pt. 1: 505–506.

30. Ibid. 32, pt. 2: 518, 566–67, 762; pt. 3: 583.

31. Ibid.

32. Ibid., pt. 3: 683.

33. Ibid., 737–38.

34. Archer Anderson to G. W. Brest, Apr. 14, 1864, Davis Papers, Tulane Univ.; copy in Law Papers, Southern Historical Collection. If Law obtained the copy during the war, he presumably hoped it would contain evidence against Longstreet; if he acquired it after the war, he was probably seeking information for an article on the Knoxville campaign. See E. M. Law to Isaac R. Pennypacker, Jan. 9, 1868, in Law Papers.

35. *O.R.* 32, pt. 3: 637–38.

36. Sanger and Hay, *James Longstreet*, 244–45.

37. Hattaway and Jones, *How the North Won*, 482–85.

38. *O.R.* 32, pt. 2: 810; pt. 3: 590, 637.

39. Hattaway and Jones, *How the North Won*, 484; *O.R.* 32, pt. 3: 637.

40. *O.R.* 32, pt. 2: 789–92, 809–810.

41. Ibid., pt. 3: 582–83.

42. Ibid., 627–28, 637–41.

43. Ibid., 674–76.

44. Ibid., 637, 641–42.

45. Ibid., 679–80.

46. Douglas Southall Freeman, Hamilton J. Eckenrode, Bryan Conrad, and Clifford Dowdey portray Longstreet as virtually consumed by ambition. Archer Jones and Thomas L. Connelly also portray him as exceedingly ambitious. See bibliography for works by these authors.

47. Quoted in Blackford, *Memoirs* 2: 206; *O.R.* 32, pt. 3: 680.

48. Quoted in Longstreet, "General Longstreet's Second Paper on Gettysburg," 268; Sanger and Hay, *James Longstreet*, 259.

49. Bean, *Stonewall's Man: Sandie Pendleton*, 197.

50. Alexander, *Military Memoirs*, 493; Dickert, *History of Kershaw's Brigade*, 42.

51. *O.R.* 32, pt. 3: 737.

52. Quoted in Badeau, *Campaigning with Grant*, 47.

53. Alexander, *Military Memoirs*, 503–506; Sanger and Hay, *James Longstreet*, 265–67.

54. James Longstreet to T. J. Goree, May 21, 1875, Goree Papers, LSU; Sorrel, *Recollections*, 241.

55. Dawson, *Reminiscences*, 116; Dickert, *History of Kershaw's Brigade*, 349; Sorrel, *Recollections*, 243–44; McDowell and Davis, "General Joseph B. Kershaw," 38–39.

56. Ranson, "Reminiscences of the Civil War," 447; Dawson, *Reminiscences*, 166; Sorrel, *Recollections*, 243–44; Sanger and Hay, *James Longstreet*, 294; Alexander, *Military Memoirs*, 506; Longstreet, *From Manassas to Appomattox*, 567.

57. Dawson, *Reminiscences*, 116; quoted in Long, *Memoirs of Robert E. Lee*, 331.

58. Stiles, *Four Years Under Marse Robert*, 247.

59. *O.R.* 51, pt. 2: 893; Ranson, "Reminiscences of the Civil War," 447; Blackford, *Memoirs* 2: 224–25; Gray and Ropes, *War Letters*, 334; Edmonston, *"Journal of a Secesh Lady,"* 557–58; Longstreet, *From Manassas to Appomattox*, 572; Sanger and Hay, *James Longstreet*, 277–78.

60. Robert E. Lee to James Longstreet, Aug. 29, 1864, Longstreet Papers, Georgia Archives.

61. T. J. Goree to S. W. Goree, fragment of letter, ca. Aug. 1864, Goree Papers, LSU.

62. Sanger and Hay, *James Longstreet*, 279–80.

63. T. J. Goree to Mary Frances Kittrell, Oct. 21, 1864, Goree Papers, LSU; *O.R.* 42, pt. 3: 1140; Longstreet, *From Manassas to Appomattox*, 572; Sanger and Hay, *James Longstreet*, 280.

64. Owen, *In Camp and Battle*, 355.

65. T. J. Goree to Mary Frances Kittrell, Oct. 21, 1864, Goree Papers, LSU.

66. Robert E. Lee to James Longstreet, Feb. 25, 1865, quoted in Sears Wilson Cabell to Nelson M. Shipp, June 10, 1940, Helen Longstreet Papers, Georgia Historical Soc.

67. Robert E. Lee to James Longstreet, Feb. 22, 1865, Lee Papers, Washington and Lee Univ.; Owen, *In Camp and Battle*, 375.

68. Sanger and Hay, *James Longstreet*, 294–95.

69. Gordon, *Reminiscences*, 433; Alexander, *Military Memoirs*, 600; quoted in Longstreet, *From Manassas to Appomattox*, 620; James Longstreet to E. P. Alexander, June 17, 1869, Alexander Papers, Southern Historical Collection, Univ. of N.C.

70. Quoted in Ranson, "General Lee as I Knew Him," 335.

71. James Longstreet to G. M. Sorrel, May 21, 1865, Goree Papers, LSU; Osmun Latrobe to William Miller Owen, April 12, 1865, Boagni Collection.

72. T. J. Goree to E. P. Alexander, Dec. 6, 1887, Goree Papers, LSU.

6. Setting the Stage

1. Thomas J. Goree diary, bound typescript copy, 15, 18ff., Goree Papers, LSU; *New York Times*, Mar. 25, 1866; William Miller Owen to Robert E.

Lee, Aug. 28, 1866, Lee Papers, Washington and Lee Univ.; James Longstreet to William Miller Owen, May 18, 1867, Boagni Collection; James Longstreet to U. S. Grant, Apr. 10, 1867, Longstreet Papers, Chicago Historical Soc.; White, *Confederate Veteran*, 55–56; James Longstreet to E. P. Alexander, Feb. 26, 1866, Alexander Papers, Southern Historical Collection, Univ. of N.C.; Insurance Policy of J. A. Chalaron, signed by Longstreet as president of the Great Southern and Western Life and Accident Insurance Company, June 9, 1866, Chalaron Papers, Tulane Univ.; quoted in Wells, "Kind Admonitions: The Education of a Louisiana Teacher," 301–302.

2. Hill, "Haversack," *Land We Love* 3: 347.

3. *New York Herald*, Sept. 9, Oct. 27, Nov. 2, 14, 1865; *New York Times*, June 20, 1866 [some of these articles were reprinted in Southern papers]; Helen Longstreet, *Lee and Longstreet at High Tide*, 105–106.

4. See, for instance, Jacobs, *Notes on the Rebel Invasion*, 23–27ff.; Murphy, *Four Years in the War*, 117–19; Houghton, *Campaigns of the Seventh Maine*, 91–97; Stevens, *Three Years in the Sixth Corps*, 242–45; Benedict, *Battle of Gettysburgh*, 4–9, 12; Conyingham, *Irish Brigade*, 417–18; Woodward, *Our Campaigns*, 266.

5. Swinton, *Campaigns of the Army of the Potomac*, 340–41.

6. *Savannah Republican*, Sept. 28, 1863; Connelly, *Marble Man*, 15.

7. R. A. Shackleford to Brother, Feb. 27, 1863, Shackleford Letters, Tennessee Archives; punctuation and capitalization added for clarity.

8. Quoted in West, *Texan in Search of a Fight*, 115.

9. Fremantle, *Three Months in the Confederate States*, 237, 266.

10. Ross, *Cities and Camps of the Confederate States*, 52, 122–25.

11. Estvan, *War Pictures from the South*, 346.

12. An English Combatant, *Battlefields of the South*, 59, 247n; Borcke, "Memoirs of the Confederate War for Independence," 280–81.

13. Alexander, "Confederate Chieftains," 37.

14. Snow, *Southern Generals*, 313–38.

15. Wilson, "Edward Alfred Pollard," 4147–50.

16. Pollard, *Lee and His Lieutenants*, 411–20.

17. McCabe, *Life and Campaigns of General Robert E. Lee*, 461.

18. Dabney, *Life and Campaigns of Lieut.-Gen. Thomas J. Jackson*, 467, 534, 611.

19. Fremantle, *Three Months in the Confederate States*, 247, 249.

20. Alexander, "Confederate Chieftains," 37–38.

21. Pollard, *Lee and His Lieutenants*, 419–20.

22. An English Combatant, *Battlefields of the South*, 333.

23. Robert E. Lee to Longstreet, Owen & Co., Jan. 26, 1866, Longstreet Papers, Georgia Archives.

24. Robert E. Lee to James Longstreet, Mar. 9, 1866, Lee Papers, Duke Univ.

25. Robert E. Lee to Dear General, July 31, 1865. This letter is marked "circular"; an identical letter addressed to Beauregard bears the same date; both in Lee Papers, Washington and Lee Univ.; Charles Marshall to Robert E. Lee, Oct. 1, Nov. 28, 1865; Robert E. Lee to P. G. T. Beauregard, Oct. 3, 1865; Robert E. Lee to Jubal A. Early, Nov. 22, 1865; James Longstreet to Robert E. Lee, Mar. 9, 1866, all in Lee Papers, Washington and Lee Univ.

26. Freeman, *R. E. Lee* 4: 261, 418–19.

27. Klein, *Edward Porter Alexander,* 143.

28. E. P. Alexander to Henry L. Benning, n.d.; J. W. Waddell to Henry L. Benning, Dec. 2, 1866, Benning Papers, Southern Historical Collection, Univ. of N.C.

29. James Longstreet to E. P. Alexander, Aug. 9, 1869, Alexander Papers, Southern Historical Collection, Univ. of N.C.; Klein, *Edward Porter Alexander,* 214–29.

30. Bean, "Memoranda of a Conversation Between General Robert E. Lee and William Preston Johnston, May 7, 1868, and March 18, 1870," 478; Eggleston, *A Rebel's Recollections,* 153.

31. Beaty, *John Esten Cooke,* 68–69, 96, 101; Davis, "John Esten Cooke and the Confederate Defeat," 66–68, 74–76.

32. Addey, *Stonewall Jackson;* Cooke, *Life of Stonewall Jackson;* Hallock, *Complete Biographical Sketch of "Stonewall" Jackson;* Ramsey, *True Eminence Founded in Holiness;* Smith, *Discourse on the Life and Character of Lt. Gen. Thos. J. Jackson;* Pate, *The Character of Stonewall Jackson;* Addey, *Life and Imprisonment;* Dabney, *Life and Campaigns of Lieut.-Gen. Thomas J. Jackson.* Jackson's frequent detached service doubtless made him more attractive to biographers. Because his service was most often directly under Lee, Longstreet would have posed a much greater challenge to biographers.

7: Scalawags, the Lost Cause, and the Sunrise Attack Controversy

1. *New Orleans Times,* Mar. 18, 1867; Richter, "James Longstreet: From Rebel to Scalawag," 216–18.

2. Raphael J. Moses to Robert E. Lee, Mar. 23, 1865, enclosing clippings from the *Richmond Enquirer,* same date; Robert E. Lee to P. G. T. Beauregard, Oct. 3, 1865, both in Lee Papers, Washington and Lee Univ.

3. *New Orleans Times,* Mar. 23, 1867; Fleming, *Civil War and Reconstruction in Alabama,* 503–504; Jarrell, *Wade Hampton and the Negro,* 16–18; Pearce, *Benjamin Hill,* 142, 150–53; Sanger and Hay, *James Longstreet,* 331.

4. *New Orleans Times,* Apr. 6, 1867; *New York Times,* Apr. 13, 1867.

5. Wade, *Augustus Baldwin Longstreet,* 355; Sanger and Hay, *James Longstreet,* 333; *New Orleans Times,* June 8, 1867.

6. Keller, *Affairs of State,* 209; Richter, "James Longstreet," 222–26.

7. James Longstreet to William Miller Owen, May 18, 1867, Boagni Collection.

8. James Longstreet to R. H. Taliaferro, July 4, 1867, Boagni Collection.

9. Ibid.

10. Undated newspaper clipping, *New Orleans Tribune*, Longstreet Papers, Duke Univ.; Richter, "James Longstreet," 225–26.

11. James Longstreet to Sarah Longstreet Ames, June 26, 1867, quoted in Williams, *Unconquered*, 346. Given the novelist's introductory remarks concerning his research, there is no reason to doubt that he is quoting an actual, not a fictional, letter.

12. Quoted in Sanger and Hay, *James Longstreet*, 335n.

13. Taylor, "New Orleans and Reconstruction," 196–97; Pitre, "Collapse of the Warmoth Regime," 162–63.

14. James Longstreet to William Miller Owen, June 18, 1867; James Longstreet to R. H. Taliaferro, July 4, 1867, Boagni Collection.

15. *New York Times*, June 20, 21, 1867.

16. Longstreet, *From Manassas to Appomattox*, 632–34. Lee applied for a pardon on June 13, 1865; see Lee to P. G. T. Beauregard, Oct. 3, 1865, Lee Papers, Washington and Lee Univ.

17. Sanger and Hay, *James Longstreet*, 340–42.

18. Ibid., 345–46; "Longstreet's Reminiscences," *New York Times*, July 24, 1885.

19. Elam, "Scalawag," 456.

20. Daniels, *Tar Heel Editor*, 129.

21. Jubal A. Early to Brother, July 15, 1867, Early Papers, Library of Congress; capitalization corrected.

22. Quoted in Stoval, *Robert Toombs*, 325.

23. Cate, *Lucius C. Q. Lamar*, 178; Hill, "Haversack," *Land We Love* 3: 347, 355.

24. Wetta, "'Bulldozing the Scalawags,'" 53.

25. Longstreet, *From Manassas to Appomattox*, vii, 635–37.

26. Sanger and Hay, *James Longstreet*, 340–42, 347.

27. Pearce, *Benjamin Hill*, 153n; Hill, "Haversack," *Land We Love* 3: 267.

28. Wilson, *Baptized in Blood*, 1–17; Osterweis, *Myth of the Lost Cause*, 120–25; Weaver, *Southern Tradition at Bay*, 270–71, 353.

29. Silver, *Confederate Morale and Church Propaganda*, 55–59; Brown, "Southern Religion, Mid-Century," 135–36; Dabbs, *Southern Heritage*, 170; Weaver, "Older Religiousness of the South," 243; Weaver, *Southern Tradition at Bay*, 181.

30. Hubble, *South in American Literature*, 717; Moore, "'A Distinctly Southern Magazine,'" 51–53; Weaver, *Southern Tradition at Bay*, 135ff.

31. Hill, untitled editorial, *Land We Love* 3: 347, 355.

32. Osterweis, *Romanticism and Nationalism in the Old South*, 115.

33. Timrod, *Collected Poems*, 129–30.

34. Anderson, *Centennial Edition of the Works of Sidney Lanier* 1: 14–15.
35. Fanny Downing, "Land We Love," *Land We Love* 1: 161–62.
36. Holman, *Immoderate Past*, 7; Osterweis, *Romanticism and Nationalism in the Old South*, 87, 91.
37. Fidler, *Augusta Evans Wilson*, 14, 41–45, 92–95, 106, 119–20.
38. Ibid., 105–109, 114.
39. Lively, *Fiction Fights the Civil War*, 46.
40. The authors, in order of citation, are Sally Rochester Ford, Sarah J. C. Whittlesey, and Sallie F. Chapin.
41. Whitson, *Gilbert St. Maurice*, 3–4.
42. Beaty, *John Esten Cooke*, 68–69, 159–61; Davis, "John Esten Cooke and the Confederate Defeat," 66; Weaver, *Southern Tradition at Bay*, 278.
43. Davis, "John Esten Cooke and the Confederate Defeat," 68–69; Harwell, "John Esten Cooke, Civil War Correspondent," 515–16.
44. Beaty, *John Esten Cooke*, 95.
45. Fishwick, *Virginians on Olympus*, 53–55; Connelly, *Marble Man*, 20–30, 42–43.
46. Early, *Campaigns of Robert E. Lee*, 30–32.
47. Bushong, *Old Jube*, 265, 286–87; Robert E. Lee to Jubal A. Early, Nov. 22, 1865, Mar. 15, 1866, Early Papers, Library of Congress. Early's book was entitled *A Memoir of the Last Year of the War for Independence in the Confederate States of America*.
48. *Richmond Enquirer and Examiner*, Nov. 5, 1870; John W. Caldwell to Jubal A. Early, Oct. 13, 1871; Edmund Kirby Smith to Jubal A. Early, Jan. 23, 1872, Early Papers, Library of Congress.
49. It is possible that Early's remarks were inspired by a statement of Charles S. Marshall as published in "Tributes to General Lee," *Southern Magazine* 8 (Jan. 1871): 30. Referring to Lee's statement at Gettysburg that the catastrophe was "all my fault," Marshall remarked, "But there, with painful consciousness that his plans had been frustrated by others, and that defeat and humiliation had overtaken his army, in the presence of his troops he openly assumed the entire responsibility of the campaign and of the lost battle. One word from him would have released him of this responsibility, but that word he refused to utter until it could be spoken without fear of doing the least injustice." But the fact that neither Early nor Marshall, who cooperated with each other against Longstreet, ever tried to use *this* statement against Longstreet is very strong evidence that it referred to Stuart, as would seem to be confirmed by Marshall's later writing, edited by Frederick Maurice as *An Aide-de-Camp of Lee*, 214–17, 248–52.
50. *New York Times*, Jan. 9, Mar. 13, Apr. 1, Oct. 20, 1872; Warmoth, *War, Politics, and Reconstruction*, 149, 197–220; Gonzales, "William Pitt Kellogg," 396–412; Harris, "Henry Clay Warmoth," 529, 604–33; Pitre, "Collapse of the Warmoth Regime," 167–68.
51. Sanger and Hay, *James Longstreet*, 14n, 367.

52. Ibid., 366–68; *New York Times,* July 28, 1884.
53. Connelly, *Marble Man,* 37–38.
54. Pendleton, "Personal Recollections of General Robert E. Lee," manuscript, 23–24, Pendleton Papers, Southern Historical Collection, Univ. of N.C.
55. *O.R.* 27, pt. 2: 346–54.
56. Pendleton, "Personal Recollections of General Robert E. Lee," manuscript, 33–37. This copy of Pendleton's actual speech is even more critical of Longstreet than the condensed, published version; see Pendleton, "Personal Recollections of General Lee," *Southern Magazine* 15 (Dec. 1874): 603–36.
57. "The Rev. Mr. Pendleton," undated newspaper clipping from the *Vicksburg Herald,* attached to letter from W. W. Lord to William Nelson Pendleton, Aug. 12, 1873; James Longstreet to William Nelson Pendleton, Apr. 4, 1875, all in Pendleton Papers, Southern Historical Collection, Univ. of N.C.
58. Sanger and Hay, *James Longstreet,* 412–13.
59. D. A. S. Vaught to John R. Ficklen, May 8, 1894, Ficklen Papers, LSU.
60. Sanger and Hay, *James Longstreet,* 370–71; Prichard, "Origins and Activities of the 'White League' in New Orleans," 530–32, 534–37; Taylor, "New Orleans and Reconstruction," 203–204.
61. James Longstreet to T. J. Goree, May 12, 1875, Goree Papers, LSU.
62. James Longstreet to William Nelson Pendleton, Apr. 4, 1875, Pendleton Papers, Southern Historical Collection, Univ. of N.C.
63. William Nelson Pendleton to James Longstreet, Apr. 14, 1875, ibid.
64. James Longstreet to William Nelson Pendleton, Apr. 19, 1875, ibid. This copy of the original was made by Pendleton.
65. Lafayette McLaws to James Longstreet, June 12, 1873, McLaws Papers, Southern Historical Collection, Univ. of N.C.; this copy of McLaws's letter was made by Garland Longstreet.
66. James Longstreet to Lafayette McLaws, July 25, 1873, ibid.
67. Walter H. Taylor to James Longstreet, Apr. 28, 1875; Charles Marshall to James Longstreet, May 7, 1875; A. L. Long to James Longstreet, May 31, 1875, Longstreet Papers, Emory Univ.
68. C. S. Venable to James Longstreet, n.d., in ibid.
69. James Longstreet to William Miller Owen, May 5, 1875, Boagni Collection; James Longstreet to E. P. Alexander, Apr. 21, May 25, 1875, Alexander Papers, Southern Historical Collection, Univ. of N.C.; James A. Seddon to James Longstreet, May 7, 1875, Longstreet Papers, Emory Univ.; James Longstreet to T. J. Goree, May 12, 21, June 2, 1875; T. J. Goree to James Longstreet, May 17, 1875, all four in Goree Papers, LSU; italics are Goree's; James Longstreet to John P. Nicholson, Apr. 19, 1875, Longstreet Papers, Huntington Library; Hood, *Advance and Retreat,* 55–59; *New York Times,* July 16, 1875.
70. *New Orleans Republican,* Jan. 25, 1876.

71. Quoted in Sanger and Hay, *James Longstreet*, 413. It should be remembered that Longstreet had taken care in his official report, by which he could expect to be judged in history, to state his opposition to the July 3 assault quite clearly.
72. *New Orleans Republican*, Jan. 25, 1876.
73. "Gettysburg," *New Orleans Republican*, Feb. 27, 1876.
74. Wade Hampton to Jubal A. Early, Mar. 27, 1876, Early Family Papers, Virginia Historical Soc.
75. Erasmus Taylor to James Longstreet, Sept. 10, 1889, Longstreet Papers, Emory Univ. Longstreet's comment to Taylor would seem to indicate that, while he wanted to give Lee his full support during the war, he wanted also to be able to have his disapproval of Lee's tactics at Gettysburg a part of the historical record.
76. "Gettysburg; General Longstreet Reviews General Early's Reply," newspaper clipping dated Mar. 26, 1876, in McLaws Papers, Southern Historical Collection, Univ. of N.C.
77. Ibid.

8. The Anti-Longstreet Faction Emerges

1. Connelly, *Marble Man*, 27–28.
2. C. S. Venable to Jubal A. Early, Apr. 5, 1872, Early Papers, Library of Congress.
3. A. L. Long to Jubal A. Early, Mar. 13, 1876; C. S. Venable to Jubal A. Early, Mar. 13, May 3, 1876; Charles Marshall to Jubal A. Early, Apr. 10, 1876, Mar. 24, 1877; Walter H. Taylor to Jubal A. Early, May 5, 1876, all in ibid.; William Nelson Pendleton to A. L. Long, Oct. 5, 22, 1875; "Genl. Long's Statement about Gettysburg," n.d., Pendleton Papers, Southern Historical Collection, Univ. of N.C.
4. Jones, *Personal Reminiscences*, 120–22.
5. See, for example, Fitzhugh Lee to J. William Jones, Feb. 17, 1875, Mar. 21, 1876, Fitzhugh Lee Papers, Univ. of Va.; George W. Peterkin to William Nelson Pendleton, Dec. 5, 1875; Coupland Page to William Nelson Pendleton, Feb. 22, 1877; T. H. B. Randolph to William Nelson Pendleton, Mar. 11, 1878, Pendleton Papers, Southern Historical Collection, Univ. of N.C.; Wade Hampton to Jubal A. Early, Mar. 27, May 7, 1876, Early Family Papers, Virginia Historical Soc.; Fitzhugh Lee to Jubal A. Early, Aug. 9, 1875, Mar. 3, 6, 20, Apr. 6, 1876; Braxton Bragg to Jubal A. Early, Mar. 28, 1876; Bradley T. Johnston to Jubal A. Early, Mar. 17, 1876; John H. New to Jubal A. Early, Mar. 23, 1870; R. E. Wilbourne to Jubal A. Early, Mar. 23, 1876, all in Early Papers, Library of Congress.
6. William H. Payne to Jubal A. Early, Mar. 16, 1875, Early Papers, Library of Congress.

7. James Longstreet to Lafayette McLaws, Feb. 28, 1876, McLaws Papers, Southern Historical Collection, Univ. of N.C.

8. McClure, *Recollections of Half a Century*, 400.

9. Taylor, "Campaign in Pennsylvania," 305–18.

10. McClure, *Recollections of Half a Century*, 399–400. Longstreet's letter to McLaws, July 25, 1873, McLaws Papers, Southern Historical Collection, Univ. of N.C., indicates that Grady merely polished the General's work, for the private letter covers most of the points in the article. Nevertheless, Grady pasted a clipping of the article in his scrapbook with the marginal notation, "Written by me—from Gen. Longstreet" (Henry W. Grady Scrapbook 4, pp. 52–65, Grady Papers, Emory Univ.).

11. James Longstreet to Buchler & Co., Oct. 27, 1877, Longstreet Papers, Chicago; James Longstreet to John P. Nicholson, Nov. 2, 1877, Longstreet Papers, Historical Soc. of Pa.; James Longstreet to John P. Nicholson, Nov. 9, 1877, Longstreet Papers, Duke Univ.; James Longstreet to John P. Nicholson, July 15, 29, Nov. 15, 1877; James Longstreet to Dear Sir, Oct. 22, 1877, all four in Longstreet Papers, Huntington Library. The implication in Sanger and Hay, *James Longstreet*, 424–25, that Longstreet was hiding his articles from Nicholson is clearly erroneous; Nicholson most likely sought to interest Longstreet in a book-length treatment of Gettysburg.

12. Longstreet, "Lee in Pennsylvania" and "The Mistakes of Gettysburg," *Annals of the War*, 414–26, 619–33.

13. James Longstreet to Lafayette McLaws, Dec. 10, 1877, McLaws Papers, Southern Historical Collection, Univ. of N.C.; James Longstreet to D. H. Hill, Nov. 27, 1877, Hill Papers, North Carolina Archives.

14. See, for example, C. M. Wilcox to J. William Jones, Nov. 18, 1877, Records of the Southern Historical Soc., Virginia Historical Soc.; S. R. Johnston to Fitzhugh Lee, Feb. 11, 1878, Mar. 15, Early Family Papers, Virginia Historical Soc.; J. William Jones to Jubal A. Early, Sept. 3, 21, Dec. 7, 1877; Mar. 26, May 2, 1878; Walter H. Taylor to Jubal A. Early, Mar. 12, 1878; C. S. Marshall to Jubal A. Early, Mar. 13, 1878, all in Early Papers, Library of Congress.

15. "Causes of the Defeat of Gen. Lee's Army at the Battle of Gettysburg—Opinions of Leading Confederate Soldiers," *SHSP* 4 (Aug. 1877): 49.

16. Ibid.; J. William Jones to Jubal A. Early, Feb. 16, 1877, Early Papers, Library of Congress.

17. Early, "Letter from Gen. J. A. Early," *SHSP* 4 (Aug. 1877): 59–68; Lee, "Letter from General Fitz. Lee," ibid., 71–72, 74; Allan, "Letter from William Allan, of Ewell's Staff," ibid., 79–80; Taylor, "Memorandum from Colonel Walter H. Taylor, of General Lee's Staff," ibid., 84–85; William Allan to Jubal A. Early, Mar. 26, 1872, Early Papers, Library of Congress.

18. C. M. Wilcox to E. P. Alexander, Feb. 2, Mar. 10, 1869, Alexander Pa-

pers, Southern Historical Collection, Univ. of N.C.; C. M. Wilcox to John W. Daniel, Jan. 25, 1876, Daniel Papers, Duke Univ.

19. E. P. Alexander to J. William Jones, Apr. 9, 1877, De Renne Confederate Manuscript Collection, Univ. of Ga.

20. J. William Jones to Jubal A. Early, Sept. 13, 1877, Early Papers, Library of Congress.

21. Early, "Leading Confederates on the Battle of Gettysburg," *SHSP* 4 (Dec. 1877): 273–74. Early had difficulty gaining the support of Stuart's foremost partisan, Henry B. McClellan, but did so by 1878. See Connelly, *Marble Man*, 88–89.

22. Early, "Leading Confederates," 293.

23. Longstreet, "General James Longstreet's Account of the Campaign and Battle," *SHSP* 5 (Jan. 1878): 54–86.

24. Lee, "A Review of the First Two Days' Operations at Gettysburg and a Reply to General Longstreet," ibid. 5 (Jan. 1878): 172–94; John Lee Carroll to Fitzhugh Lee, Apr. 15, 1876; Fitzhugh Lee to Jubal A. Early, Apr. 29, 1876; J. William Jones to Jubal A. Early, May 1, 1876, Early Papers, Library of Congress.

25. Longstreet, "General Longstreet's Second Paper on Gettysburg," *SHSP* 5 (June 1878); 257–69; Early, "Reply to General Longstreet's Second Paper," ibid., 270–87; Wilcox, "General C. M. Wilcox on the Battle of Gettysburg," ibid. 6 (Sept. 1878): 92–124; Oates, "Gettysburg—The Battle on the Right," ibid 6 (Oct. 1878): 172–82.

26. J. William Jones to William Nelson Pendleton, Aug. 14, 1878, Pendleton Papers, Southern Historical Collection, Univ. of N.C.

9: A Georgia Republican Courting Clio

1. *New York Tribune*, June 12, 1881.

2. Quoted in *New York Times*, June 28, 1875; capitalization corrected.

3. Ibid., Dec. 16, 1888; Helen Longstreet, *Lee and Longstreet at High Tide*, 123.

4. Sanger and Hay, *James Longstreet*, 378–82, 384.

5. Longstreet left no records of his diplomatic service, but details of the Turkish post at this time are recounted in Straus, *Under Four Administrations* 1: 43, 60–65, 102.

6. James Longstreet to Charles Eliot Norton, Sept. 9, 1881, Longstreet Papers, Harvard Univ.; Norton, *Letters of Charles Eliot Norton* 2: 115–17; Sanger and Hay, *James Longstreet*, 384n.

7. James Longstreet to William Miller Owen, May 19, 1880 [error: 1881], Boagni Collection; James Longstreet to Fitz Randolph Longstreet, Apr. 27, 1881, Longstreet Papers, Georgia Archives; Longstreet, "Lee's Right Wing at Gettysburg," 353–54.

8. Ward, "Republican Party in Bourbon Georgia," 197–98; Sanger and Hay, *James Longstreet*, 383.

9. Shadgett, *Republican Party in Georgia*, 70–71, 92–97.
10. Quoted in Perros, "Letters of James Longstreet Relative to His Position of United States Marshal in Georgia," 302.
11. Shadgett, *Republican Party in Georgia*, 97–100.
12. *New York Times*, June 1, 1880; Dec. 19, 1882; July 3, Sept. 16, 1883; Jan. 17, 20, July 21, 22, 28, 1884; Feb. 26, 1885.
13. Rowland, *Jefferson Davis* 9: 175–76.
14. Hesseltine and Gara, "Georgia's Confederate Leaders After Appomattox," 10–11; Woodward, *Origins of the New South*, 14–15.
15. Tankersley, *John B. Gordon*, vii, 267, 342, 349–50, 377; Kendrick and Arnett, *South Looks at Its Past*, 112–14.
16. Quoted in *New York Times*, July 29, 1879.
17. Ibid.
18. James Longstreet to William Miller Owen, Mar. 9, 1883, Boagni Collection; *New York Herald*, June 19, 1881; *Atlanta Constitution*, Aug. 2, 1881; *New York Times*, July 24, 27, 1881.
19. Taylor, *Destruction and Reconstruction*, 231.
20. Jones, *Army of Northern Virginia Memorial Volume*, 122.
21. Ibid.
22. Davis, *Rise and Fall of the Confederate Government* 2: 441–42; Rowland, *Jefferson Davis* 8: 5–23, 56, 73–74, 82–105, 136–37, 300, 488–89; 9: 141–42, 197, 379–80; 10: 112–13; Connelly, *Marble Man*, 42. While Davis downplayed the importance of Gettysburg, his comments reinforced Longstreet's negative image.
23. James Longstreet to Henry B. McClellan, Jan. 30, July 28, 1878, McClellan Papers, Virginia Historical Soc.; D. H. Hill to James Longstreet, Feb. 4, 1879; Robert Toombs to James Longstreet, Feb. 5, 1879; John Bell Hood to James Longstreet, Mar. 11, 1879; Joseph E. Johnston to James Longstreet, Feb. 3, 1879, all in Longstreet Papers, Georgia Archives; D. H. Hill to Longstreet, Apr. 15, Aug. 29, 1879; Lafayette McLaws to James Longstreet, Apr. 9, 1879; G. M. Sorrel to James Longstreet, July 21, 1879, all in Longstreet Papers, Duke Univ.; Longstreet to T. J. Goree, Feb. 22, 1883, Goree Papers, LSU.
24. D. H. Hill to James Longstreet, Feb. 11, 1885, Longstreet Papers, Duke Univ.
25. D. H. Hill to James Longstreet, May 21, 1885, ibid.
26. Johnson, *Remembered Yesterdays*, 189–90.
27. Ibid., 190–203; Garland, *Roadside Meetings*, 335, 338, 340–43; Buck, *Road to Reunion*, 248.
28. James Longstreet to Editors of *Century*, Apr. 11, June 2, 10, July 31, 1884; Joseph E. Johnston to Editors of *Century*, July 8, 1884, *Century* Collection, New York Public Library.
29. James Longstreet to Robert U. Johnson, July 31, Oct. 1, 1884; James Longstreet to Editors of *Century*, Dec. 22, 1884; Jan. 24, 1886, all in ibid.
30. James Longstreet to Editors of *Century*, Mar. 21, Apr. 22, May 3, Dec.

20, 1885; Jan. 24, 1886; James Longstreet to Josiah Carter, July 10, Aug. 21, 1885, all in ibid.

31. Longstreet, "Seven Days Fighting About Richmond," 470–74, 476; the sentence quoted appears in parentheses in the original.

32. James Longstreet to John P. Nicholson, July 12, 1885, Longstreet Papers, Harvard Univ.

33. Longstreet, "Our March Against Pope," 601–14; "Invasion of Maryland," 309–15.

34. Longstreet, "Battle of Fredericksburg," 609–26; James Longstreet to Editors of *Century,* Oct. 1, 1884, *Century* Collection, New York Public Library.

35. Longstreet, "Lee's Invasion of Pennsylvania," 936–43.

36. D. H. Hill to James Longstreet, June 5, 1885; Feb. 5, Mar. 12, 1887, Longstreet Papers, Duke Univ.

37. Lafayette McLaws to Dear General, Nov. 30, 1885, Longstreet Papers, Emory Univ.

38. Allan, "A Reply to General Longstreet," *B&L* 3: 355–56; Mosby and Robertson, "Confederate Cavalry in the Gettysburg Campaign," ibid., 251–52; Ransom, "Ransom's Division at Fredericksburg," ibid., 94–95; Smith, "Two Days of Battle at Seven Pines (Fair Oaks)," ibid., 229–63.

39. Johnson, *Remembered Yesterdays,* 196; Fitzhugh Lee to Jubal A. Early, June 29, 1883, Early Papers, Library of Congress.

40. Davis, "Robert E. Lee," 65.

41. Quoted in Rowland, *Jefferson Davis* 10: 26–31.

42. See also Mosby, *Mosby's War Reminiscences and Stuart's Cavalry Campaigns;* Allan, *Army of Northern Virginia in 1862;* Smith, *Battle of Seven Pines;* Allan, "First Maryland Campaign"; Jones, "Visit to Beauvoir."

43. Wolseley, "English View of the Civil War," *North American Review* 149 (Aug. 1889): 174; 149 (Sept. 1889): 279–80, 283, 286–89.

44. Ibid. 149 (Sept. 1889): 289.

10: A Procrustean Ending

1. Abbott M. Gibney, taped interview with William Longstreet, Gettysburg, Pa., 1968.

2. Helen Longstreet, *Lee and Longstreet at High Tide,* 123–24; *New York Times,* July 24, 1885; Dec. 16, 1888; Aug. 19, 1894.

3. *New York Times,* Dec. 16, 1888; Aug. 19, 1894; Sanger and Hay, *James Longstreet,* 397–98.

4. James Longstreet to William Miller Owen, June 6, 25, 1889, Boagni Collection; *Atlanta Constitution,* Jan. 15, 1888; *New York Times,* Jan. 20, 1888.

5. *New York Times,* July 24, Aug. 12, 1885.

6. Ibid., Apr. 16, 1889; Helen Longstreet, *Lee and Longstreet at High Tide,*

123–24; Borcke, *Memoirs of the Confederate War for Independence,* 22–23.

7. *Atlanta Constitution,* June 5, 1890.

8. For references to Longstreet's health, see James Longstreet to Lafayette McLaws, Sept. 24, 1886, McLaws Papers, Southern Historical Collection, Univ. of N.C.; James Longstreet to William Miller Owen, May 16, 1889; May 19, June 25, 1890, Boagni Collection; James Longstreet to Louis A. Adams, Jan. 18, 1890, Assoc. of the Army of Northern Virginia Papers, Tulane Univ.

9. Moses, "Autobiography," 57, Moses Papers, Southern Historical Collection, Univ. of N.C.

10. James Longstreet to Osmun Latrobe, Mar. 27, May 28, 1886, attached to Latrobe diary, Virginia Historical Soc.; James Longstreet to Thomas T. Munford, Nov. 2, 8, 1891, Munford-Ellis Family Papers, Duke Univ.; Marcus J. Wright to James Longstreet, Aug. 21, 1897, Longstreet Papers, Huntington Library; *New York Times,* Dec. 16, 1888.

11. James Longstreet to Marcus J. Wright, May 7, Aug. 22, 1892; Longstreet to E. A. Carmon, Feb. 11, 1897, Longstreet Papers, Huntington Library; James Longstreet to Thomas T. Munford, Aug. 26, 1894, Munford-Ellis Family Papers, Duke Univ.

12. *Washington Post,* June 11, 1893; *New York Times,* Aug. 19, 1894.

13. James Longstreet to Lafayette McLaws, Dec. 11, 1887, McLaws Papers, Southern Historical Collection, Univ. of N.C.

14. Hassler, "The 'Ghost' of General Longstreet," 25–27.

15. James Longstreet to Thomas T. Munford, Apr. 23, 1895, Munford-Ellis Family Papers, Duke Univ.

16. Sanger and Hay, *James Longstreet,* 432.

17. Longstreet, *From Manassas to Appomattox,* 17–18, 60, 212–16, 543, 554, 565, 573, 600, 605, 614, 627–28, 630, 633–34.

18. Ibid., 548.

19. Ibid., 573; this passage may well have been a criticism of Wade Hampton also.

20. Ibid., 196.

21. Ibid., 78, 375.

22. Ibid., 332.

23. Ibid., 401n.

24. Ibid., 573.

25. G. M. Sorrel to T. J. Goree, June 19, 1886, Goree Papers, LSU; Sanger and Hay, *James Longstreet,* 434–35.

26. Bushong, *Old Jube,* 304–306; Charles S. Venable to Walter H. Taylor, Feb. 11, 1896, Taylor Papers, Virginia State Library; Walter H. Taylor to Jed. Hotchkiss, June 23, 1896, McGuire Papers, Virginia Historical Soc.; *Richmond Times,* June 14, 1896; *Richmond Dispatch,* Feb. 16, 1896; Jones, "Longstreet-Gettysburg Controversy," 342–48.

27. Johnston, *Long Roll,* 403–404, 589.

28.   *New York Times*, Sept. 25, 1883.

29.   James Longstreet to Lafayette McLaws, Sept. 24, 1886, McLaws Papers, Southern Historical Collection, Univ. of N.C.

30.   *New York Times*, July 2, 3, 1888.

31.   Daniel E. Sickles, "Introduction," *From Manassas to Appomattox*, 18–20.

32.   Longstreet, ibid., 20; Sanger and Hay, *James Longstreet*, 407; *Philadelphia Weekly Times*, Apr. 28, May 1, 1893; *New York Times*, July 3, 1893.

33.   James Longstreet to Robert Coston, Jan. 21, 1897, Longstreet Papers, Univ. of Ga.; James Longstreet to C. E. S. Wingate, Apr. 7, 1897, Longstreet Papers, Harvard Univ.; Sanger and Hay, *James Longstreet*, 408; *New York Times*, Apr. 28, 1869.

34.   Thomas, *General James "Pete" Longstreet*, 292; "Confederate General's Widow," *Life* 15 (Dec. 1943), 37–40; *New York Times*, Sept. 5, 7, 9, 1897; Sanger and Hay, *James Longstreet*, 438–40. The Helen Longstreet Papers in the Georgia Historical Soc. Library provide an almost pathetic chronicle of Mrs. Longstreet's long campaign on the General's behalf. She endured poverty and great mental anguish in her attempts to restore his reputation.

35.   J. H. Stine to James Longstreet, Apr. 11, 1900, Gibney Collection.

36.   Alexander, *Confederate Veteran*, 3–4.

37.   James Longstreet to Horatio C. King, Aug. 9, 1902, Longstreet Papers, Huntington Library; James Longstreet to Daniel E. Sickles, Sept. 19, 1902, Longstreet Papers, Historical Soc. of Pa.

38.   Helen Longstreet to Miss——Longstreet, Dec. 26, 1939, Helen Longstreet Papers, Georgia Historical Soc.

39.   White, *Confederate Veteran*, 10–13, 18–20; Wilson, *Baptized in Blood*, 33.

40.   White, *Confederate Veteran*, 27–28; Osterweis, *Myth of the Lost Cause*, 93; Hattaway, "Clio's Southern Soldiers," 214. The *Confederate Veteran* magazine was not officially connected with the UCV but endorsed it in the strongest possible manner.

41.   Osterweis, *Myth of the Lost Cause*, 111–17; White, *Confederate Veteran*, 43–44.

42.   Muldowny, "Jefferson Davis: The Postwar Years," 31; Woodward, *Origins of the New South*, 155; Tankersley, *John B. Gordon*, 330.

43.   *Atlanta Constitution*, May 1, 2, 1886; Tankersley, *John B. Gordon*, 332.

44.   *Atlanta Constitution*, May 1, 2, 1886; Tankersley, *John B. Gordon*, 332; James Longstreet to William Miller Owen, Oct. 20, 1889, Boagni Collection. Longstreet confuses the date of Ben Hill Day with that of the Piedmont Exposition of the following year.

45.   James Longstreet to William Miller Owen, May 12, 1890, Boagni Collection; James Longstreet to T. J. Goree, Sept. 7, 1894, Goree Papers, LSU.

46.   James Longstreet to William Miller Owen, May 19, 1890, Boagni Collection.

47.   James Longstreet to T. J. Goree, July 7, 1894; G. M. Sorrel to T. J.

Goree, Aug. 17, 1896, Goree Papers, LSU; Sanger and Hay, *James Long-street*, 405.

48. James Longstreet to T. J. Goree, July 7, 1894, Goree Papers, LSU.
49. Ibid.
50. Ibid.
51. *Atlanta Constitution*, Jan. 15, 1888.
52. *New York Times*, Dec. 12, 1888; Feb. 20, Mar. 19, Apr. 6, 7, 1897; *Gen'l. Longstreet's Speech on McKinley and the Gold Standard versus Bryan, the Sil-ver Standard, and the Mobocrats*, copy in Helen Longstreet Papers, Geor-gia Historical Soc. Mrs. Longstreet is probably the author.
53. *New York Times*, Dec. 31, 1893; Oct. 23, 1897; Helen Longstreet, *Lee and Longstreet at High Tide*, 117.
54. James Longstreet to James Longstreet, Jr., Jan. 27, 1903, Longstreet Papers, Emory Univ.; *New York Times*, Nov. 27, 1898; Helen Longstreet, *Lee and Longstreet at High Tide*, 108.
55. Gordon, "Gettysburg," 2–24; Gordon, *Reminiscences*, 160–61.
56. Gordon, *Reminiscences*, 166.
57. James Longstreet to James Longstreet, Jr., Jan. 27, 1903, Longstreet Papers, Emory Univ.; *New York Herald*, Sept. 27, 1903; *Boston Herald*, Jan. 3, 1904; *Vicksburg Herald*, Jan. 5, 1904; Alvarez, "Death of the 'Old War Horse' Longstreet," 71; Helen Longstreet to Sears Wilson Cabell, Oct. 29, 1940, Helen Longstreet Papers, Georgia Historical Soc.
58. Alvarez, "Death of the 'Old War Horse' Longstreet," 71; Helen Long-street to James Longstreet Sibley, Jan. 26, 1940, Helen Longstreet Pa-pers, Georgia Historical Soc.
59. Alvarez, "Death of the 'Old War Horse' Longstreet," 72–73; *Atlanta Constitution*, Jan. 7, 1904.
60. Quoted in Helen Longstreet, *Lee and Longstreet at High Tide*, 342.
61. Alvarez, "Death of the 'Old War Horse' Longstreet," 74; *New York Times*, Jan. 6, 1904.

11: Longstreet Postmortem

1. Jones, *Life and Letters of Robert E. Lee*, 253–76; italics are Jones's. Jeffer-son Davis refused to endorse a similar statement by Jones; see Rowland, *Jefferson Davis* 9: 531.
2. Taylor, *General Lee*, 193–209.
3. Early, *Autobiographical Sketch*, 270–274.
4. Maurice, *An Aide-de-Camp of Lee*, 174, 180–81, 232–34, 238–40.
5. See, for example, Jones, "Confederate Generals Are All Passing Away," 189–92; Crocker, "My Personal Experiences," 111–34; McKim, "Get-tysburg Campaign," 225–30; Thompson, "Who Lost Gettysburg?" 257–58.

6. "Historical Department, U.D.C."; Osterweis, *Myth of the Lost Cause,* 93–94.
7. Chandler and Chitwood, *Makers of American History,* 208; Hall, *Half-Hours in Southern History,* 247–48; Stephenson, *An American History,* 445–46; Andrews, *History of the United States,* 306; *American History and Government,* 338; Fish, *History of American Government,* 377.
8. See, for instance, Lee, *New Primary History of the United States;* Thompson, *A History of the United States;* White, *A School History of the United States.*
9. Oates, *War Between the Union and the Confederacy,* 222–25, 240–43, 245–46, 339. Oates deeply resented Longstreet's conduct toward his friend E. M. Law; this may have affected Oates's version of Gettysburg.
10. Hunter, *Johnny Reb and Billy Yank,* 402–15; Royall, *Some Reminiscences,* 10–24; Morgan, *Personal Reminiscences,* 168; Dunaway, *Reminiscences of a Rebel,* 93–94.
11. Stiles, *Four Years Under Marse Robert,* 247; Alexander, *Military Memoirs,* 388–433; Sorrel, *Recollections,* 167–74.
12. Page, *Robert E. Lee the Southerner,* 177–78.
13. Bradford, *Lee the American,* 139.
14. Ibid., 177; Whipple, *Heart of Lee,* 169; Maurice, *Robert E. Lee the Soldier,* 142–43, 174–75, 186–89, 192–212; Young, *Marse Robert,* 236, 245–48, 273; Brooks, *Lee of Virginia;* Winston, *Robert E. Lee,* 255–57, 267.
15. Freeman, *R. E. Lee* 2: 325, 348.
16. Ibid., 501, 501n.
17. Ibid. 3: 15.
18. Ibid. 2: 484; Connelly, *Marble Man,* 150.
19. Freeman, *R. E. Lee* 3: 85.
20. Ibid. 3: 86–90, 132, 554. Longstreet's innocent swig of rum came from the flask Fremantle gave him. See Fremantle, *Three Months in the Confederate States,* 267.
21. Hackett, *70 Years of Best Sellers, 1895–1965,* 151; "Virginians," *Time,* Oct. 18, 1948, p. 111.
22. Eckenrode and Conrad, *James Longstreet,* 366.
23. Ibid., 163, 208.
24. Ibid., 367–68.
25. Ibid., 49–55, 81–83, 105–106, 119–35, 219, 243, 301–10, 361–62.
26. Fuller, *Decisive Battles of the U.S.A.,* 234–47; Randall, *Civil War and Reconstruction,* 518–32; Coulter, *William G. Brownlow,* 389; Milton, *Conflict: The American Civil War,* 234–47; Eliot, *West Point in the Confederacy,* 199–244.
27. Huffman, *Ups and Downs of a Confederate Soldier,* 77; Douglas, *I Rode with Stonewall,* 248, 251; Blackford, *War Years with Jeb Stuart,* 47.
28. Freeman, *Lee's Lieutenants* 3: 110, 113–22, 140, 143–48, 151–58, 161–67, 169–89.

29. Freeman may have recanted his views on Longstreet late in his life. In a letter to the author dated Oct. 15, 1979, Freeman's acquaintance Marion B. Roberts, M.D., relates: "I talked with Dr. Freeman a few months before his death, when he told me, 'When I finish my [biography of] Washington I intend to rewrite the R. E. Lee because I feel I have done some deserving men injustice, especially Longstreet.'"

30. Faulkner, *Intruder in the Dust,* 194–95.

31. Hergesheimer, *Swords and Roses,* 3; Dixon, *Man in Gray;* Boyd, *Marching On;* McGhee, *Journey Proud;* Hackett, *70 Years of Best Sellers, 1895–1965,* 153, 157, 176, 179, 190, 201; De Voto, "Fiction Fights the Civil War," 3–4, 15–16; Bloom, "Battle of Gettysburg in Fiction," 309–27; Cobb, *Redd Likker;* Johnson, *By Reason of Strength.*

32. Hackett, *70 Years of Best Sellers, 1895–1965,* 149, 153, 155.

33. Dwight, *Linn Dickson, Confederate,* 209, 212, 233–34.

34. Griswold, *A Sea Island Lady,* 475.

35. Dowdey, *Bugles Blow No More,* 170, 276–77, 280, 298, 300, 307, 310–11, 385.

36. Williams, *House Divided,* xxii–xxiii, 31–32, 321, 418–19, passim; Hackett, *Seventy Years of Best Sellers, 1895–1965,* 176.

37. Williams, *House Divided,* 357, 815, 886, 955.

38. Williams, *Unconquered,* 279–81, 289–90, passim.

39. Sanger and Hay, *James Longstreet,* v, 3–4, 315–16; Sanger, "Was Longstreet a Scapegoat?" 39–46.

40. Sanger and Hay, *James Longstreet,* 3, 85–88, 144–49.

41. Ibid., 168–88.

42. Ibid., 172, 175–76, 416, 435–36.

43. Tucker, *High Tide at Gettysburg,* 214–17, 235–36, 247.

44. Tucker, "Longstreet: Culprit or Scapegoat?" 5–6, 39–40.

45. Tucker, *Lee and Longstreet at Gettysburg,* 14–48, 159–73.

46. Stewart, *Pickett's Charge,* 17, 285–86; Dupuy and Dupuy, *Compact History of the Civil War,* 231; Burger and Buttersworth, *South of Appomattox,* 273–301.

47. Tucker, "Longstreet: Culprit or Scapegoat?" 5; Gibney, *War Horse of the Confederacy,* 99–115, 167–78; Herman Leonard to Abbott M. Gibney, May 31, 1967, courtesy of Mr. Gibney, Birmingham, Mich.

48. Catton, *Terrible Swift Sword,* 326, 341; Catton, "Who Really Won at Gettysburg?" *Saturday Review,* June 15, 1957, pp. 13–15, 48; *New York Times,* Aug. 6, 1978.

49. The collection is entitled *The Wartime Papers of R. E. Lee.*

50. Dowdey, *Death of a Nation,* 30, 80, 157, 164, 173, 177, 180, 207.

51. See, for example, Bushong, *Old Jube,* 159; Vandiver, *Mighty Stonewall,* 295, 345–46; Davis, *They Called Him Stonewall,* 208, 254, 302, 320; Davis, *Gray Fox,* 123, 208–209, 227–28, 232, 246–47, 286; Davis, *Jeb Stuart,* 334–35.

52.   Mitchell, *Decisive Battles of the Civil War,* 153–54, 157; Henderson, *Civil War,* 238, 242, 246; Mapp, *Frockcoats and Epaulets,* 188, 194–200; Foote, *Civil War* 2: 488–92, 498, 581.

53.   Eaton, *History of the Southern Confederacy,* 201, 203; Wellman, *Rebel Boast,* 127; Stackpole, *They Met at Gettysburg,* 76, 177–79, 181, 199–204, 227; Downey, *Guns of Gettysburg,* 125.

54.   South Carolina Confederate War Centennial Commission, *Confederate Centennial,* 9, 19–20.

Bibliography

Manuscripts

Collection of Edward M. Boagni, M.D., Baton Rouge, La.
Chicago Historical Society, Chicago, Ill.
    James Longstreet Papers
College of William and Mary, Williamsburg, Va.
    Joseph E. Johnston Papers
Duke University, Durham, N.C.
    Braxton Bragg Papers
    Clement Claiborne Clay Papers
    John W. Daniel Papers
    Jefferson Davis Papers
    Jubal A. Early Papers
    John B. Gordon Papers
    D. H. Hill Papers
    John Bell Hood Papers
    Micah Jenkins Papers
    Joseph E. Johnston Papers
    E. M. Law Papers
    Fitzhugh Lee Papers
    Augustus Baldwin Longstreet Papers
    James Longstreet Papers
    James Longstreet Letters, microfilm
    John S. Mosby Papers
    Munford-Ellis Family Papers
    William Nelson Pendleton Papers
Emory University, Atlanta, Ga.
    Jefferson Davis Papers
    Henry W. Grady Papers
    James Longstreet Papers
Georgia Historical Society, Savannah, Ga.
    Helen Dortch Longstreet Papers
    James Longstreet Papers
Georgia State Department of Archives and History, Atlanta, Ga.
    James Longstreet Papers
Collection of Abbott M. Gibney, Birmingham, Mich.
Harvard University, Cambridge, Mass.
    James Longstreet Papers
Henry E. Huntington Library, San Marino, Calif.
    James Longstreet Papers

Historical Society of Pennsylvania, Philadelphia, Pa.
    James Longstreet Papers
Library of Congress, Washington, D.C.
    Jubal Anderson Early Papers   S. R. Johnston Papers
    Douglas Southall Freeman Papers   Louis T. Wigfall Papers
Louisiana State University, Baton Rouge, La.
    Jubal A. Early Papers   Thomas J. Goree Papers
    John R. Ficklen Papers   William H. Ker Letters
Museum of the Confederacy, Richmond, Va.
    D. H. Hill Papers   James Longstreet Papers
    Robert E. Lee Papers   William Nelson Pendleton Papers
New York Public Library, New York, N.Y.
    The Century Collection
North Carolina Department of Cultural Resources, Division of Archives and
    History, Raleigh, N.C.
    D. H. Hill Papers
Rutherford B. Hayes Memorial Library, Fremont, Ohio
    James Longstreet Papers
Tennessee State Library and Archives, Nashville, Tenn.
    R. A. Shackleford Letters
Collection of Wilbur M. Thomas, Washington, D.C.
Tulane University, New Orleans, La.
    Mrs. Mason Barrett Collection of the Papers of Albert Sidney and
    William Preston Johnston
    George H. and Katherine M. Davis Collection
    Louisiana Historical Society Collection
        Association of the Army of Northern Virginia Papers
        J. A. Chalaron Papers
        James B. Walton Papers
        W. Chaldron White Papers
University of Georgia, Athens, Ga.
    James Longstreet Papers
    De Renne Confederate Manuscript Collection
University of North Carolina, Chapel Hill, N.C.
    Southern Historical Collection
        E. P. Alexander Papers   James Longstreet Papers
        Henry L. Benning Papers   Lafayette McLaws Papers
        Benjamin F. Cheatham Papers   Raphael Moses Papers
        Peter W. Hairston Papers   William Nelson Pendleton Papers
        John Cheves Haskell   William B. Pettit Papers
        Reminiscences   Donald Bridgman Sanger Papers
        Ann Bachman Hyde Papers   Glenn Tucker Papers
        A. L. Long Papers   Charles S. Venable Papers

University of Virginia, Charlottesville, Va.
    Douglas Southall Freeman Papers
    Letters of Confederate Soldiers Collection: Fitzhugh Lee Papers
Virginia Historical Society, Richmond, Va.
    Virginia Historical Collection
        Early Family Papers   Henry B. McClellan Papers
        Douglas Southall Freeman Papers Hunter Holmes McGuire Papers
        Osmun Latrobe Papers   Charles S. Venable Papers
        Robert E. Lee Papers
Virginia State Library, Richmond, Va.
        Jubal A. Early Papers   William Nelson Pendleton Papers
        Hill-Dabney Letters   Walter H. Taylor Papers
        John William Jones Papers
Western Reserve Historical Society, Cleveland, Ohio
    Braxton Bragg Papers
Washington and Lee University, Lexington, Va.
        Jefferson Davis Papers   William Preston Johnston Papers
        Joseph E. Johnston Papers   Robert E. Lee Papers

Newspapers

Atlanta Constitution
Augusta Chronicle
Augusta Chronicle and Georgia Advertiser
Boston Herald
Nashville Banner
New Orleans Republican
New Orleans Times
New Orleans Tribune
New York Herald
New York Times
New York Tribune
Philadelphia Weekly Press
Philadelphia Weekly Times
Richmond Dispatch
Richmond Enquirer and Examiner
Richmond Times
Savannah Republican
Vicksburg Daily Herald
Washington Post

Printed Primary Sources

BOOKS

Alexander, E. P. *The Confederate Veteran.* Cedar Rapids, Iowa: Republican Printing, 1902.
―――. *The Military Memoirs of a Confederate.* New York: Scribner's, 1907.
Badeau, Adam. *Campaigning with Grant.* Edited by Wayne C. Temple. New York: Bonanza Books, 1961.

Batchelor, Benjamin Franklin. *Batchelor-Turner Letters, 1861–1864.* Annotated by H. J. H. Rugley. Austin, Tex.: Steck, 1961.

Benedict, G. G. *The Battle of Gettysburgh, and the Part Taken Therein by Vermont Troops.* Burlington, Ver.: Free Press Print, 1867.

Berkley, Henry Robinson. *Four Years in the Confederate Artillery.* Edited by William H. Runge. Chapel Hill: University of North Carolina Press, 1961.

Blackford, Susan Leigh. *Memoirs of Life In and Out of the Army in Virginia During the War Between the States.* 2 vols. Lynchburg, Va.: J. P. Bell, 1894.

Blackford, William W. *War Years with Jeb Stuart.* New York: Scribner's, 1945.

Borcke, Heros von. *Memoirs of the Confederate War for Independence.* Philadelphia: Lippincott, 1867.

Conyingham, David Porter. *The Irish Brigade and Its Campaigns.* New York: W. McSorley, 1867.

Cooke, John Esten, *Hammer and Rapier.* New York: G. W. Carleton, 1870.

――――. *Wearing of the Gray, Being Personal Portraits, Scenes, and Adventures of the War.* New York: E. B. Trent, 1867.

Cumming, Kate. *Kate: The Journal of a Confederate Nurse.* Edited by Richard Barksdale Harwell. Baton Rouge: Louisiana State University Press, 1959.

Curry, Jabez Lamar Monroe. *Civil History of the Confederate States with Some Personal Reminiscences.* Richmond, Va.: B. F. Johnson, 1901.

Daniel, John Monclure. *The Richmond Examiner During the War.* New York: By the author, 1868.

Daniels, Josephus. *Tar Heel Editor.* Chapel Hill: University of North Carolina Press, 1939.

Davis, Jefferson. *The Rise and Fall of the Confederate Government.* 2 vols. New York: Appleton, 1881.

Dawson, Francis. *Reminiscences of Confederate Service.* Charleston, S.C.: News and Courier Book Presses, 1882.

Dickert, D. Augustus. *History of Kershaw's Brigade.* Newberry, S.C.: Elbert H. Aull, 1899.

Douglas, Henry Kyd. *I Rode with Stonewall.* Chapel Hill: University of North Carolina Press, 1940.

Dowdey, Clifford, ed. *The Wartime Papers of R. E. Lee.* Boston: Little, Brown, 1961.

Dunaway, Wayland Fuller. *Reminiscences of a Rebel.* New York: Neale, 1913.

Early, Jubal A. *Autobiographical Sketch and Narrative of the War Between the States.* Philadelphia: Lippincott, 1912.

――――. *A Memoir of the Last Year of the War for Independence in the Confederate States of America.* Toronto: Lovell and Gibson, 1866.

Edmonston, Catherine. *"Journal of a Secesh Lady": The Diary of Catherine Ann Devereux Edmonston, 1860–1866.* Edited by Beth G. Crabtree and James W. Patton. Raleigh, N.C.: Department of Archives and History, 1979.

Eggleston, George Cary. *A Rebel's Recollections.* New York: Hurd and Houghton, 1875.

English Combatant, An. *Battlefields of the South, from Bull Run to Fredericksburg.* New York: John Bradburn, 1864.

Estvan, Bella. *War Pictures from the South.* New York: Appleton, 1863.

Freeman, Douglas Southall, ed. *Lee's Dispatches.* New York: Putnam's, 1915.

Fremantle, A. J. L. *Three Months in the Confederate States: April–June 1863.* New York: John Bradburn, 1864.

Gaillard, Franklin. *Franklin Gaillard's Civil War Letters.* Compiled by Charles C. Gaillard, Clair Gaillard Bissell, and Fred E. Gaillard. N.p., 1941, 1969.

Girard, Charles. *A Visit to the Confederate States of America in 1863.* Paris: E. Dentu, 1864.

Gordon, John Brown. *Reminiscences of the Civil War.* New York: Scribner's, 1903.

Grant, Ulysses Simpson. *Personal Memoirs of U. S. Grant.* 2 vols. New York: Charles L. Webster, 1885.

Gray, John Chipman, and Ropes, John Codman. *War Letters, 1862–1865.* Boston: Houghton Mifflin, 1927.

Haskell, John Cheves. *The Haskell Memoirs.* Edited by Gilbert E. Govan and James W. Livingood. New York: Putnam's, 1960.

Heartsill, W. W. *Fourteen Hundred and 91 Days in the Confederate Army.* Edited by Bell I. Wiley. Jackson, Tenn.: McCowat-Mercer Press, 1953.

Hood, John Bell. *Advance and Retreat: Personal Experiences in the United States and Confederate States Armies.* Philadelphia: Burk and M'Fetridge, 1880.

Houghton, Edward B. *Campaigns of the Seventeenth Maine.* Portland, Me.: Short and Loring, 1866.

Huffman, Jones. *Ups and Downs of a Confederate Soldier.* New York: William E. Rudges' Sons, 1940.

Hunter, Alexander. *Johnny Reb and Billy Yank.* New York: Neale, 1905.

Hunton, Eppa. *Autobiography of Eppa Hunton.* Richmond, Va.: William Byrd Press, 1933.

Inman, Arthur Crew, ed. *Soldier of the South: General Pickett's War Letters to His Wife.* Boston: Houghton Mifflin, 1928.

Jacobs, Michael. *Notes on the Rebel Invasion of Maryland and Pennsylvania.* Philadelphia: Lippincott, 1864.

Johnson, Robert Underwood. *Remembered Yesterdays.* Boston: Little, Brown, 1923.

Johnston, Joseph E. *Narrative of Military Operations.* New York: Appleton, 1874.

Kean, Robert G. H. *Inside the Confederate Government: The Diary of Robert Garlick Hill Kean.* Edited by Edward Younger. New York: Oxford University Press, 1957.

Lane, Mills, ed. *"Dear Mother: Don't grieve about me. If I get killed I'll only be dead":*

Letters from Georgia Soldiers in the Civil War. Savannah, Ga.: Beehive Press, 1972.

Longstreet, James. *From Manassas to Appomattox.* Philadelphia: Lippincott, 1896.

McClure, Alexander Kelly. *Colonel Alexander K. McClure's Recollections of Half a Century.* Salem, Mass.: Salem Press, 1902.

Mackall, William W. *A Son's Recollections of His Father.* New York: Dutton, 1930.

Maurice, Frederick, ed. *An Aide-de-Camp of Lee, Being the Papers of Colonel Charles Marshall, Sometime Aide-de-Camp, Military Secretary, and Assistant Adjutant General on the Staff of Robert E. Lee, 1862–1865.* Boston: Little, Brown, 1927.

Moore, Robert A. *A Life for the Confederacy As Recorded in the Pocket Diaries of Pvt. Robert A. Moore.* Edited by James W. Silver. Jackson, Tenn.: McCowat-Mercer Press, 1959.

Morgan, William Henry. *Personal Reminiscences of the War of 1861–5.* Lynchburg, Va.: J. P. Bell, 1911.

Mosby, John Singleton. *Mosby's War Reminiscences and Stuart's Cavalry Campaigns.* Boston: G. A. Jones, 1887.

Murphy, Thomas G. *Four Years in the War: History of the First Regiment of Delaware Volunteers, (Infantry).* Philadelphia: James S. Claxton, 1886.

Norton, Charles Eliot. *Letters of Charles Eliot Norton with Biographical Comment by His daughter, Sarah Norton and M. A. De Wolfe Howe.* 2 vols. Boston: Houghton Mifflin, 1913.

Oates, William Calvin. *The War Between the Union and the Confederacy and Its Lost Opportunities, with a History of the 15th Alabama Regiment. . . .* New York: Neale, 1905.

Owen, William Miller. *In Camp and Battle with the Washington Artillery of New Orleans.* Boston: Ticknor, 1885.

Pryor, Mrs. Roger A. *Reminiscences of War and Peace.* New York: Macmillan, 1904.

Roman, Alfred. *The Military Operations of General Beauregard in the War Between the States 1861 to 1865.* 2 vols. New York: Harper, 1884.

Ross, Fitzgerald. *Cities and Camps of the Confederate States.* Edited by Richard Barksdale Harwell. Urbana: University of Illinois Press, 1958.

Rowland, Dunbar, ed. *Jefferson Davis, Constitutionalist: His Letters, Papers and Speeches.* 10 vols. New York: J. J. Little and Ives, 1923.

Royall, William Lawrence. *Some Reminiscences.* New York: Neale, 1909.

Scheibert, Justus. *Seven Months in the Rebel States During the North American War 1863.* Translated by Joseph C. Haynes. Edited by Wm. Stanley Hoole. Tuscaloosa, Ala.: Confederate Publishing, 1867.

Scott, Winfield. *Memoirs of Lieut.-General Scott, Ll.D.* 2 vols. New York: Sheldon, 1864.

Shaver, Lewellyn A. *History of the Sixteenth Alabama Regiment.* Montgomery, Ala.: Barrett and Brown, 1867.

Smith, Ephraim Kirby. *To Mexico with Scott: Letters of Captain E. Kirby Smith to His Wife*. Cambridge: Harvard University Press, 1917.

Smith, Gustavus Woodson. *The Battle of Seven Pines*. New York: C. G. Crawford, 1891.

Sorrel, G. Moxley. *Recollections of a Confederate Staff Officer*. New York: Neale, 1905.

Stevens, George Thomas. *Three Years in the Sixth Corps*. Albany, N.Y.: S. R. Gray, 1866.

Stiles, Robert. *Four Years Under Marse Robert*. New York: Neale, 1904.

Straus, Oscar. *Under Four Administrations from Cleveland to Taft*. Boston: Houghton Mifflin, 1922.

Strong, George Temple. *The Diary of George Temple Strong*. Edited by Allen Nevins. New York: Macmillan, 1967.

Taylor, Richard. *Destruction and Reconstruction: Personal Experiences of the Late War*. New York: Appleton, 1879.

War Department. *The War of the Rebellion: A Compilation of the Official Records of the Union and Confederate Armies*. 128 vols. Washington, D.C.: Government Printing Office, 1880–1901.

West, John C. *A Texan in Search of a Fight*. Waco, Tex.: J. S. Hill, 1901.

Woodward, Evan Morrison. *Our Campaigns*. Philadelphia: J. E. Potter, 1865.

ARTICLES

Alexander, Edward Porter. "The Great Charge and Artillery Fighting at Gettysburg." *B&L* 3: 357–68.

———. "Letter from E. P. Alexander, late Chief of Artillery First Corps, A.N.V." *SHSP* 4 (Sept. 1877): 97–111.

———. "Longstreet at Knoxville." *B&L* 3: 745–51.

———. "Sketch of Longstreet's Division: Winter of 1861–62." *SHSP* 9 (Oct.–Dec. 1881): 512–18; 10 (Jan.–Feb. 1882): 32–45.

Alexander, P. W. "Confederate Chieftains." *Southern Literary Messenger* 25 (Jan. 1863): 34–38.

Allan, William. "First Maryland Campaign: Review of General Longstreet by Colonel W. Allan." *SHSP* 14 (Jan.–Dec. 1886): 102–18.

———. "Letter from William Allan, of Ewell's Staff." *SHSP* 4 (Aug. 1877): 76–80.

———. "A Reply to General Longstreet." *B&L* 3: 355–56.

Anderson, Archer. "The Campaign and Battle of Chickamauga." *SHSP* 9 (Sept. 1881): 385–418.

Bean, W. G., ed. "Memoranda of Conversations Between General Robert E. Lee and William Preston Johnston, May 7, 1868, and March 16, 1870." *VMHB* 73 (Oct. 1965): 474–84.

Beauregard, P. G. T. "The First Battle of Bull Run." *B&L* 1: 196–227.

Borcke, Heros von. "Memoirs of the Confederate War for Independence, Part I." *Blackwood's Edinburgh Magazine* 98 (Sept. 1865): 269–88.

Crocker, James F. "My Personal Experiences in Taking Up Arms and in the Battle of Malvern Hill/Gettysburg-Pickett's Charge." *SHSP* 33 (Jan.–Dec. 1905): 111–34.

Early, Jubal A. "Leading Confederates on the Battle of Gettysburg: A Review by General Early." *SHSP* 4 (Dec. 1877): 241–302.

———. "Letter from Gen. J. A. Early." *SHSP* 4 (Aug. 1877): 50–68.

———. "Reply to General Longstreet's Second Paper." *SHSP* 5 (June 1878): 270–87.

Goggin, James M. "Chickamauga—A Reply to Major Sykes." *SHSP* 11 (May 1884): 219–24.

Gordon, John B. "Gettysburg." *Scribner's Monthly* 34 (July 1903): 2–24.

Hassler, William W., ed. "The Civil War Letters of General William Dorsey Pender to His Wife." *Georgia Review* 17 (Spring 1963): 57–75.

Hill, Daniel Harvey. "Chickamauga—The Great Battle in the West." *B&L* 3: 638–62.

Hunt, Henry J. "The First Day at Gettysburg." *B&L* 3: 255–84.

Kershaw, James B. "Kershaw's Brigade at Gettysburg." *B&L* 3: 331–38.

Law, Evander McIvor. "The Struggle for 'Round Top.'" *B&L* 3: 318–30.

Lee, Fitzhugh. "Letter from General Fitz. Lee." *SHSP* 4 (Aug. 1877): 69–76.

———. "A Review of the First Two Days' Operations at Gettysburg and a Reply to General Longstreet." *SHSP* 5 (Apr. 1878): 162–94.

Lee, Stephen D. "The Artillery at Second Manassas—Rejoinder of General S. D. Lee to General Longstreet." *SHSP* 6 (Dec. 1878): 250–54.

———. "The Second Battle of Manassas—A Reply to General Longstreet." *SHSP* 6 (July 1878): 59–70.

Long, Armistead L. "Letter from General A. L. Long, Military Secretary to General R. E. Lee." *SHSP* 4 (Sept. 1877): 118–23.

Longstreet, James. "The Artillery at Second Manassas—General Longstreet's Reply to General S. D. Lee." *SHSP* 6 (Oct. 1878): 215–17.

———. "The Battle of Fredericksburg." *Century* 32 (Aug. 1886): 609–26; *B&L* 3: 70–85.

———. "General James Longstreet's Account of the Campaign and Battle." *SHSP* 5 (Jan. 1878): 54–86.

———. "General Longstreet's Second Paper on Gettysburg." *SHSP* 5 (June 1878): 257–69.

———. "The Invasion of Maryland." *Century* 32 (June 1886): 309–15; *B&L* 2: 663–74.

———. "Lee in Pennsylvania." *Annals of the War*, 414–46.

———. "Lee's Invasion of Pennsylvania." *Century* 33 (Feb. 1887): 622–36; *B&L* 3: 244–51.

———. "Lee's Right Wing at Gettysburg." *B&L* 3: 339–54.

———. "Letter from General Longstreet." *SHSP* 5 (Jan.-Feb. 1878), 52–53.

_____. "The Mistakes of Gettysburg." *Annals of the War*, 619–33.

_____. "Our March Against Pope." *Century* 31 (Feb. 1886): 601–614; *B&L* 2: 512–26.

_____. "The Seven Days Fighting About Richmond." *Century* 30 (July 1885): 468–77.

McLaws, Lafayette. "The Battle of Gettysburg." *Philadelphia Weekly Press*, Apr. 21, 1886.

_____. "The Confederate Left at Fredericksburg." *B&L* 3: 86–94.

_____. "Gettysburg." *SHSP* 7 (Jan. 1879): 64–90.

Morrison, James L., Jr., ed. "The Memoirs of Henry Heth." *Civil War History* 8 (Mar. 1962): 5–24; (Sept. 1962): 300–326.

Mosby, John S. "Personal Recollections of General Lee." *Munsey's Magazine* 45 (Apr. 1911): 65–69.

Mosby, John S., and Robertson, Beverly H. "The Confederate Cavalry in the Gettysburg Campaign." *B&L* 3: 251–53.

Oates, William C. "Gettysburg—Battle on the Right." *SHSP* 6 (Oct. 1878): 172–82.

Owen, William Miller. "A Hot Day on Mayre's Heights." *B&L* 3: 97–99.

Pendleton, William Nelson. "Personal Recollections of General Lee." *Southern Magazine* 15 (Dec. 1874): 603–36.

Perros, George P. "Letters of James Longstreet Relative to His Position of United States Marshal in Georgia." *Georgia Historical Quarterly* 41 (Sept. 1957): 300–308.

Phillips, Ulrich B. "The Correspondence of Robert Toombs, Alexander H. Stephens, and Howell Cobb." *Annual Report of the American Historical Association for the Year 1911*, 2: 4–743.

Polley, J. B. "Reminiscences of Chickamauga." *Confederate Veteran* 5 (Jan. 1897): 11–13.

Prichard, Walter, ed. "The Origins and Activities of the 'White League' in New Orleans (Reminiscences of a Participant in the Movement)." *Louisiana Historical Quarterly* 22 (Apr. 1940): 525–43.

Ranson, A. R. H. "Reminiscences of the Civil War by a Confederate Staff Officer." *Sewanee Review* 22 (1914): 444–57.

_____. "General Lee as I Knew Him." *Harper's Monthly Magazine* 122 (Feb. 1911): 327–36.

Ransom, Robert. "Ransom's Division at Fredericksburg." *B&L* 3: 94–95.

Reed, Merl E. "The Gettysburg Campaign—a Louisiana Lieutenant's Eye-Witness Account." *Pennsylvania History* 30 (April 1963): 184–91.

Scheibert, Justus. "Letter from Maj. Scheibert, of the Prussian Royal Engineers." *SHSP* 5 (Jan.-Feb. 1878): 90–93.

Smith, Gustavus Woodson. "The Second Day at Seven Pines." *Century* 8 (May 1885): 122–30.

_____. "Two Days of Battle at Seven Pines (Fair Oaks)." *B&L* 2: 220–63.

Smith, J. B. "The Charge of Pickett, Pettigrew, and Trimble." *B&L* 3: 354.

Taylor, Walter H. "The Campaign in Pennsylvania." *Annals of the War*, 305–18.
————. "Memorandum from Colonel Walter H. Taylor, of General Lee's Staff." *SHSP* 4 (Aug. 1877): 80–87.
————. "Second Paper by Col. Walter H. Taylor, of General Lee's Staff." *SHSP* 4 (Sept. 1877): 124–39.
Trimble, Isaac R. "The Battle and Campaign of Gettysburg." *SHSP* 26 (Jan.-Dec. 1898): 116–28).
————. "The Campaign and Battle of Gettysburg." *Confederate Veteran* 25 (May 1917): 209–13.
Trundle, Joseph H. "Gettysburg as Described in Two Letters from a Maryland Confederate." *Maryland Historical Magazine* 54 (June 1959): 210–12.
Wilcox, Cadmus M. "General C. M. Wilcox on the Battle of Gettysburg." *SHSP* 5 (Sept. 1878): 97–124.
Youngblood, William. "Unwritten History of the Gettysburg Campaign." *SHSP* 38 (Jan.-Dec. 1910): 312–18.

Printed Secondary Sources

BOOKS

Abele, Rudolph Radama von. *Alexander H. Stephens*. New York: Knopf, 1946.
Addey, Markinfield. *Life and Imprisonment of Jefferson Davis: Together with the Life and Military Career of Stonewall Jackson. . . .* New York: M. Doolay, 1866.
————. *"Stonewall Jackson": The Life and Military Career of Thomas Jonathan Jackson, Lieutenant-General in the Confederate Army.* New York: Charles T. Evans, 1863.
Allan, William. *The Army of Northern Virginia in 1862*. Boston: Houghton, Mifflin, 1892.
Anderson, Charles A., ed. *The Centennial Edition of the Works of Sidney Lanier.* Vol. 1, *Poems and Poem Outlines.* Baltimore: Johns Hopkins University Press, 1945.
Andrews, J. Cutler. *The South Reports the Civil War.* Princeton: Princeton University Press, 1970.
Andrews, Mathew Page. *American History and Government.* Philadelphia: Lippincott, 1921.
————. *History of the United States.* Philadelphia: Lippincott, 1914.
————. *United States History for Young Americans.* Philadelphia: Lippincott, 1916.
Bean, W. G. *Stonewall's Man: Sandie Pendleton.* Chapel Hill: University of North Carolina Press, 1959.
Beaty, John O. *John Esten Cooke.* New York: Columbia University Press, 1922.
Boyd, James. *Marching On.* New York: Scribner's, 1927.
Bradford, Gamaliel. *Lee the American.* Boston: Houghton Mifflin, 1912.

Brooks, William E. *Lee of Virginia.* New York: Bobbs-Merrill, 1932.

Buck, Paul. *The Road to Reunion.* Boston: Little, Brown, 1937.

Burger, Nash K., and Buttersworth, John K. *South of Appomattox.* New York: Harcourt, Brace, 1959.

Bushong, Millard Kessler. *Old Jube: A Biography of General Jubal A. Early.* Boyce, Va.: Carr, 1955.

Cabel, George W. *Kincaid's Battery.* New York: Scribner's, 1905.

Cabell, Sears Wilson. *The "Bulldog" Longstreet at Gettysburg and Chickamauga.* N.p., n.d.

Caldwell, J. F. J. *The History of a Brigade of South Carolinians, Known First as "Gregg's" and Subsequently as "McGowan's Brigade."* Philadelphia: King and Baird, 1866.

Cate, Wirt Armistead. *Lucius Q. C. Lamar: Secession and Reunion.* Chapel Hill: University of North Carolina Press, 1935.

Catton, Bruce. *Glory Road.* Garden City, N.Y.: Doubleday, 1952.

———. *Never Call Retreat.* New York: Pocket Books, 1965.

———. *Terrible Swift Sword.* Garden City, N.Y.: Doubleday, 1963.

Chamberlayne, John Hampden. *Ham Chamberlayne—Virginian.* Richmond, Va.: Press of Dietz Printing, 1932.

Chandler, J. A. C., and Chitwood, O. P. *Makers of American History.* New York: Silver Burdett, 1904.

Chapin, Sallie F. *Fitz-Hugh St. Clair: The South Carolina Rebel Boy: Or It is No Crime to Be Born a Gentleman.* Charleston. S.C.: John M. Greer, 1872.

Cobb, Irvins. *Red Likker.* New York: Cosmopolitan Book, 1929.

Coddington, Edward B. *The Gettysburg Campaign.* New York: Scribner's, 1968.

Connelly, Thomas L. *Autumn of Glory: The Army of Tennessee, 1862–1865.* Baton Rouge: Louisiana State University Press, 1971.

———. *The Marble Man: Robert E. Lee and His Image in American Society.* New York: Knopf, 1977.

Connelly, Thomas L., and Jones, Archer. *The Politics of Command: Factions and Ideas in Confederate Strategy.* Baton Rouge: Louisiana State University Press, 1973.

Cooke, John Esten. *Hilt to Hilt.* New York: G. W. Carleton, 1869.

———. *A Life of Gen. Robert E. Lee.* New York: Appleton, 1871.

———. *The Life of Stonewall Jackson.* New York: Charles B. Richardson, 1853.

———. *Mohun; or The Last Days of Lee and His Paladins.* New York: F. J. Huntington, 1869.

———. *Surry of Eagle's-Nest or The Memoirs of a Staff Officer Serving in Virginia.* New York: Bruce and Huntington, 1866.

———. *The Virginia Comedians.* 2 vols. New York: Appleton, 1854.

Coulter, E. Merton. *William G. Brownlow, Fighting Parson of the Southern Highlands.* Knoxville: University of Tennessee Press, 1971.

Cruse, Mary Ann. *Cameron Hall: A Story of the Civil War.* Philadelphia: Lippincott, 1867.

Dabbs, James McBride. *The Southern Heritage.* New York: Knopf, 1958.

Dabney, Robert Lewis. *Life and Campaigns of Lieut.-Gen. Thomas J. Jackson, (Stonewall Jackson.).* New York: Blelock, 1866.

Davis, Burke. *Gray Fox: Robert E. Lee and the Civil War.* New York: Rinehart, 1956.

———. *Jeb Stuart: The Last Cavalier.* New York: Rinehart, 1957.

———. *They Called Him Stonewall.* New York: Rinehart, 1954.

Dixon, Thomas. *The Clansman.* New York: Doubleday, Page, 1905.

———. *The Man in Gray.* New York: Appleton, 1922.

Dowdey, Clifford. *Bugles Blow No More.* Boston: Little, Brown, 1937.

———. *Death of a Nation: The Story of Lee and His Men at Gettysburg.* New York: Knopf, 1958.

Downey, Fairfax. *The Guns of Gettysburg.* New York: David McKay, 1958.

Dufour, Charles L. *The Night the War Was Lost.* Garden City, N.Y.: Doubleday, 1960.

Dupuy, R. Ernest, and Dupuy, Trevor N. *The Compact History of the Civil War.* New York: Hawthorn Books, 1960.

Dwight, Allan. *Linn Dickson, Confederate.* New York: Macmillan, 1934.

Early, Jubal A. *The Campaigns of Gen. Robert E. Lee: An Address by Lieut. Gen. Jubal A. Early before Washington and Lee University, January 19, 1872.* Baltimore: John Murphy, 1872.

Eaton, Clement. *A History of the Southern Confederacy.* New York: Macmillan, 1954.

———. *Jefferson Davis.* New York: Free Press, 1971.

Eckenrode, Hamilton J., and Conrad, Bryan. *James Longstreet, Lee's War Horse.* Chapel Hill: University of North Carolina Press, 1936.

Eliot, Ellsworth, Jr. *West Point in the Confederacy.* New York: G. H. Baker, 1941.

Faulkner, William. *Intruder in the Dust.* New York: Random House, 1948.

Fidler, William Perry. *Augusta Evans Wilson, 1835–1909.* University: University of Alabama Press, 1951.

Fish, Carl Russell. *History of America.* New York: American Book, 1925.

Fishwick, Marshall William. *Virginians on Olympus: A Cultural Analysis of Four Great Men.* Richmond, Va.: n.p., 1951.

Fleming, Walter L. *Civil War and Reconstruction in Alabama.* New York: Columbia University Press, 1905.

Foote, Shelby. *The Civil War: A Narrative.* 3 vols. New York: Random House, 1958–74.

Ford, Sally Rochester. *Raids and Romances of Morgan and His Men.* New York: Charles B. Richardson, 1864.

Freeman, Douglas Southall. *Lee's Lieutenants: A Study in Command.* 3 vols. New York: Scribner's, 1942–44.

———. *R. E. Lee: A Biography.* 4 vols. New York: Scribner's, 1934–1935.

Fuller, J. F. C. *Decisive Battles of the U.S.A.* New York: Yoseloff, 1942.

Garland, Hamlin. *Roadside Meetings.* New York: Macmillan, 1930.

Glasgow, Ellen. *The Battle-Ground.* New York: Doubleday, Page, 1902.

———. *The Deliverance.* New York: Doubleday, Page, 1904.

———. *The Voice of the People.* New York: Doubleday, Page, 1900.

Govan, Gilbert E., and Livingood, James W. *A Different Valor: The Story of General Joseph E. Johnston, C.S.A.* New York: Bobbs-Merrill, 1956.

Griswold, Francis. *A Sea Island Lady.* New York: Morrow, 1939.

Hackett, Alice Payne. *70 Years of Best Sellers, 1895–1965.* New York: Bowker, 1967.

Hall, Jonathan Leslie. *Half-Hours in Southern History.* Richmond, Va.: B. F. Johnson, 1907.

Hallock, Charles. *A Complete Biographical Sketch of "Stonewall" Jackson. . . .* Augusta, Ga.: Steam Power Press Chronicle and Sentinel, 1863.

Hamlin, Percy Gatlin. *"Old Bald Head" (General R. S. Ewell): The Portrait of a Soldier.* Strasburg, Va.: Shenandoah Publishing House, 1940.

Harris, Joel Chandler. *Free Joe and Other Georgian Sketches.* New York: Scribner's, 1887.

———. *Gabriel Tolliver: A Story of Reconstruction.* New York: McClure, Phillips, 1902.

Hattaway, Herman, and Jones, Archer. *How the North Won: A Military History of the Civil War.* Urbana, Ill.: University of Chicago Press, 1983.

Henderson, G. F. R. *The Civil War: A Soldier's View.* Edited by Jay Luvaas. Chicago: University of Chicago Press, 1958.

Hergesheimer, Joseph. *Swords and Roses.* New York: Knopf, 1929.

Holman, C. Hugh. *The Immoderate Past: The Southern Writer and History.* Athens: University of Georgia Press, 1977.

Hubble, Jay B. *The South in American Literature, 1607–1900.* Durham, N.C.: Duke University Press, 1954.

Jarrell, Hampton McNeely. *Wade Hampton and the Negro: The Road Not Taken.* Columbia: University of South Carolina Press, 1949.

Johnson, Gerald W. *By Reason of Strength.* New York: Minton, Balch, 1930.

Johnston, Mary. *Cease Firing.* Boston: Houghton Mifflin, 1912.

———. *The Long Roll.* Boston: Houghton Mifflin, 1911.

Jones, Charles C., Jr. *A Roster of General Officers, Heads of Departments, Senators, Representatives, Military Organizations, &c., &c., in Confederate Service During the War Between the States.* Richmond, Va.: Southern Historical Society, 1876.

Jones, John William. *Army of Northern Virginia Memorial Volume.* Richmond, Va.: J. W. Randolph and English, 1880.

———. *Life and Letters of Robert E. Lee, Soldier and Man.* New York: Neale, 1906.

———. *Personal Reminiscences, Anecdotes and Letters of General Robert E. Lee.* New York: Appleton, 1874.

Keller, Morton. *Affairs of State; Public Life in Late Nineteenth Century America.* Cambridge: Harvard University Press, Belknap Press, 1977.

Kendrick, Benjamin Burks, and Arnett, Alex Mathews. *The South Looks at Its Past*. Chapel Hill: University of North Carolina Press, 1935.

King, Alvy. *Louis T. Wigfall, Southern Fire-eater*. Baton Rouge: Louisiana State University Press, 1970.

Klein, Maury. *Edward Porter Alexander*. Athens: University of Georgia Press, 1971.

Lee, Fitzhugh. *General Lee*. New York: Appleton, 1894.

Lee, Robert E., Jr. *Recollections and Letters of General Robert E. Lee*. New York: Doubleday, Page, 1904.

Lee, Susan P. *Memoirs of William Nelson Pendleton, DD*. Philadelphia: Lippincott, 1893.

———. *New Primary History of the United States*. Richmond, Va.: B. F. Johnson, 1905.

Lively, Robert A. *Fiction Fights the Civil War*. Chapel Hill: University of North Carolina Press, 1957.

Long, Armistead L. *Memoirs of Robert E. Lee: His Military and Personal History*. New York: J. M. Stoddart, 1886.

Longstreet, Helen Dortch. *Gen'l. Longstreet's Speech on McKinley and the Gold Standard versus Bryan, The Silver Standard, and the Mobocrats*. N.p., 1896.

———. *Lee and Longstreet at High Tide*. Gainesville, Ga.: By the author, 1905.

Lonn, Ella. *Foreigners in the Confederacy*. Chapel Hill: University of North Carolina Press, 1940.

McCabe, James Dabney. *The Aide-de-Camp: A Romance of the War*. Richmond, Va.: W. A. J. Smith, 1863.

———. *Life and Campaigns of Robert E. Lee*. Atlanta: National Publishing, 1866.

———. *The Life of Thomas J. Jackson*. Richmond, Va.: James E. Goode, 1864.

McGhee, Thomasine. *Journey Proud*. New York: Macmillan, 1934.

McMaster, Richard K. *Musket, Saber, and Missile: A History of Fort Bliss*. El Paso, Tex.: Complete Letter and Printing Service, 1963.

McWhiney, Grady, and Jamieson, Perry D. *Attack and Die: Civil War Military Tactics and the Southern Heritage*. University: University of Alabama Press, 1982.

Magill, Mary Tucker. *Women: Or, Chronicles of the Late War*. Baltimore: Turnbill Press, 1871.

Mapp, Alf. J., Jr. *Frockcoats and Epaulets*. New York: Yoseloff, 1963.

Marks, James Junius. *The Peninsular Campaign in Virginia*. Philadelphia: Lippincott, 1864.

Maurice, Frederick. *Robert E. Lee the Soldier*. Boston: Houghton Mifflin, 1925.

Mayes, Edward D. *Lucius Q. C. Lamar: His Life, Times, and Speeches*. Nashville, Tenn.: Publishing House of the Methodist Episcopal Church, South, 1896.

Milton, George F. *Conflict; The American Civil War*. New York: Coward-McCann, 1941.

Mitchell, Joseph B. *Decisive Battles of the Civil War*. New York: Putnam's, 1955.

Mitchell, Margaret. *Gone with the Wind.* New York: Macmillan, 1934.

Murfin, James V. *The Gleam of Bayonets: The Battle of Antietam and the Maryland Campaign of 1862.* New York: Bonanza Books, 1965.

Murphy, James B. *L. Q. C. Lamar: Pragmatic Patriot.* Baton Rouge: Louisiana State University Press, 1973.

Nelson, Larry E. *Bullets, Ballots, and Rhetoric: Confederate Policy for the United States Presidential Contest of 1864.* University: University of Alabama Press, 1980.

Osterweis, Rollin G. *The Myth of the Lost Cause, 1865–1900.* New York: Archon Books, 1973.

————. *Romanticism and Nationalism in the Old South.* Baton Rouge: Louisiana State University Press, 1967.

Page, Thomas Nelson. *Among the Camps: or Young People's Stories of the War.* New York: Scribner's, 1891.

————. *Red Rock: A Chronicle of Reconstruction.* New York: Scribner's, 1898.

————. *Robert E. Lee the Southerner.* New York: Scribner's, 1909.

————. *Two Little Confederates.* New York: Scribner's, 1888.

Paris, Louis Philippe Albert d'Orléans, Comte de. *History of the Civil War in America.* 4 vols. Philadelphia: J. H. Coates, 1875–88.

Pate, O. K. *The Character of Stonewall Jackson, a lecture delivered in the hall of the House of Delegates, Richmond, Virginia, January 28, 1865.* Richmond: "Southern Star" Office, 1865.

Pearce, Haywood J., Jr. *Benjamin Hill: Secession and Reconstruction.* Chicago: University of Chicago Press, 1928.

Pickett, La Salle Corbell. *Pickett and His Men.* Atlanta: Foote and Davies, 1899.

Polk, William Mecklenburg. *Leonidas Polk, Bishop and General.* 2 vols. New York: Longmans, Green, 1915.

Pollard, Edward A. *Lee and His Lieutenants.* New York: E. B. Treat, 1867.

Polley, J. B. *Hood's Texas Brigade.* New York: Neale, 1910.

Ramsey, James Beverlin. *True Eminence Founded in Holiness: A Discourse Occasioned by the Death of Lieut. Gen. T. J. Jackson, Preached in the First Presbyterian Church of Lynchburg, May 24, 1863.* Lynchburg, Va.: Virginian Print, 1863.

Randall, James G. *The Civil War and Reconstruction.* Boston: Heath, 1937.

Reid, J. W. *History of the Fourth Regiment of South Carolina Volunteers from the Commencement of the War Until Lee's Surrender.* Greenville, S.C.: Shannon, 1892.

Rice, Jessie Pearl. *J. M. L. Curry: Southerner, Statesman, and Educator.* New York: King's Crown Press, 1949.

Rodenbough, Theophilus Francis, and Haskins, William L., eds. *The Army of the United States: Historical Sketches of Staff and Line with Portraits of Generals-in-chief.* New York: Maynard, Merrill, 1898.

Sanger, Donald Bridgman. *The Story of Old Fort Bliss.* El Paso, Tex.: Hughes, Buie, 1933.

Sanger, Donald Bridgman, and Hay, Thomas Robson. *James Longstreet: Soldier, Politician, Officeholder, and Writer*. Baton Rouge: Louisiana State University Press, 1952.

Shadgett, Olive Hall. *The Republican Party in Georgia From Reconstruction through 1900*. Athens: University of Georgia Press, 1964.

Silver, James W. *Confederate Morale and Church Propaganda*. New York: Norton, 1957.

Simpson, Harold B. *Hood's Texas Brigade: Lee's Grenadier Guard*. Waco, Tex.: Texian Press, 1970.

Smith, Francis Henry. *Discourse on the Life and Character of Lt. Gen. Thos. J. Jackson. . . .* Richmond: Ritchie and Dunnavant, 1863.

Smith, Justin H. *The War with Mexico*. 2 vols. New York: Macmillan, 1919.

Snow, William Parker. *Southern Generals: Their Lives and Campaigns*. New York: Charles B. Richardson, 1866.

South Carolina Confederate War Centennial Commission. *The Confederate War Centennial: An Opportunity for All South Carolinians*. Columbia, S.C.: South Carolina Confederate War Centennial Commission, n.d.

Stackpole, Edward J. *They Met at Gettysburg*. Harrisburg, Pa.: Eagle Books, 1956.

Stephenson, Nathaniel Wright. *An American History*. Boston: Ginn, 1913.

Stewart, George R. *Pickett's Charge: A Microhistory of the Final Attack at Gettysburg, July 3, 1863*. Boston: Houghton Mifflin, 1957.

Stovall, Pleasant A. *Robert Toombs*. New York: Cassell, 1892.

Swinton, William. *Campaigns of the Army of the Potomac*. New York: Charles B. Richardson, 1866.

Tankersley, Allen P. *John B. Gordon: A Study in Gallantry*. Atlanta: Whitehall Press, 1955.

Taylor, Walter H. *General Lee, His Campaigns in Virginia, 1861–1865, with Personal Reminiscences*. Norfolk: Nusbaum Book and News Co., 1906.

Thomas, Wilbur. *General James "Pete" Longstreet, Lee's "Old War Horse," Scapegoat for Gettysburg*. Parsons, W. Va.: McClain Printing Co., 1979.

Thompson, Waddy. *A History of the United States*. Boston: Heath, 1904.

Thompson, William Y. *Robert Toombs of Georgia*. Baton Rouge: Louisiana State University Press, 1966.

Timrod, Henry. *The Collected Poems of Henry Timrod: A Variorum Edition*. Edited by Edd Winfield Parks and Aileen Wells Parks. Athens: University of Georgia Press, 1965.

Tucker, Glenn. *High Tide at Gettysburg*. Rev. ed. Dayton, Ohio: Press of the Morningside Bookshop, 1973.

———. *Lee and Longstreet at Gettysburg*. New York: Bobbs-Merrill, 1968.

Utley, Robert M. *Frontiersmen in Blue: The United States Army and the Indian, 1848–1865*. New York: Macmillan, 1967.

Vandiver, Frank E., Jr. *Mighty Stonewall*. New York: McGraw-Hill, 1957.

Wade, John Donald. *Augustus Baldwin Longstreet: A Study of the Development of Culture in the South*. Athens: University of Georgia Press, 1969.

Warmoth, Henry C. *War, Politics, and Reconstruction: Stormy Days in Louisiana.* New York: Macmillan, 1930.

Weaver, Richard M. *The Southern Tradition at Bay.* New Rochelle, N.Y.: Arlington House, 1968.

Wellman, Manly Wade. *Rebel Boast: First at Bethel—Last at Appomattox.* New York: Holt, 1956.

Whipple, Wayne. *The Heart of Lee.* Philadelphia: G. W. Jacobs, 1918.

White, Henry Alexander. *A School History of the United States.* New York: Silver, Burdett, 1904.

White, William W. *The Confederate Veteran.* Tuscaloosa: Confederate Publishing Co., 1963.

Whitson, Mrs. Lorenzo Don. *Gilbert St. Maurice.* Louisville, Ky.: Bradley and Gilbert, 1875.

Whittesley, Sarah J. C. *Bertha the Beauty: A Story of the Southern Revolution.* Philadelphia: Claxton, Remsen and Heffelfinger, 1872.

Wilhelm, Thomas. *A Synopsis History of the Eighth U.S. Infantry and Military Record of Officers Assigned to the Regiment From Its Organization July, 1838, to Sept. 1871.* New York: Eighth Infantry Headquarters, 1871.

Williams, Ben Ames. *House Divided.* Boston: Houghton Mifflin, 1947.

————. *The Unconquered.* Boston: Houghton Mifflin, 1953.

Williams, T. Harry. *P. G. T. Beauregard, Napoleon in Gray.* Baton Rouge: University of Louisiana Press, 1934.

Wilson, Augusta Evans. *Macaria: Or Altars of Sacrifice.* New York: John Bradburn, 1864.

Wilson, Charles Regan. *Baptized in Blood: The Religion of the Lost Cause, 1865–1920.* Athens: University of Georgia Press, 1980.

Winston, Robert A. *Robert E. Lee.* New York: Morrow, 1934.

Wise, Jennings Cropper. *The Long Arm of Lee.* Lynchburg, Va.: J. P. Bell, 1915.

Woodward, C. Vann. *Origins of the New South.* Baton Rouge: Louisiana State University Press, 1971.

Young, James C. *Marse Robert, Knight of the Confederacy.* New York: Rae D. Henkle, 1929.

Young, Stark. *So Red the Rose.* New York: Scribner's, 1934.

ARTICLES

Alvarez, Eugene. "The Death of the 'Old War Horse' Longstreet." *Georgia Historical Quarterly* 52 (Mar. 1968): 70–77.

Anderson, John Coleman. "Lee and Longstreet at Gettysburg." *Confederate Veteran* 12 (Oct. 1904): 488.

Andrews, J. Cutler. "The Press Reports the Battle of Gettysburg." *Pennsylvania History* 31 (Apr. 1954): 176–98.

Ashe, A. S. "The Pickett-Pettigrew Charge, Gettysburg, July 3, 1863." *N.C. Regts.* 5: 137–59.

Bloom, Robert L. "The Battle of Gettysburg in Fiction." *Pennsylvania History* 42 (Oct. 1976): 309–27.

Bradford, Gamaliel, Jr. "James Longstreet." *Atlantic Monthly* 110 (Dec. 1912): 834–45.

Bright, Robert A. "Pickett's Charge at Gettysburg." *Confederate Veteran* 38 (July 1930): 263–66.

Brown, Robert Raymond. "Southern Religion in Mid-Century." In *The Lasting South,* edited by Louis D. Rubin, Jr., and James Kilpatrick, 129–44. Chicago: Regnery, 1957.

Catton, Bruce. "Who Really Won at Gettysburg?" *Saturday Review,* June 15, 1957, pp. 13–15, 48.

Christian, George L., et al. "North Carolina and Virginia." *SHSP* 31 (Jan.-Dec. 1903): 340–46.

"Confederate General's Widow." *Life,* Dec. 27, 1943, pp. 37–40.

Connelly, Thomas L. "Robert E. Lee and the Western Confederacy: A Critique of Lee's Strategic Ability." *Civil War History* 15 (June 1969): 116–32.

Davis, Jefferson. "Robert E. Lee." *North American Review* 150 (Jan. 1890): 55–66.

Davis, Steve. "John Esten Cooke and the Confederate Defeat." *Civil War History* 24 (Mar. 1978): 66–100.

De Voto, Bernard. "Fiction Fights the Civil War." *Saturday Review of Literature,* Dec. 18, 1937, pp. 3–4, 15–16.

Downing, Fanny. "The Land We Love." *Land We Love* 1 (July 1886): 161–62.

Elam, W. C. "A Scalawag." *Southern Magazine* 8 (Apr. 1871): 456–59.

Evans, Clement A. "Genl. Gordon and Genl. Longstreet." *Independent,* Feb. 11, 1904, pp. 311–16.

Floyd, Silas X. "Longstreet and Gordon." *Independent,* Jan. 21, 1904, p. 123.

Gonzales, John Edmund. "William Pitt Kellogg, Reconstruction Governor of Louisiana." *Louisiana Historical Quarterly* 29 (Apr. 1946): 394–95.

Hall, James O. "The Spy Harrison." *Civil War Times Illustrated* 24 (Feb. 1986): 19–25.

Harris, Francis Byers. "Henry Clay Warmoth, Reconstruction Governor of Louisiana." *Louisiana Historical Quarterly* 30 (Apr. 1947): 523–653.

Harwell, Richard Barksdale. "John Esten Cooke, Civil War Correspondent." *Journal of Southern History* 19 (Nov. 1953): 501–16.

Hassler, William W. "'Fighting Dick' Anderson." *Civil War Times Illustrated* 12 (Feb. 1974): 4–10, 40–43.

————. "The 'Ghost' of General Longstreet." *Georgia Historical Quarterly* 65 (Spring 1981): 22–27.

Hattaway, Herman. "Clio's Southern Soldiers: The United Confederate Veterans and History." *Louisiana History* 21 (Summer 1971): 213–42.

Hattaway, Herman, and Jones, Archer. "Lincoln as Military Strategist." *Civil War History* 26 (Dec. 1980): 293–303.

Henderson, G. F. R. "Review of General Longstreet's Book, 'From Manassas to Appomattox.'" *SHSP*, n.s. 1 (Apr. 1914): 104–115.

Hesseltine, William G., and Gara, Larry. "Georgia's Confederate Leaders After Appomattox." *Georgia Historical Quarterly* 35 (Mar. 1951): 1–15.

"Historical Department, U.D.C." *Confederate Veteran* 32 (Apr. 1924): 151.

Jones, John William. "Confederate Generals Are All Passing Away." *SHSP* 31 (Jan.-Dec. 1903): 189–92.

_____. "The Longstreet-Gettysburg Controversy—Who commenced it?" *SHSP* 23 (Jan.-Dec. 1885): 342–47.

_____. "A Visit to Beauvoir—President Davis and Family at Home." *SHSP* 14 (Jan.-Dec. 1886): 447–54.

Klein, Maury. "The Knoxville Campaign." *Civil War Times Illustrated* 10 (Oct. 1971): 4–10, 40–47.

Luvaas, Jay. "Joseph E. Johnston." *Civil War Times Illustrated* 4 (Jan. 1966): 5–6, 28–30.

_____. "A Prussian Observer with Lee." *Military Affairs* 21 (Fall 1957): 105–117.

McDowell, John E., and Davis, William C. "General Joseph B. Kershaw." *Civil War Times Illustrated* 8 (Feb. 1970): 36–39.

McKim, Randolph H. "The Gettysburg Campaign." *SHSP*, n.s. 2 (Sept. 1915): 253–300.

Marshall, Charles. "Tributes to General Lee." *Southern Magazine* 7 (Jan. 1871): 30.

Moore, Rayburn. "'A Distinctly Southern Magazine': *The Southern Bivouac.*" *Southern Literary Journal* 2 (Spring 1970): 51–65.

Mosby, John S. "A Review of Gen. Longstreet's Criticisms of Gen. J. E. B. Stuart's Conduct at Gettysburg." *SHSP* 23 (Jan.–Dec. 1895): 238–47.

_____. "Stuart and Gettysburg—Defense of the Cavalry Leader." *SHSP* 23 (Jan.–Dec. 1895): 348–53.

Muldowny, John. "Jefferson Davis: The Postwar Years." *Mississippi Quarterly* 13 (Winter 1969–70): 17–33.

"The Opposing Forces at Gettysburg." *B&L* 3: 437–39.

Page, Thomas Nelson. "Unc' Edinburg's Drowndin'." *Harper's New Monthly Magazine* 72 (Jan. 1886): 304–15.

Patterson, S. S. P. "Longstreet and the War Between the States." *Sewanee Review* 4 (May 1896): 326–32.

Pearce, Haywood Jefferson. "Longstreet's Responsibility on the Second Day at Gettysburg." *Georgia Historical Quarterly* 10 (Mar. 1926): 26–45.

Pendleton, William Nelson. "Personal Recollections of General Lee." *Southern Magazine* 15 (Dec. 1874): 603–636.

Pickett, La Salle Corbell. "Wartime Story of General Pickett." *Cosmopolitan* 55 (Nov. 1913): 752–60; 56 (Dec. 1913): 33–42; 56 (Jan. 1914): 178–85; 56 (Feb. 1914): 332–39; 56 (Mar. 1914), 437–81; 56 (Apr. 1914): 611–

22; 56 (May 1914): 762–69; 57 (June 1914): 35–43; 57 (July 1914): 196–205; 57 (Aug. 1914): 369–77.

Pitre, Althea D. "The Collapse of the Warmoth Regime, 1870–72." *Louisiana History* 6 (Spring 1965): 161–87.

Purifoy, John. "Longstreet's Attack at Gettysburg, July 3, 1863." *Confederate Veteran* 32 (Feb. 1924): 54–56.

———. "Longstreet's Attack at Gettysburg, July 2, 1863." *Confederate Veteran* 31 (Aug. 1923): 292–94.

Richter, William L. "James Longstreet: From Rebel to Scalawag." *Louisiana History* 11 (Summer 1970): 215–30.

Riley, Harris D., Jr. "Robert E. Lee's Battle with Disease." *Civil War Times Illustrated* 18 (Dec. 1979): 12–22.

Robbins, W. M. "Longstreet's Assault at Gettysburg." *N.C. Regts.* 5: 101–12.

Robertson, James I. "The Continuing Battle of Gettysburg: An Essay Review." *Georgia Historical Quarterly* 68 (Summer 1974): 278–82.

Sanger, Donald Bridgman. "Was Longstreet a Scapegoat?" *Infantry Journal* 26 (1936): 39–46.

Sefton, James E. "Gettysburg: An Exercise in the Evaluation of Historical Evidence." *Military Affairs* 28 (Fall 1966): 64–72.

Squires, Charles W. " 'Boy Officer' of the Washington Artillery." *Civil War Times Illustrated* 14 (May 1975): 10–23.

Swanson, Guy R., and Johnson, Timothy D. "Conflict in East Tennessee: Generals Law, Jenkins, and Longstreet." *Civil War History* 31 (June 1985): 101–10.

Taylor, Joe Gray. "New Orleans and Reconstruction." *Louisiana History* 9 (Summer 1968): 189–208.

Taylor, Walter H. "Lee and Longstreet." *SHSP* 14 (Jan.–Dec. 1896): 73–79.

Thompson, O. G. "Longstreet and Gettysburg." *Confederate Veteran* 23 (Oct. 1915): 453–54.

Thompson, Will H. "Who Lost Gettysburg?" *Confederate Veteran* 23 (June 1915): 257–58.

Tucker, Glenn. "Longstreet: Culprit or Scapegoat?" *Civil War Times Illustrated* 1 (Apr. 1962): 5–9, 41–42.

"The Virginians." *Time*, Oct. 18, 1948, pp. 108–11, 115–17.

Ward, Judson C., Jr. "The Republican Party in Bourbon Georgia." *Journal of Southern History* 9 (May 1943): 196–209.

Weaver, Richard M. "The Older Religiousness of the South." *Sewanee Review* 51 (1943): 237–49.

Wells, Carol. "Kind Admonitions: The Education of a Louisiana Teacher." *Louisiana History* 17 (Summer 1976): 299–319.

Wert, Jeffery D. " 'Old Artillery': William Nelson Pendleton." *Civil War Times Illustrated* 13 (June 1974): 10–18.

Wetta, Frank J. " 'Bulldozing the Scalawags': Some Examples of Persecution of Southern White Republicans in Louisiana During Reconstruction." *Louisiana History* 21 (Winter 1980): 43–58.

Wilson, Clyde N., Jr. "'The Most Promising Man of the South': James J. Pettigrew." *Civil War Times Illustrated* 11 (Feb. 1973): 11–23.
Wilson, James S. "Edward Alfred Pollard." In *Library of Southern Literature*, edited by Edwin Anderson Alderman, Joel Chandler Harris, and Charles William Kent, vol. 9, pp. 4147–50. Atlanta: Martin and Hoyt, 1907.
Wise, John S. "Two Great Confederates." *American Monthly Review of Reviews* 29 (Feb. 1904): 199–208.
Wolseley, Garnet. "An English View of the Civil War." *North American Review* 148 (May 1889): 538–63; 149 (July 1889): 30–43; 149 (Aug. 1889): 164–81; 149 (Sept. 1889): 278–92; 149 (Oct. 1889): 446–59; 149 (Nov. 1889): 594–606; 149 (Dec. 1889): 713–27.

DISSERTATION

Winton, George Peterson, Jr. "Ante-Bellum Military Instruction of West Point Officers, and Its Influence upon Confederate Military Organization and Operations." Ph.D. dissertation, University of South Carolina, 1977.

Index